FORT THOMAS HIGHLANDS FOOTBALL

I0792524

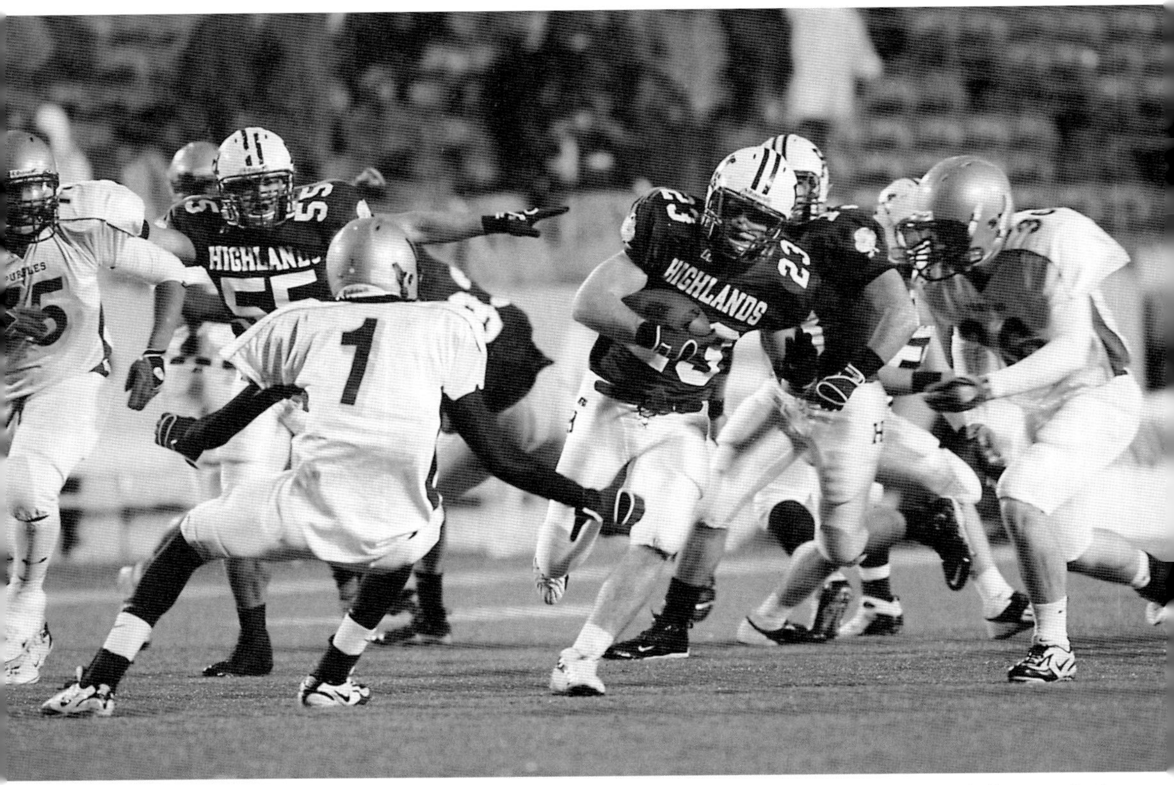

Highlands' junior running back Josh Conner bursts through the Bowling Green defense to help Highlands win the 2007 Class 5A Kentucky state championship by a score of 28-7. (Courtesy of Mark Majors.)

FRONT COVER: All State tailback Rick Hoffman holds the 1968 state championship trophy while surrounded by teammates at Stoll Field on the campus of the University of Kentucky. Hoffman went on to play for Indiana University. (Courtesy of the author.)

COVER BACKGROUND: Highlands' first football team in 1915 poses for a picture in front of the Mess Hall in Tower Park. (Courtesy of Jean Mettens.)

BACK COVER: Jake Crothers (No. 6), Matt Reed (No. 8), and other members of the Highlands' football team celebrate with the 2007 Class 5A Kentucky state championship trophy after defeating Bowling Green in Louisville. (Courtesy of Mark Majors.)

FORT THOMAS HIGHLANDS FOOTBALL

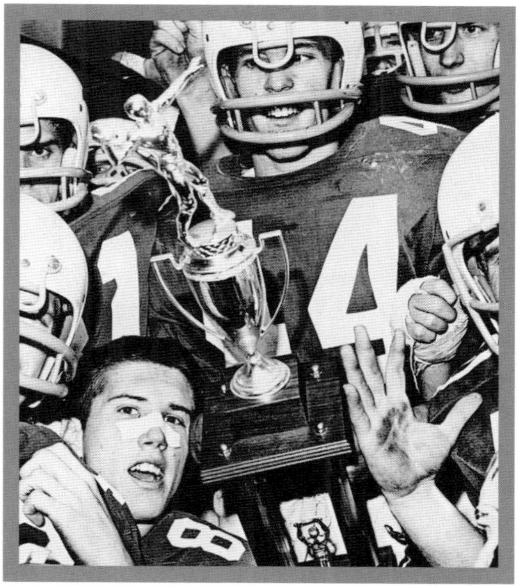

Bill Thomas

ARCADIA PUBLISHING

ISBN 978-0-7385-5391-7

Published by Arcadia Publishing
Charleston SC, Chicago IL, Portsmouth NH, San Francisco CA

Printed in the United States of America

Library of Congress Catalog Card Number: 2007942778

For all general information contact Arcadia Publishing at:
Telephone 843-853-2070
Fax 843-853-0044
E-mail sales@arcadiapublishing.com
For customer service and orders:
Toll-Free 1-888-313-2665

Visit us on the Internet at www.arcadiapublishing.com

To Coach Dale Mueller and
the senior class members of the 2007 Class 5A
Kentucky state champions

CONTENTS

ACKNOWLEDGMENTS

Many residents of Fort Thomas were kind enough to assist the author in the compilation of photographs and information for this book. They include Dick Thompson, Dave Newman, Ed Harber, Ken Honchell, Mark Majors, Tanner Johnson, Bill Mappin, Jon Englehard, Hank Pogue, Joan Mettens, and Bev Stegman. Terry Boehmker of the *Kentucky Post* and Pablo Alcala of the *Lexington Herald-Leader* also provided photographs. The author also wishes to thank the Kenton County Public Library and Highlands High School for generously providing access to their collections of photographs.

This book would not have been possible without the cooperation and enthusiasm of Highlands coach Dale Mueller. Coach Mueller gave the author total access to his team throughout the season. Also, the author wishes to thank Carol Marnell for her computer skills and artistic eye.

INTRODUCTION

I can still remember the last game of the 1956 football season when Highlands High School lost a heartbreaker to Dixie Heights by a score of 21-20. In an attempt to cheer me up after the game, my father told me that the game would prove to be a turning point and that Highlands was about to enter a new era of achievement. He knew what he was talking about.

In 1957, Highlands, under the direction of legendary coach Homer Rice, went undefeated and was the top ranked team in Kentucky. In 1959, the first year of the playoff system in Kentucky, Highlands was the Class 2A state runner-up. The Bluebirds went undefeated in 1960 and 1961, and captured Class 2A state championships in Lexington both years. Coach Rice and his teams would win 50 consecutive regular season games during this stretch of seasons.

Highlands hasn't slowed down since. The Bluebirds have won 17 state championships since 1960. They are fifth in the nation in total victories.

The 2007 team finished the season with a perfect 15-0 record and captured the first Class 5A state championship in Kentucky history. This achievement is even more impressive when one takes into account that Highlands has elected to play up two levels in competition. There are only 400 boys to draw upon in the freshmen through senior classes.

During the 2007 regular season, Highlands defeated the Class 3A and Class 4A state champions, and also defeated Trotwood Madison, an Ohio powerhouse, in a game at Nippert Stadium on the campus of the University of Cincinnati.

Highlands has a number of National Football League (NFL) connections. Austin Collinsworth, son of former All Pro Cris Collinsworth, started at defensive back as a sophomore and was named second team All State. Milton Peko, a senior defensive lineman, is the nephew of Domata Peko, a starting defensive tackle with the Cincinnati Bengals.

Highlands graduate Jared Lorenzen is the backup quarterback for the New York Giants, and another graduate, Rob Smith, is an offensive lineman with the Kansas City Chiefs. Gino Guidugli, a quarterback who led Highlands to two state championships, is playing quarterback in the Canadian Football League, and Sean Sester, an offensive lineman at Purdue, and Michael Mitchell, a safety at Ohio University, could be drafted by NFL teams in 2008 or 2009.

Highlands' football team holds a number of state records, including most undefeated teams (11), most offensive points in a season (801 in 1998), most touchdowns in a season (113 in 1998), most touchdowns passed in a game (9 versus Scott High School in 2000), and most touchdown receptions in a game (6 by Brett Hamblen in 2000).

There are many reasons why Highlands has had such a rich football tradition over the years. It can be attributed in part to the unique quality of the school and the makeup of the community. Academically, Highlands High School is considered one of the top schools in the United States. It was awarded the No Child Left Behind–National Blue Ribbon School designation in 2007 and was recently recognized by *Newsweek* and *U.S. News & World Report* as one of the country's best public schools. In addition, Fort Thomas schools have led the state of Kentucky in standardized test scores for 13 consecutive years. This school year, 11 seniors were named National Merit Finalists or Commended students, and 49 students were recognized as Advanced Placement Students.

The football team includes a good mix of excellent athletes and top students, as well as a highly dedicated coaching staff. The players work extremely hard in the off-season and during the summer months. They buy into the Highlands tradition and want to be a part of it. Football is a year-round program at Highlands, and these players work far beyond what seems possible in the weight room during the winter months. Speed is a major characteristic of each team under coach Dale Mueller, and it is developed and improved upon during drills throughout the year.

Fort Thomas is a close-knit community of 16,000, and there is great pride in the Highlands football program. Children begin instructional league play early on in grade school in the Fort Thomas Junior Football League. The league was founded in part by Homer Rice and George Ratterman, a Cincinnati native who played quarterback for Notre Dame and for the Cleveland Browns.

The Highlands tradition has been passed down through the generations. Clay Cecil, quarterback of the 2007 team, followed in the footsteps of his grandfather, a number of uncles, his father, and two brothers. Drew Bathiany, a safety, is another third-generation player at Highlands. His grandfather played in the 1940s, his father played on the 1970 state championship team, and his brother started at defensive back on the 2004 state championship team.

This book provides the reader with an inside look at the 2007 season, and it also gives the reader some of the history of the Highlands football program. A number of the greatest players through the decades are featured, and the author made a good faith effort to include as many players as space permitted.

1

2007 State Champions

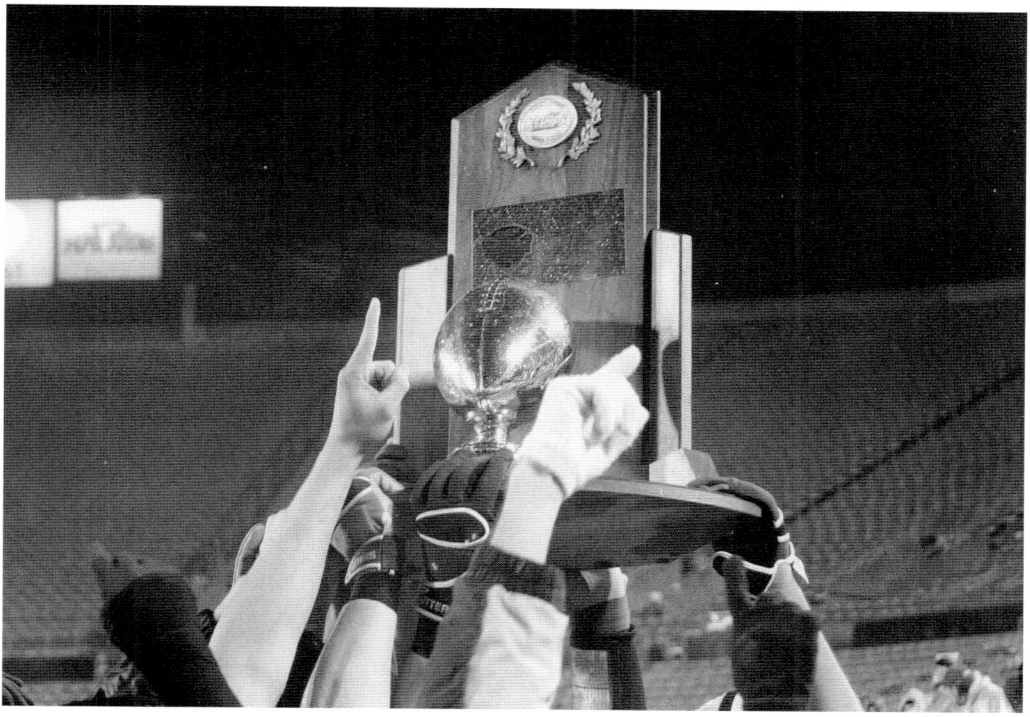

Highlands players hoist their arms and the state championship trophy into the air in celebration after defeating Bowling Green 28-7 at Papa John Stadium in Louisville. The Bluebirds finished the season with a perfect 15-0 record, won Kentucky's first-ever Class 5A state championship, and were nationally ranked by MaxPreps, a computerized scouting service. (Courtesy of Ed Harber.)

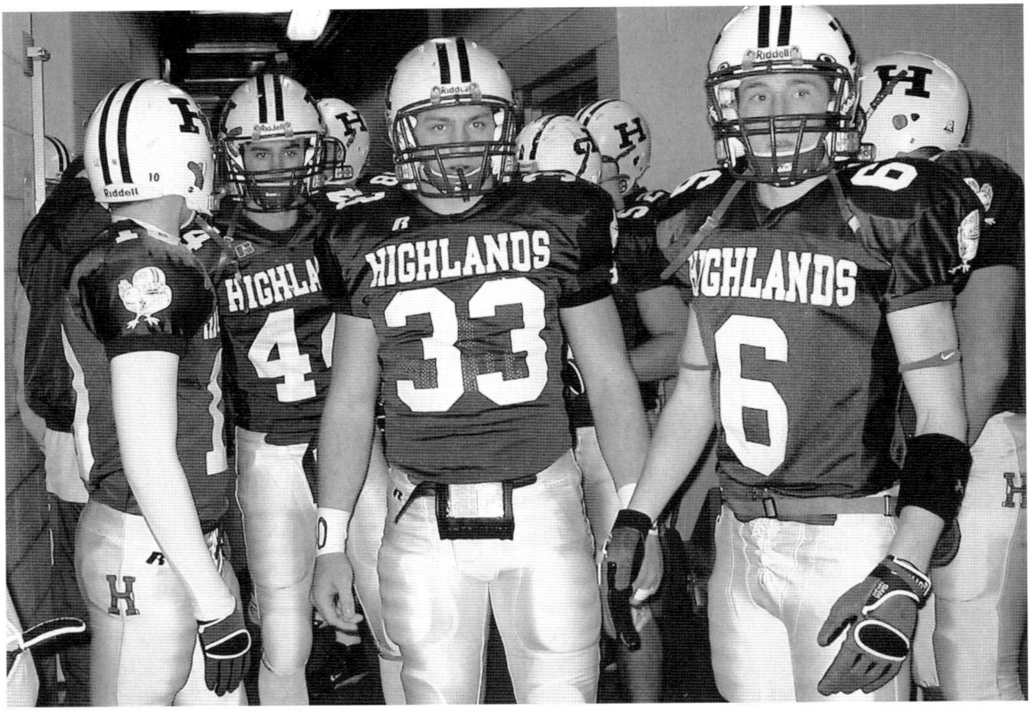

Highlands kicking team prepares to take the field for warm-ups prior to the championship game against Bowling Green. Leading the team from left to right are the following players: Drew Bathiany, Drew Simons, Zach Hurtt, and Jake Crothers.

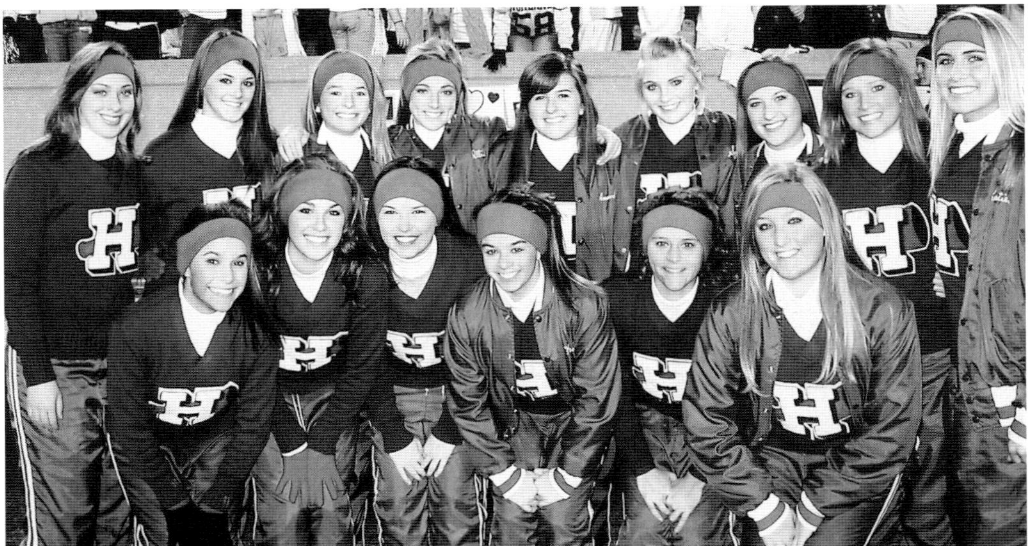

The cheerleaders and Highlands student body assembled on the field and in the stands an hour before the game in Louisville. The cheerleaders, under the direction of teacher Sally Walters, played an important role all season, cheering at games and preparing banners that the team would burst through when taking the field before games.

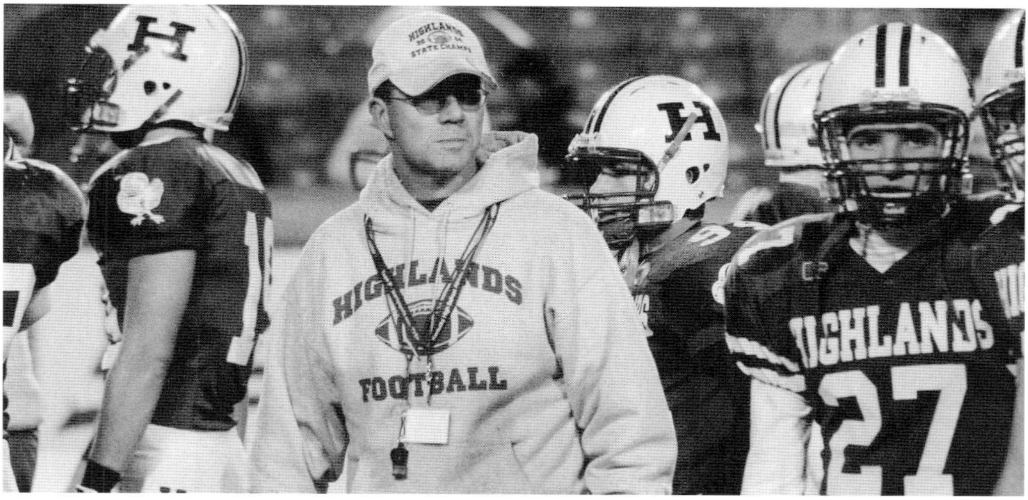

Head coach Dale Mueller is all business on the sidelines before the start of the state championship game against Bowling Green, a team that entered the Class 5A state championship game with a 13-1 record. Coach Mueller played middle linebacker and offensive guard at Highlands in the early 1970s and graduated from Cornell University with a degree in engineering. He was also an outstanding baseball catcher at Highlands and Cornell. Coach Mueller has coached at Highlands for 14 years and has won six Kentucky state championships. (Courtesy of Ed Harber.)

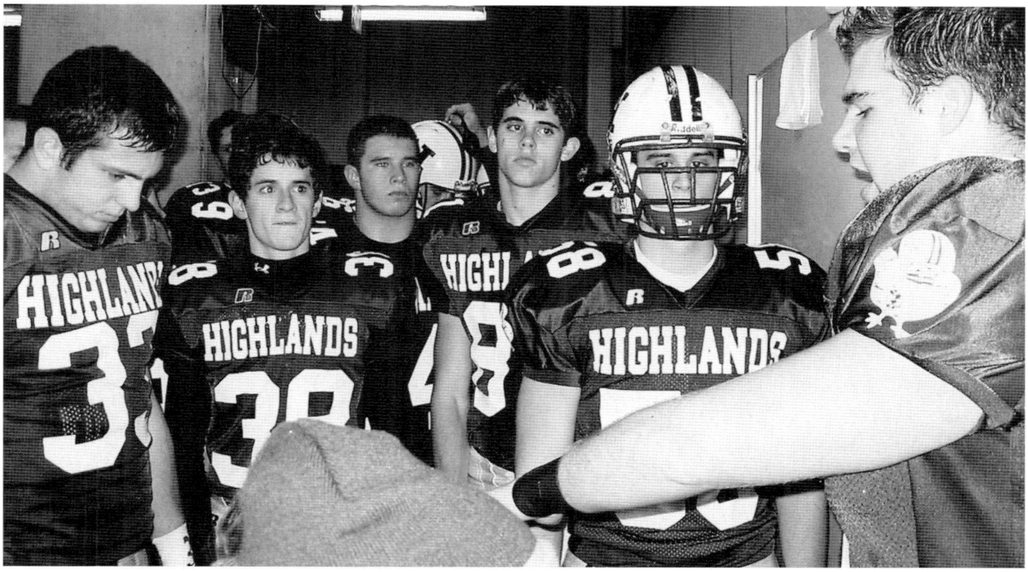

Senior center Brady Dowling was a team motivator in the locker room throughout the season. In this photograph, Dowling is firing up his teammates with a pep talk before they take the field to play Bowling Green in the state championship game. He made similar speeches before all of the playoff games. Before the Covington Catholic game, he reminded the seniors that this was their last game against their arch-rival and that "there is no way Covington Catholic is going to come to Fort Thomas and beat us." Before the state semi-finals game, he reminded the seniors that this would be the last time they would ever play on their home field.

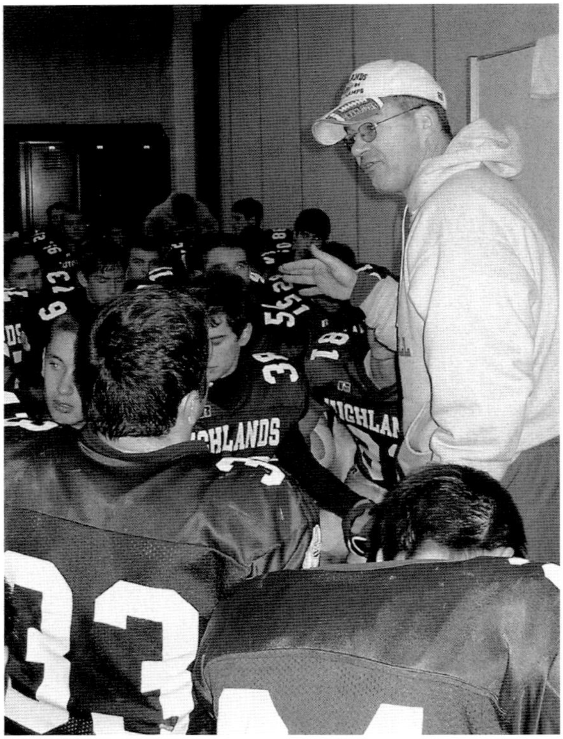

Coach Dale Mueller addresses his team in the cramped locker room at Papa John Stadium in Louisville before they take the field to play Bowling Green. Coach Mueller emphasized that everyone had a job to do on the field and that he wasn't asking any of the players to be superstars. "If you stay totally focused on every play, if you do your job, we win the game," he said. Coach Mueller also reminded his team to protect the football and avoid foolish mistakes and unsportsmanlike conduct.

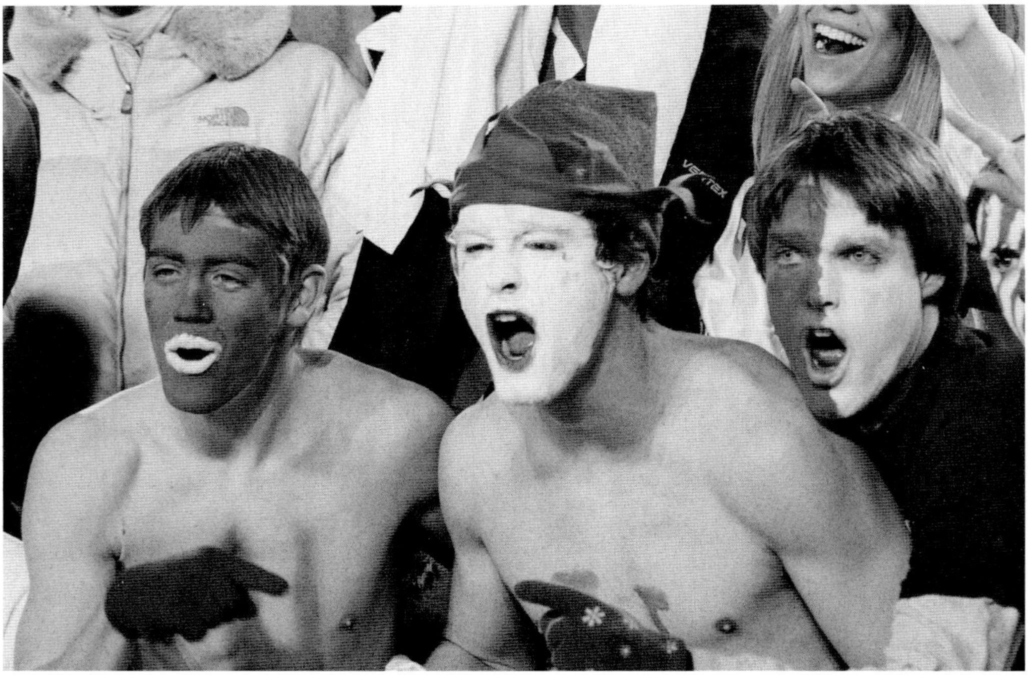

Students at Highlands painted their faces and dressed up for the state championship game. Many of the boys went shirtless for the entire game despite cold weather and a steady rain. (Courtesy of Ed Harber.)

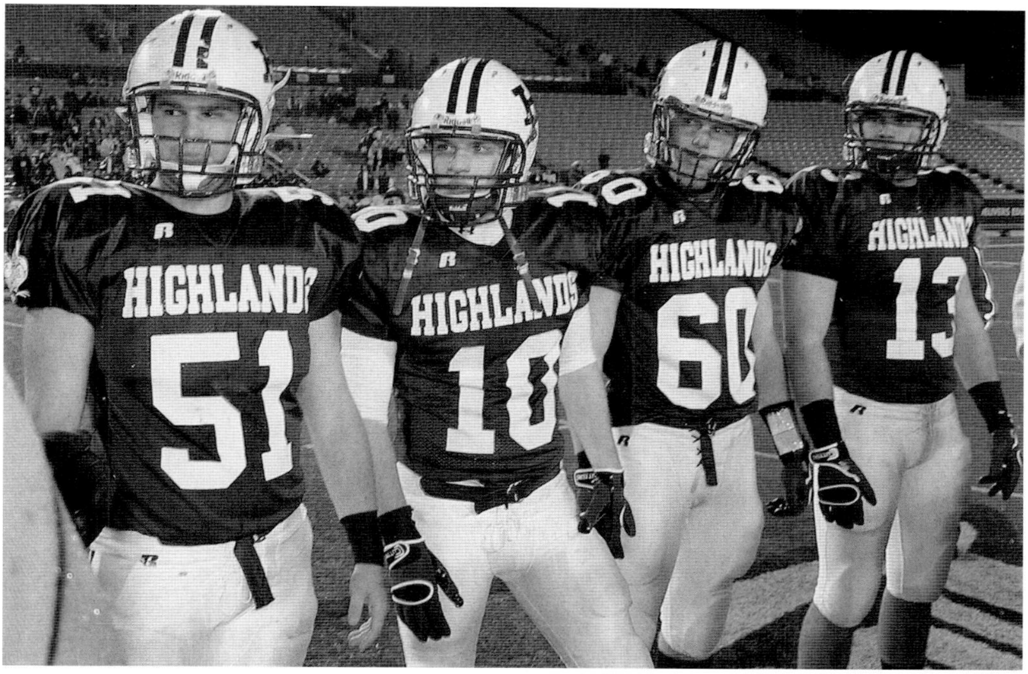

Highlands' captains arrive at the center of the field for the coin toss before the start of the Class 5A state championship game against Bowling Green. The captains are, from left to right, center Brady Dowling (No. 51), safety Drew Bathiany (No. 10), middle linebacker Joe Fitzgerald (No. 60), and tight end Trey Jurgens (No. 13). Highlands lost the coin toss, and Bowling Green chose to kick to the Bluebirds to start the game.

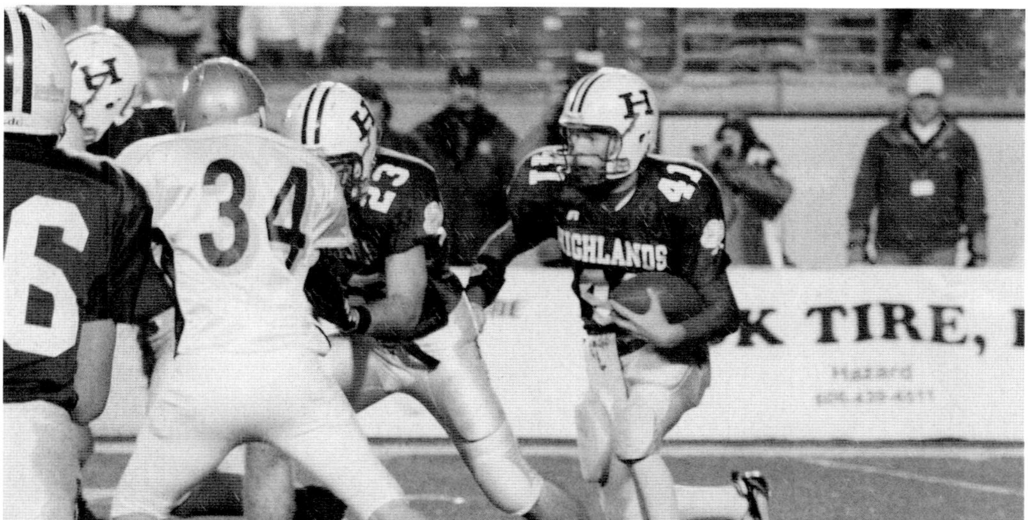

Highlands quarterback Clay Cecil gets a block from running back Josh Conner (No. 23) en route to a big gain against Bowling Green. Cecil rushed for 88 yards and threw for 93 yards and a touchdown against Bowling Green. (Courtesy of Ed Harber.)

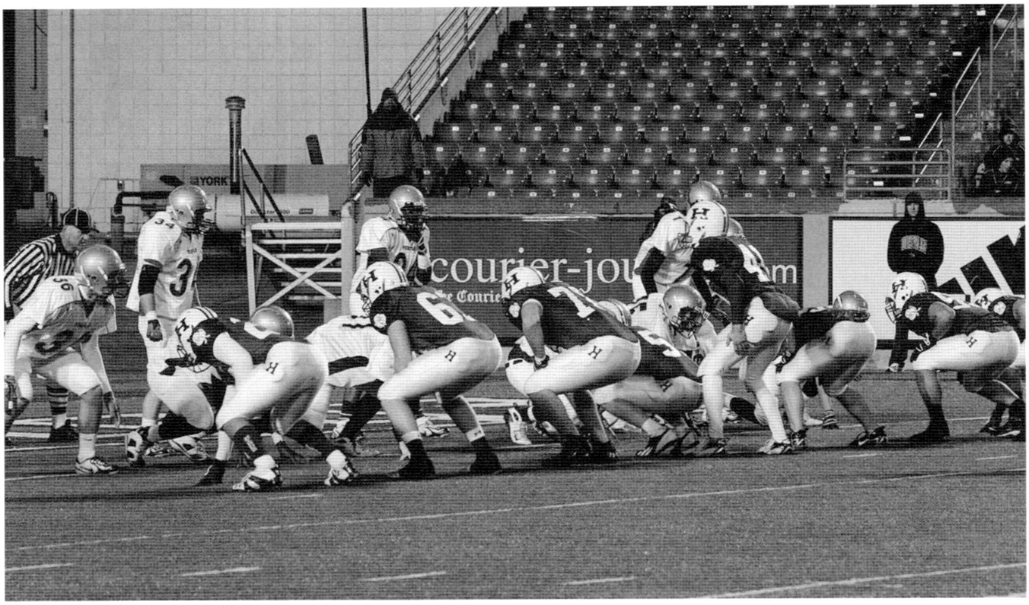

Highlands quarterback Clay Cecil is over center as the Bluebirds go into their goal line offense en route to a touchdown. Highlands' running attack was unstoppable all season long thanks to the blocking of the offensive line. They are, from left to right, Terry O'Brien, Adam Dempsey, Alex Hempfling, Brady Dowling, Ryan Ball, Luke Stein, and Trey Jurgens. (Courtesy of Ed Harber.)

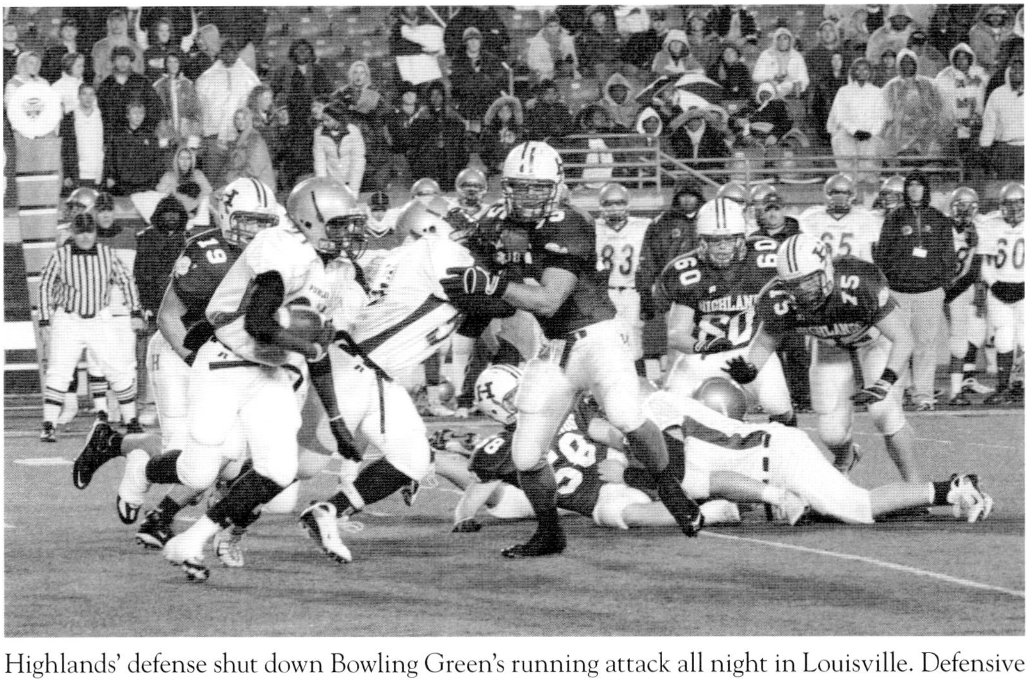

Highlands' defense shut down Bowling Green's running attack all night in Louisville. Defensive players in this photograph are, from left to right, sophomore linebacker Brandon Roller (No. 19), senior nose guard Adam Reis (No. 58), senior linebacker Luke Stein (No. 55), senior linebacker Joe Fitzgerald (No. 60), and junior lineman Kody Rosenhagen (No. 75). (Courtesy of Ed Harber.)

Wide receiver Terry O'Brien is in the locker room at halftime shortly after catching a long "Hail Terry" touchdown pass from quarterback Clay Cecil as time expired to end the half. The touchdown reception gave Highlands a 21-0 lead at the half. Unfortunately, O'Brien broke his foot early in the second half.

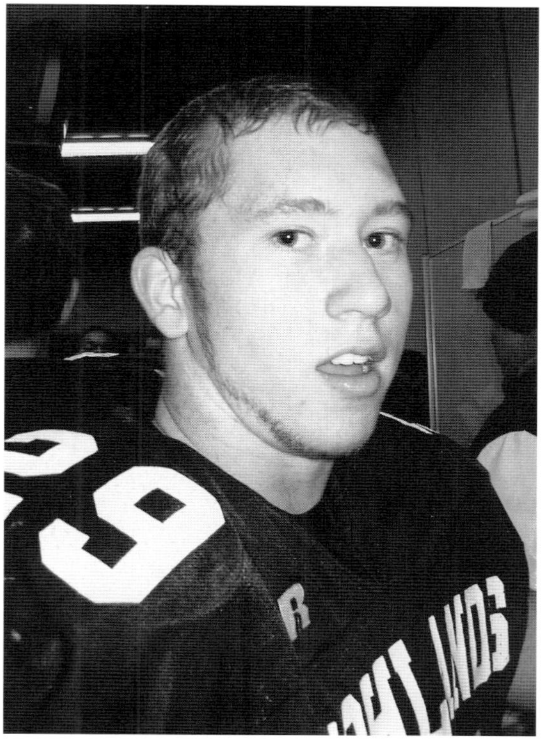

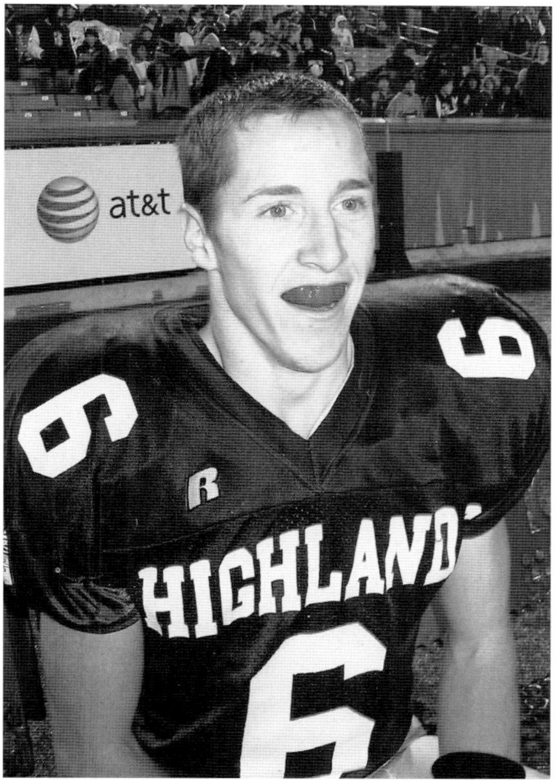

Jake Crothers, a senior defensive back, came up with a big second-half interception for Highlands to help stop a Bowling Green drive against the Bluebirds. This photograph was taken on the sidelines shortly after he was congratulated by his teammates.

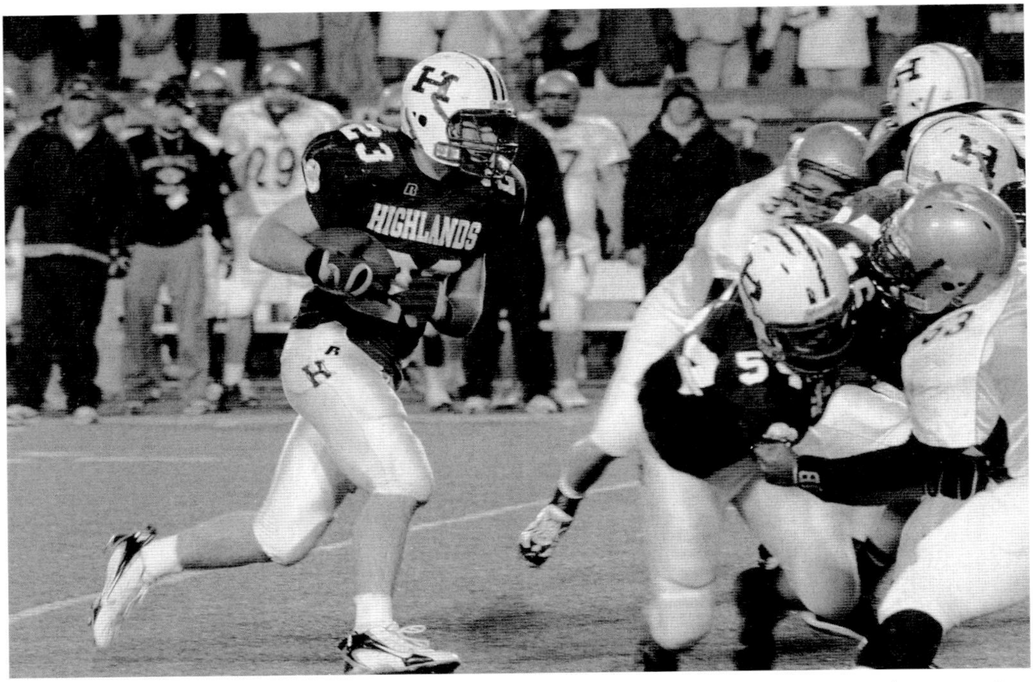

Running back Josh Conner hits a hole opened by his offensive line in the state championship game. Conner, a junior, rushed for 131 hard-earned yards on 27 carries and scored two touchdowns against Bowling Green. He also hauled in a big third-down pass from Clay Cecil to keep a drive going in the first half of the game.

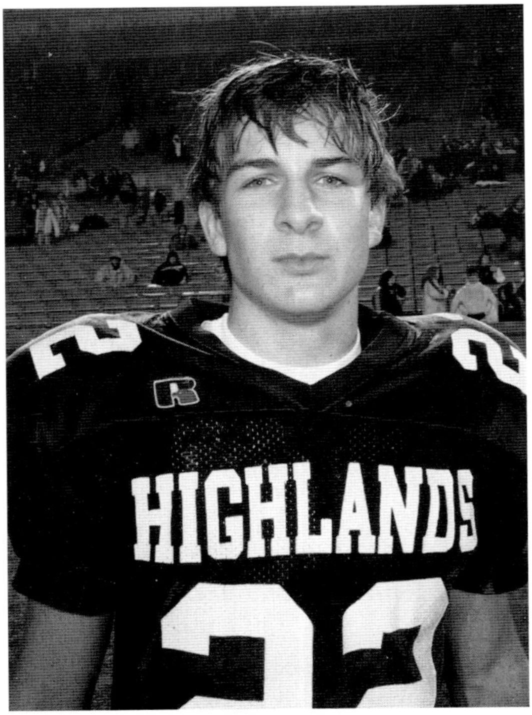

Sophomore defensive back Austin Collinsworth pauses on the sideline after coming up with an interception in the second half against Bowling Green. Collinsworth, the son of former All Pro wide receiver Cris Collinsworth, led Highlands with six interceptions in the 2007 season. He was named to the Associated Press All State team.

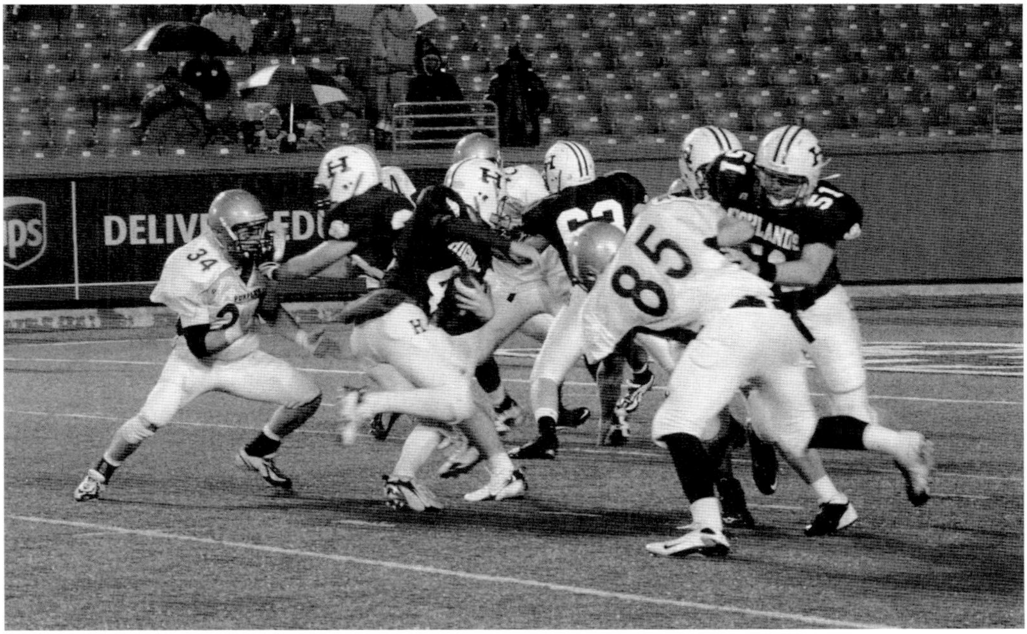

Clay Cecil heads for the end zone thanks to perfect blocking by Highlands' offensive line. Highlands' offense averaged 41 points a game for the 2007 season and also averaged 270 rushing yards each game. (Courtesy of Ed Harber.)

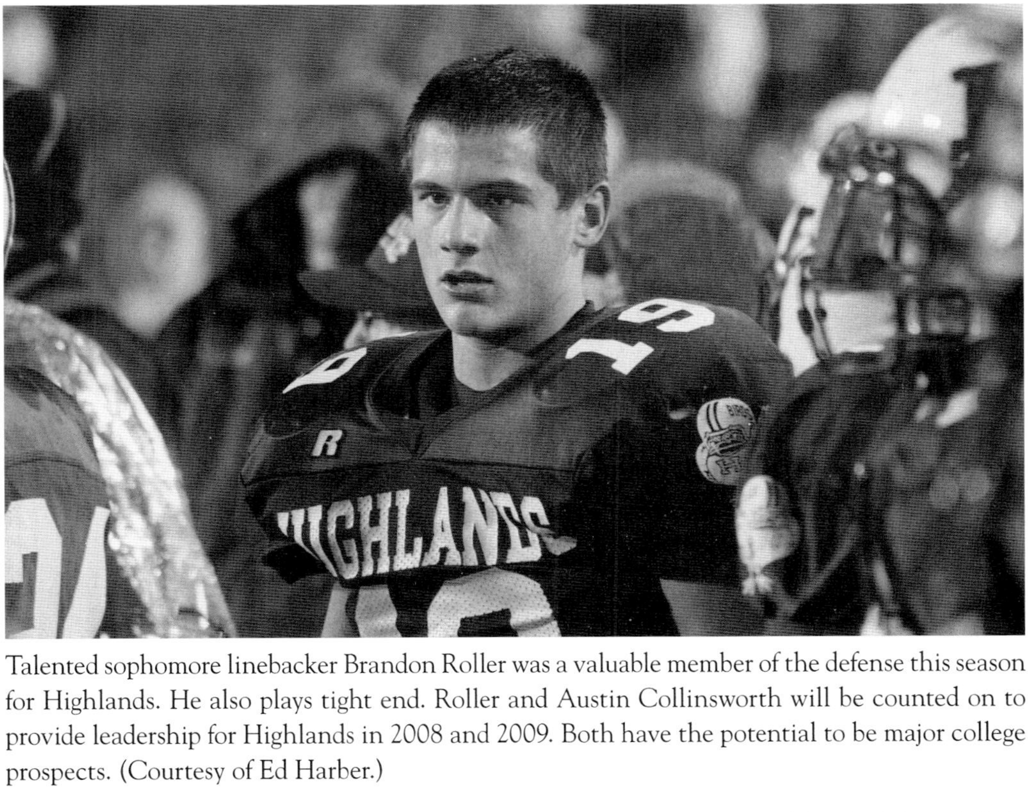

Talented sophomore linebacker Brandon Roller was a valuable member of the defense this season for Highlands. He also plays tight end. Roller and Austin Collinsworth will be counted on to provide leadership for Highlands in 2008 and 2009. Both have the potential to be major college prospects. (Courtesy of Ed Harber.)

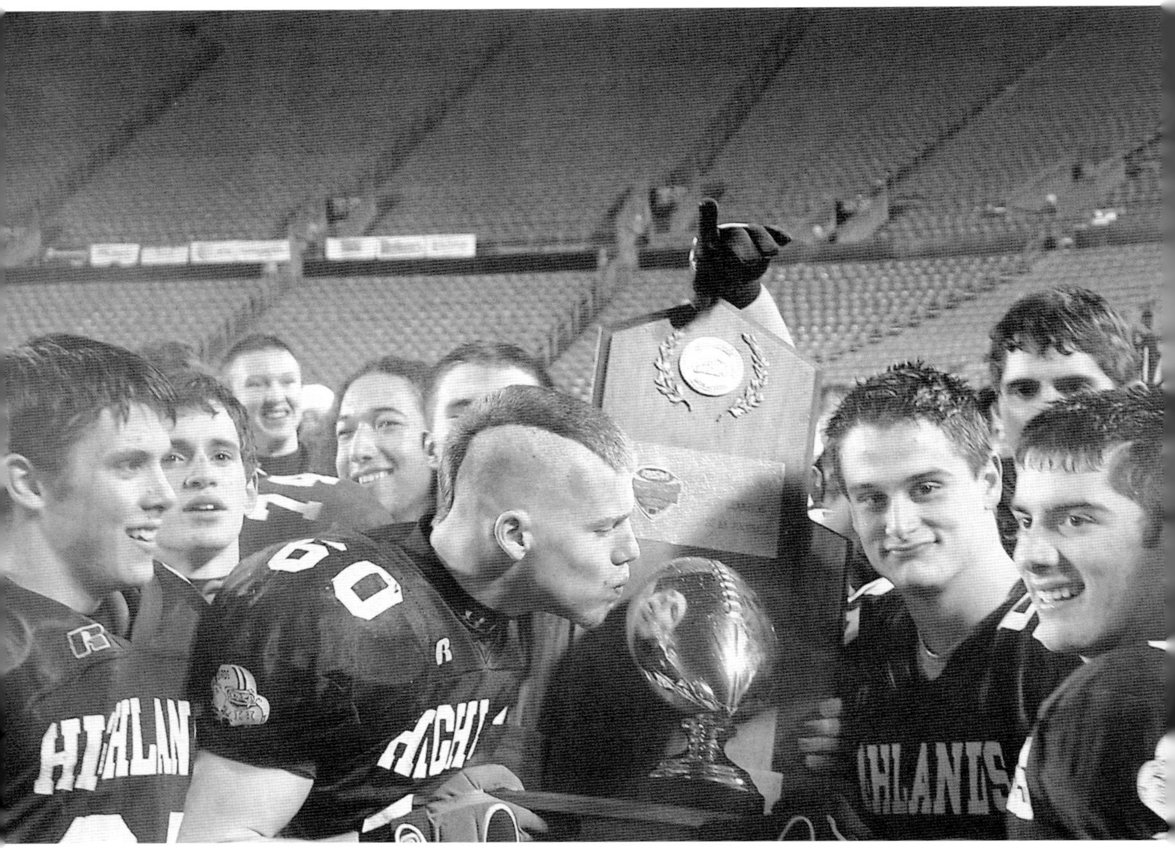

Joe Fitzgerald leans in to kiss the Class 5A state championship trophy at the conclusion of the game at Papa John Stadium in Louisville. Fitzgerald, a National Merit Commended Student, was one of a handful of Highlands' players that shaved their heads for the big game. Other players on the first row, from left to right, are Will Coleman, Adam Reis, and Matt Reed. (Courtesy of Ed Harber.)

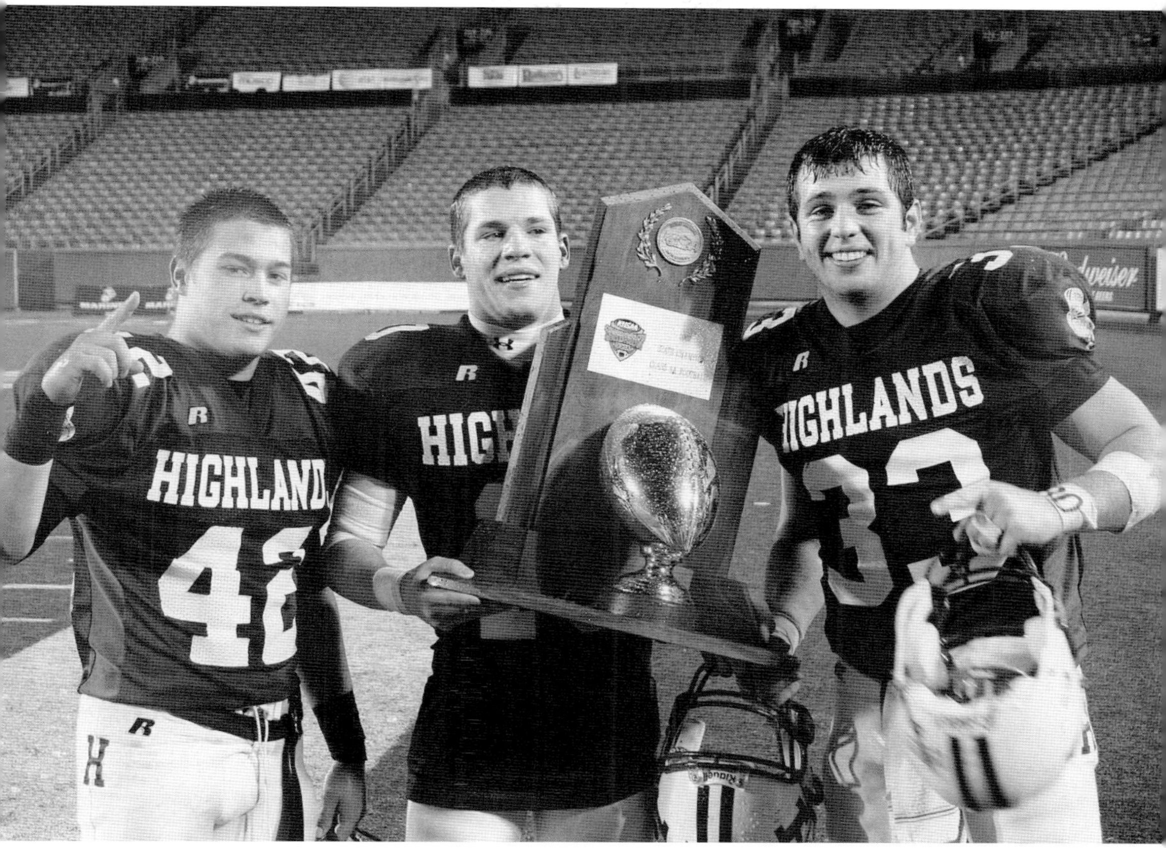

Three cousins celebrate on the field with the state championship trophy. They are, from left to right, Oliver Head, Drew Bathiany, and Zach Hurtt. Bert Bathiany, their grandfather, played for Highlands back in the 1940s. Oliver's father, Billy Head, and Drew's father, Bert Bathiany, also played for Highlands. Zach Hurtt's father was a star linebacker at Bellevue High School. Oliver Head was a solid contributor to Highlands' special teams and also played running back, defensive back, and safety for the Bluebirds. Drew Bathiany started at defensive back, and Zach Hurtt started at running back and inside linebacker. (Courtesy Ed Harber.)

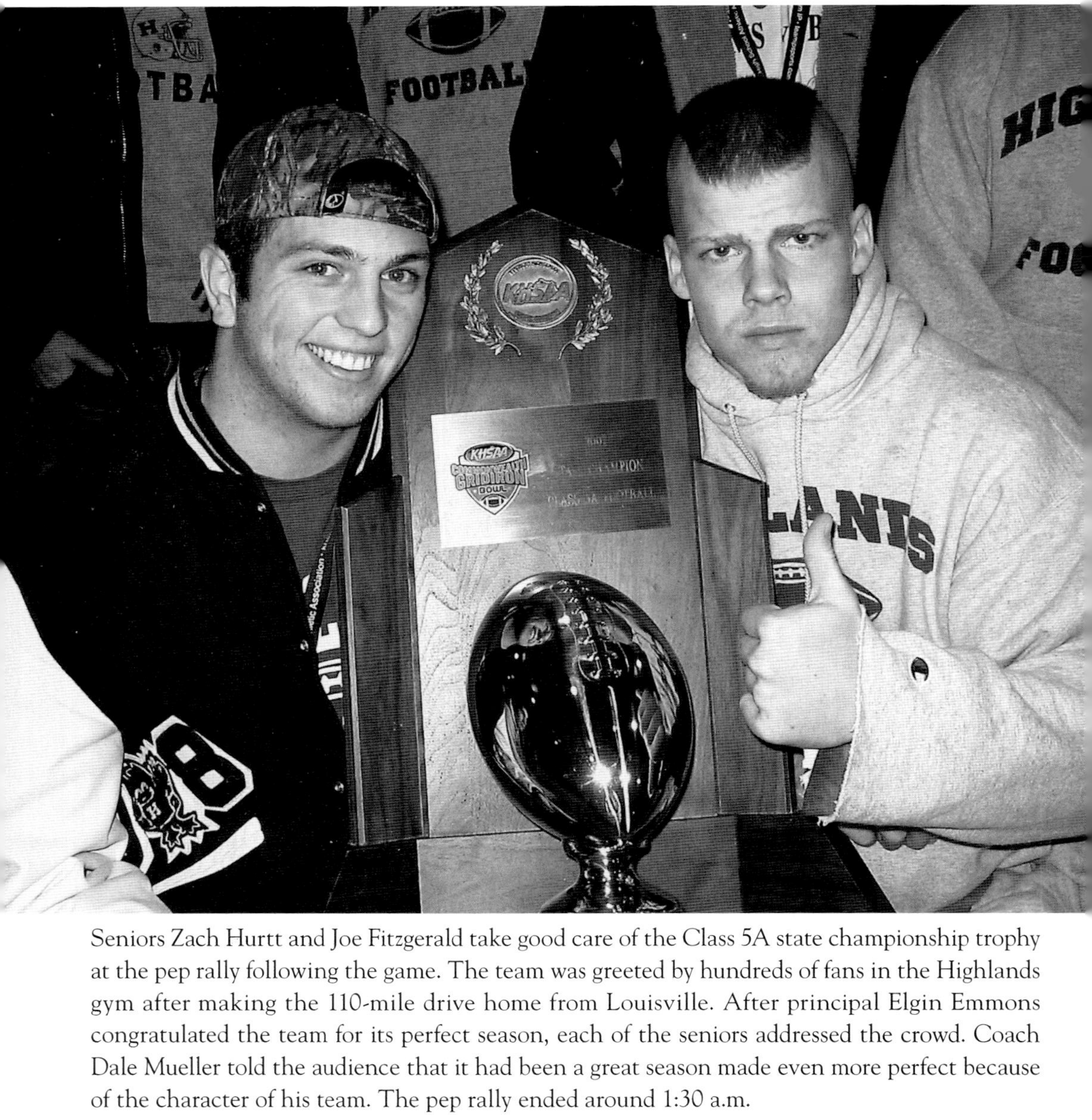

Seniors Zach Hurtt and Joe Fitzgerald take good care of the Class 5A state championship trophy at the pep rally following the game. The team was greeted by hundreds of fans in the Highlands gym after making the 110-mile drive home from Louisville. After principal Elgin Emmons congratulated the team for its perfect season, each of the seniors addressed the crowd. Coach Dale Mueller told the audience that it had been a great season made even more perfect because of the character of his team. The pep rally ended around 1:30 a.m.

2

THE WINTER WEIGHTLIFTING PROGRAM

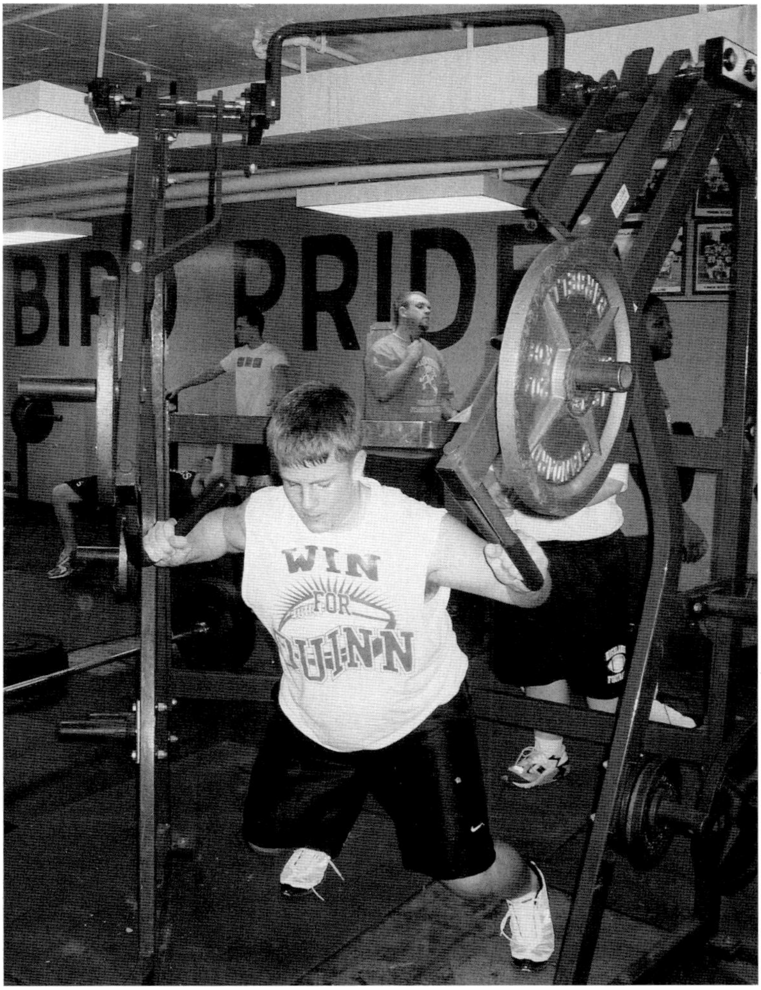

Sophomore Hunter Schlosser works out on the push press machine. Schlosser is a talented offensive and defensive lineman who is expected to step into the starting lineup in 2008. His father, Jeff Schlosser, was an All State linebacker on the Highlands football team that won a state Class 3A championship in 1975.

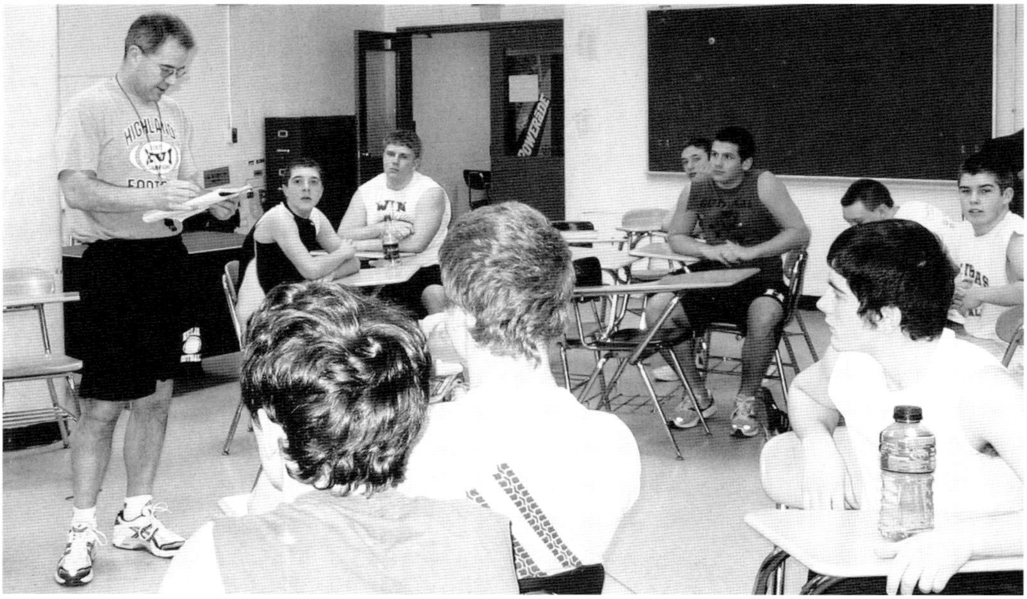

Coach Dale Mueller takes roll before the start of a winter workout in January. Most members of the team who aren't playing another sport workout three times a week throughout the winter and spring. Opposing coaches would be amazed at the quality of the facilities for indoor training at Highlands. The weight room is cramped and lacks air-conditioning. Running and quickness drills are done on concrete floors and stairways and in the aisles of the locker room or film room. Workouts last a full three hours and go well beyond what this writer thought possible for high school boys. Each coach runs a different weight lifting or running station, and each pushes the players at his station to their absolute physical limits.

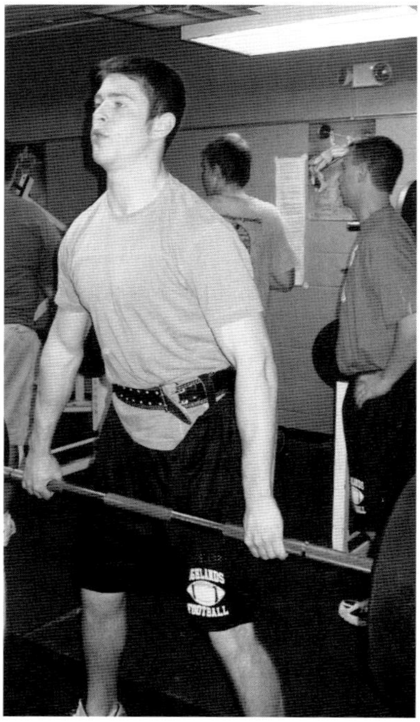

Clay Cecil does the clean weightlifting exercise in the Highlands weight room. His two older brothers played football at Highlands, and he has a younger brother who played on the freshman team. His oldest brother, Drew, is a student at the Naval Academy in Annapolis, and another brother, Chase, was Highlands quarterback when the Bluebirds captured the Class 3A state championship against Boyle County in 2004. Clay Cecil will play football at the University of Kentucky.

Senior tight end Trey Jurgens works out on a rowing machine in the weight room. Jurgens's solid play at tight end was critical to the success of the team in 2007 because it allowed coach Mueller to move another tight end, Luke Stein, to offensive tackle. Stein went on to win All Northern Kentucky and All State honors and will play college football for Gardner Webb. Jurgens was a great blocker and pass receiver, and also handled long-snapping duties for the Bluebirds. He was named homecoming king at halftime of the game against Scott High School and will also play college football.

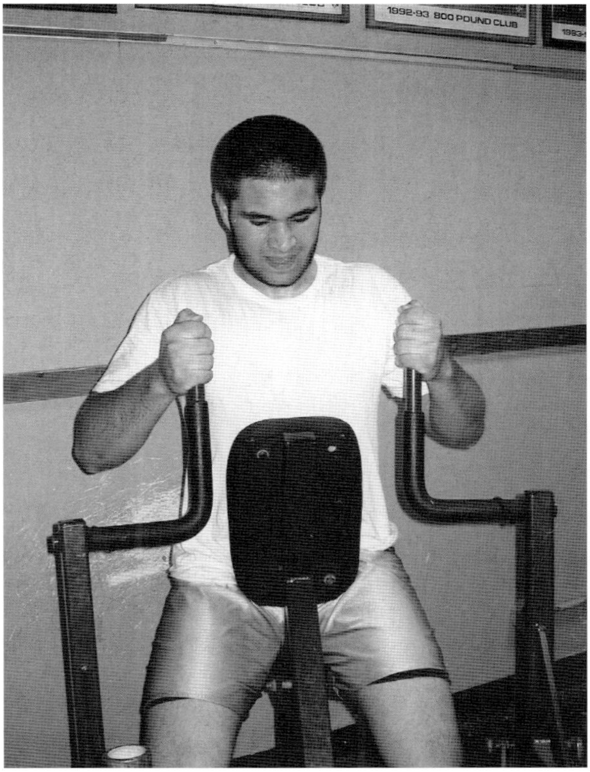

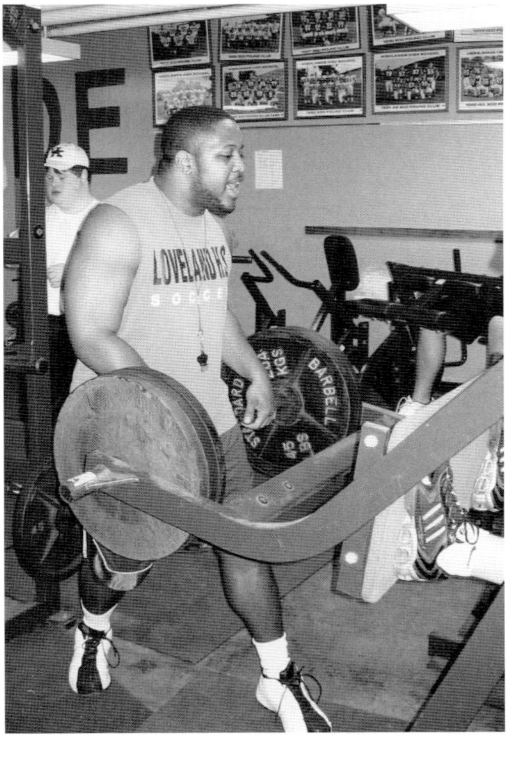

Running-backs coach Nick Jackson works with a player on the leg press machine. Jackson attended Loveland High School in Cincinnati and was a running back at Mount St. Joseph College. He teaches at Highlands Middle School and is in charge of the Fellowship of Christian Athletes Club at Highlands. Coach Jackson also assists Dave Meadows with the defensive backs during the summer and football season. He is intense and supportive in the weight room.

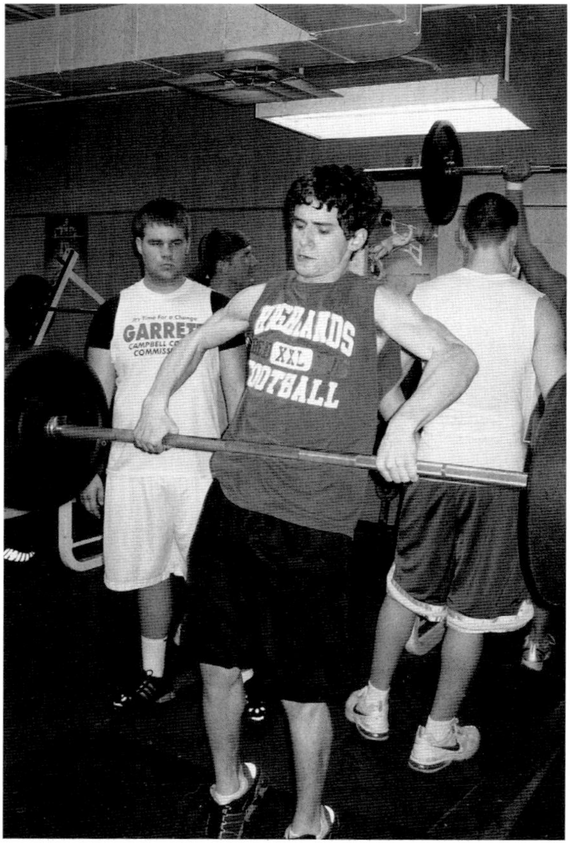

Senior Jeremy Hickman does the clean weightlifting exercise in the weight room. A typical winter workout includes numerous running and quickness drills, as well as a rigorous weightlifting regimen. It is not unusual for players to get sick during the three-hour workout. Coach Dale Mueller is such a hands-on coach that he does all of the weightlifting and running drills with his team. He pushes his players to excel. At a workout in February, coach Mueller stopped everything and asked why the weight room was so silent. "We're here today to beat Covington Catholic next season, and I don't hear anybody yelling at his partner. Attack the weights. Get intense. Push each other." That afternoon, the team ran, did exercises, broke into smaller groups for speed work, hit the weight room for two hours, divided into groups for more speed work, and returned again to the weight room for more lifting.

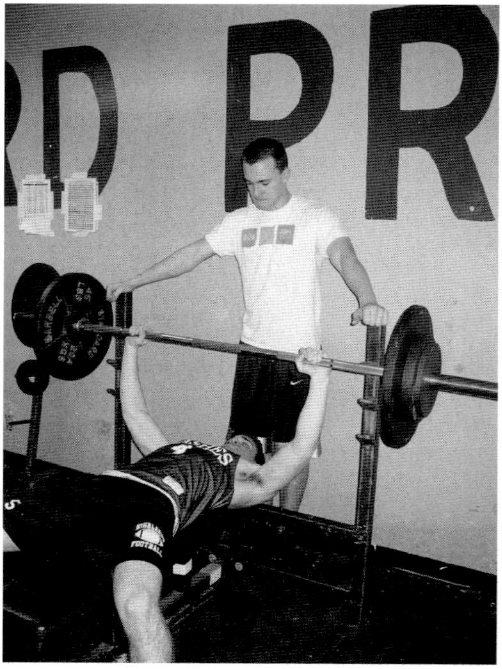

Senior wide receiver Jay Draper is spotting for senior outside linebacker Jimmy Hall in this photograph. Draper switched from quarterback to wide receiver his junior year and became a solid blocker and Clay Cecil's favorite big target on long passes. Jimmy Hall switched from wide receiver to outside linebacker his senior year, and the move helped the offense because Cecil could concentrate on playing quarterback instead of playing quarterback and outside linebacker.

3

Spring Football

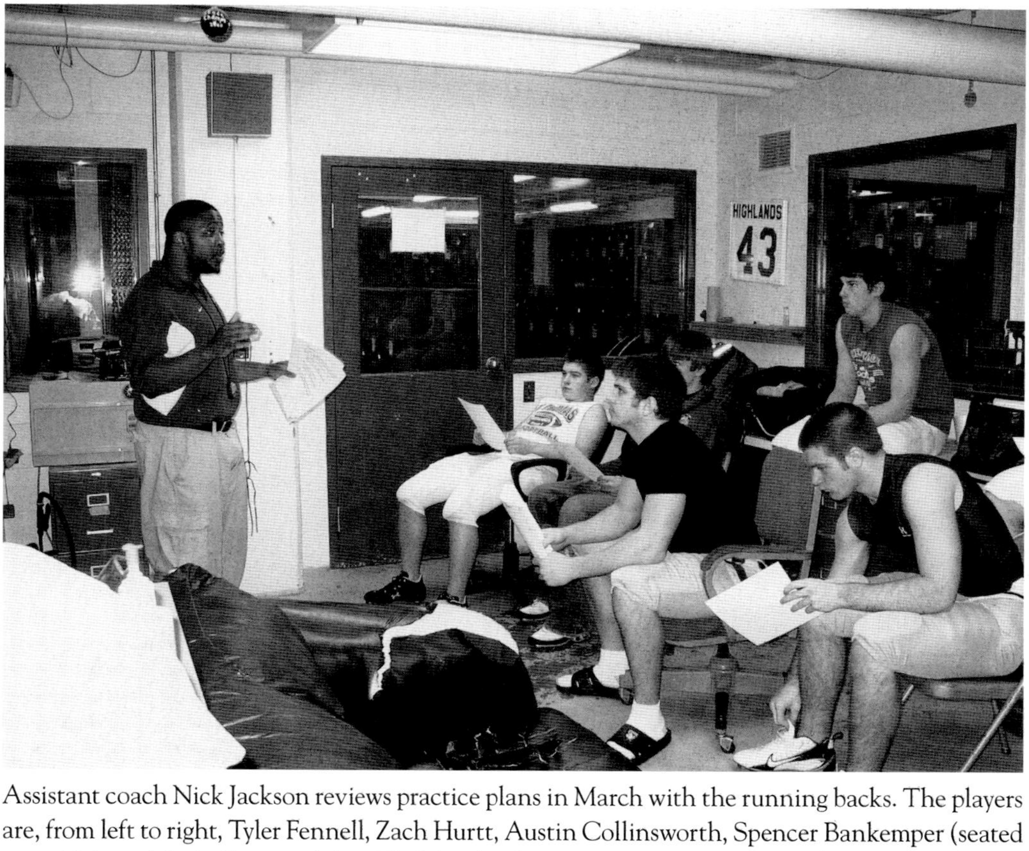

Assistant coach Nick Jackson reviews practice plans in March with the running backs. The players are, from left to right, Tyler Fennell, Zach Hurtt, Austin Collinsworth, Spencer Bankemper (seated on table), and Josh Conner. Most Highlands players participate in spring football, and coach Dale Mueller uses these practice sessions to experiment with players in new positions. This is also the period of time when his players engage in the most contact drills and scrimmages. There is much less contact during the summer because coach Mueller wants to make sure his players are healthy with the start of the regular season approaching. Spring football concludes with the annual full-scrimmage, blue-white game.

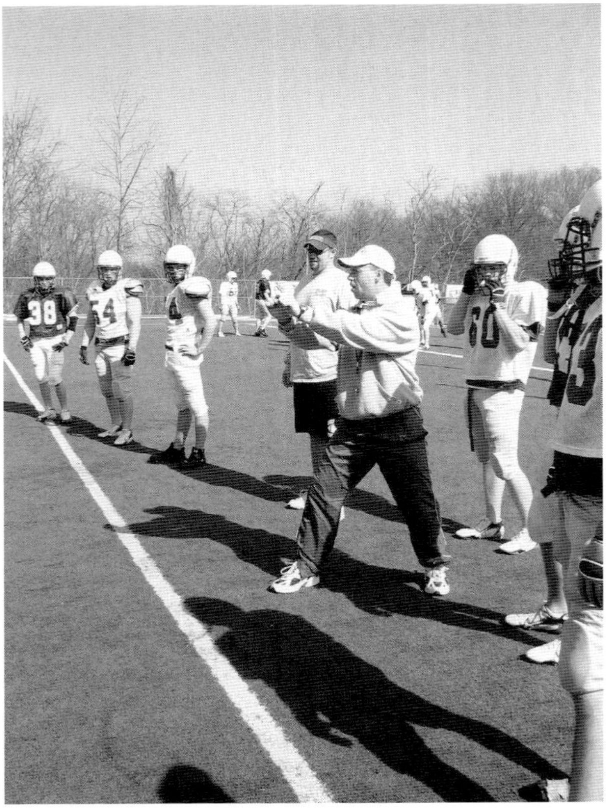

Coach Brian Weinrich works with the linebackers at a spring practice in March. Coach Weinrich is a Highlands graduate who played football at Campbellsville College in Kentucky. He is the assistant head coach and defensive coordinator at Highlands. Coach Weinrich makes all of the defensive decisions with regard to personnel and assignments and is also in charge of punt and kickoff returns. Coach Mueller concentrates completely on offense.

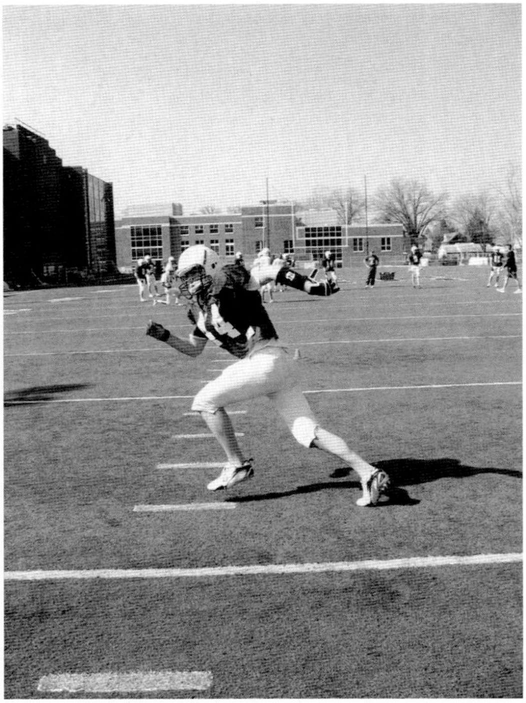

Senior outside linebacker Drew Simons works on zone drop pass coverage at a spring football practice. Simons had started since he was a sophomore and was one of the most fundamentally sound players on the team. His quickness and toughness were big factors in the win over Bowling Green in the Class 5A state football championship game.

Coach Dave Meadows works with Clay Cecil on man technique during spring football. Coach Meadows is a Highlands graduate and coaches the defensive backs on a volunteer basis. He served as a defensive coordinator at Bellevue High School before coming to Highlands. His wife teaches Spanish at Highlands.

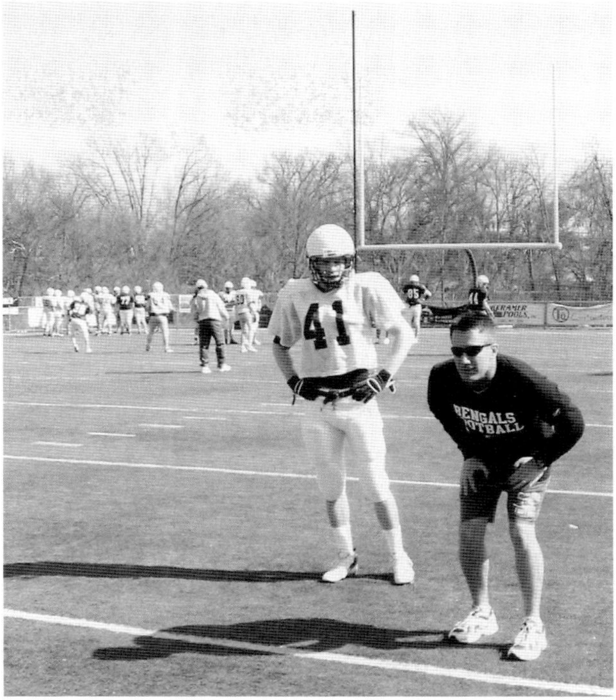

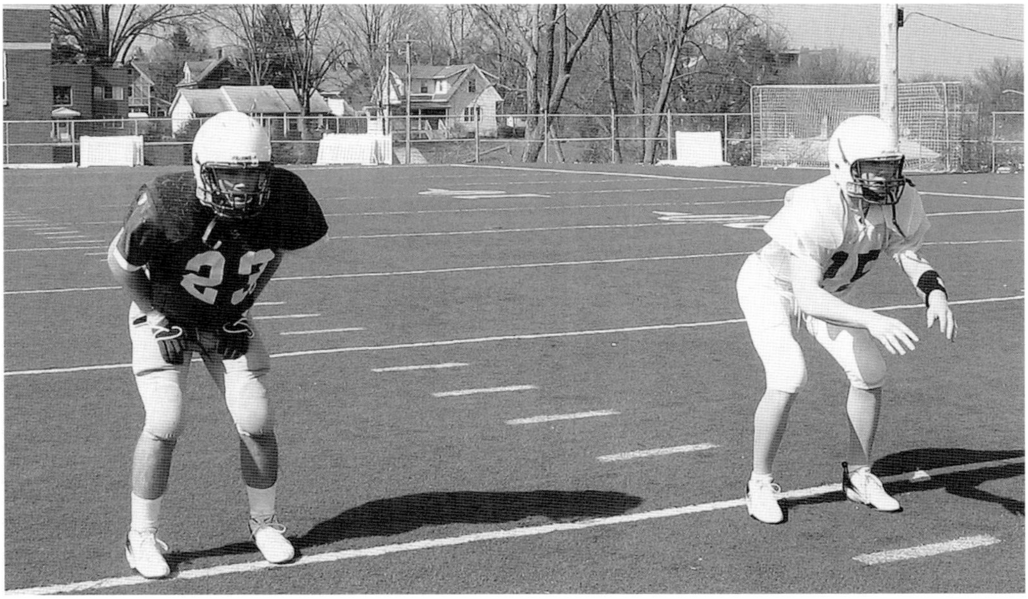

Junior quarterback Tony Guidugli (No. 15) and junior running back Josh Conner (No. 23) get ready to run a play during spring football practice. Guidugli is the youngest of four brothers to play football at Highlands. His oldest brother, Gino, was a star quarterback at the University of Cincinnati and now plays in the Canadian Football League. Tony Guidugli had an excellent spring and summer, and gained valuable experience during the 2007 season. He is expected to start at quarterback for the Bluebirds in 2008. Coach Mueller calls him a top college prospect.

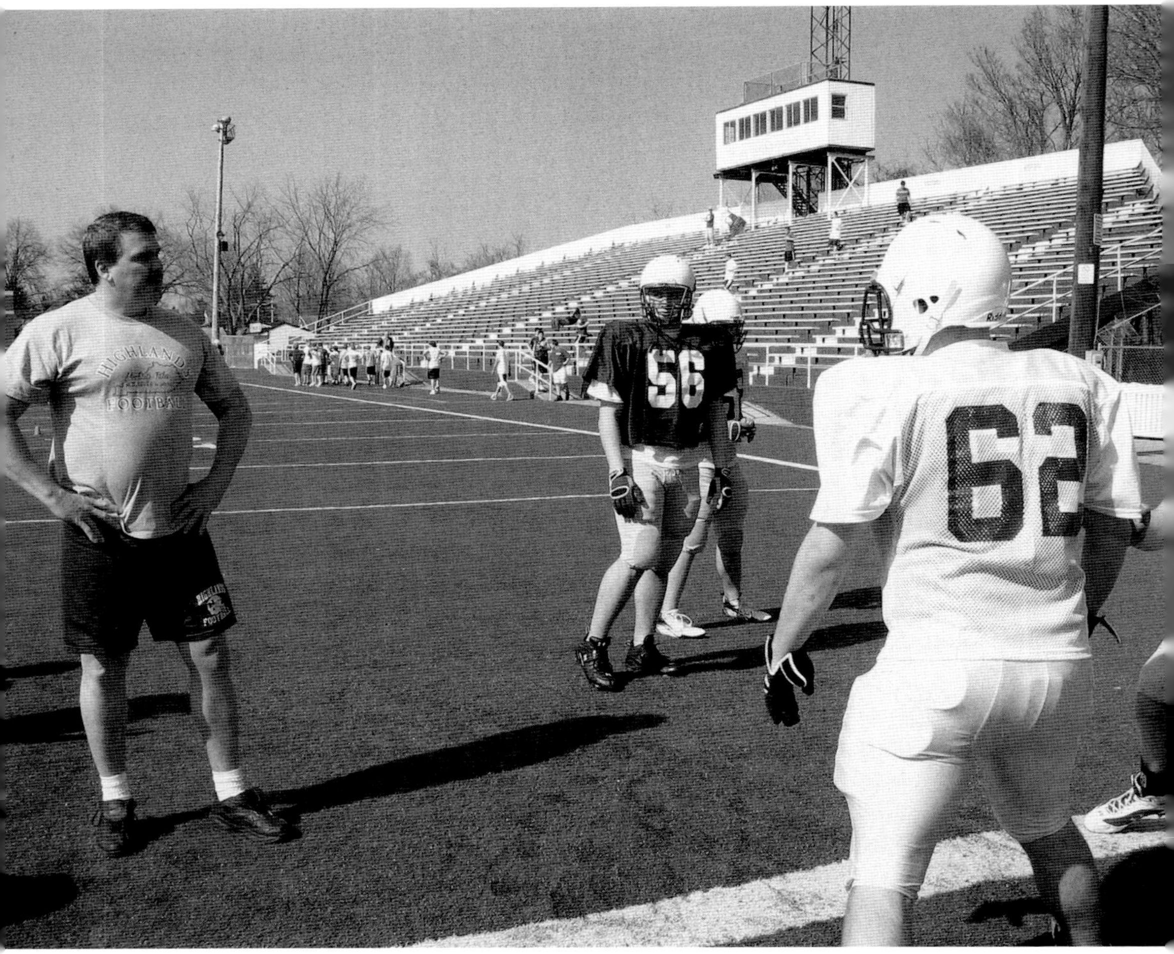

Coach Mark Dill shouts instructions to the defensive line during a spring football practice. Coach Dill is a volunteer coach and a lieutenant on the Fort Thomas police force. The freshman football team can be seen running stadium laps in the background. The varsity players in this photograph are junior Jarred Frank (No. 56) and sophomore Hunter Schlosser (No. 62).

4

SUMMER PRACTICES

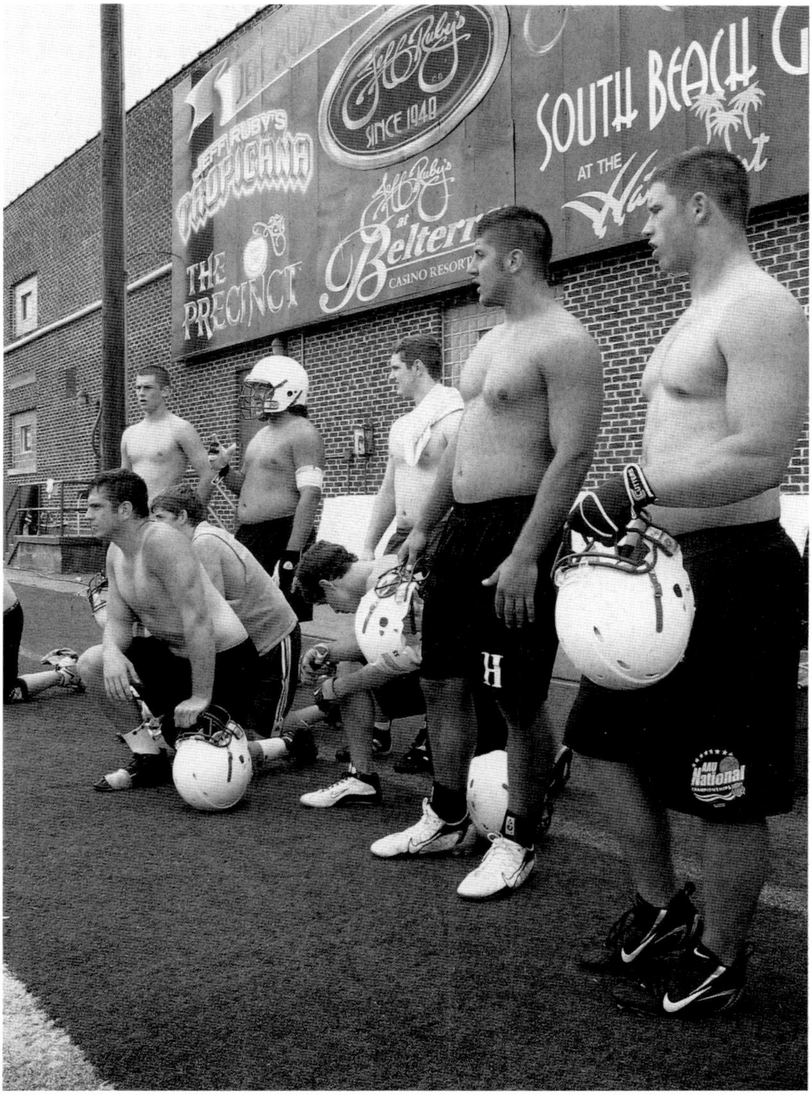

Highlands' defensive players watch from the sideline as Highlands competes with Cincinnati Withrow in a 7-vs.-7 passing scrimmage. Highlands spent much of the early summer competing against Cincinnati schools in non-contact passing scrimmages. Players in this photograph, from left to right, are Spencer Bankemper, Zach Hurtt, Milton Peko, Josh Frost, Luke Stein, and Ryan Ball.

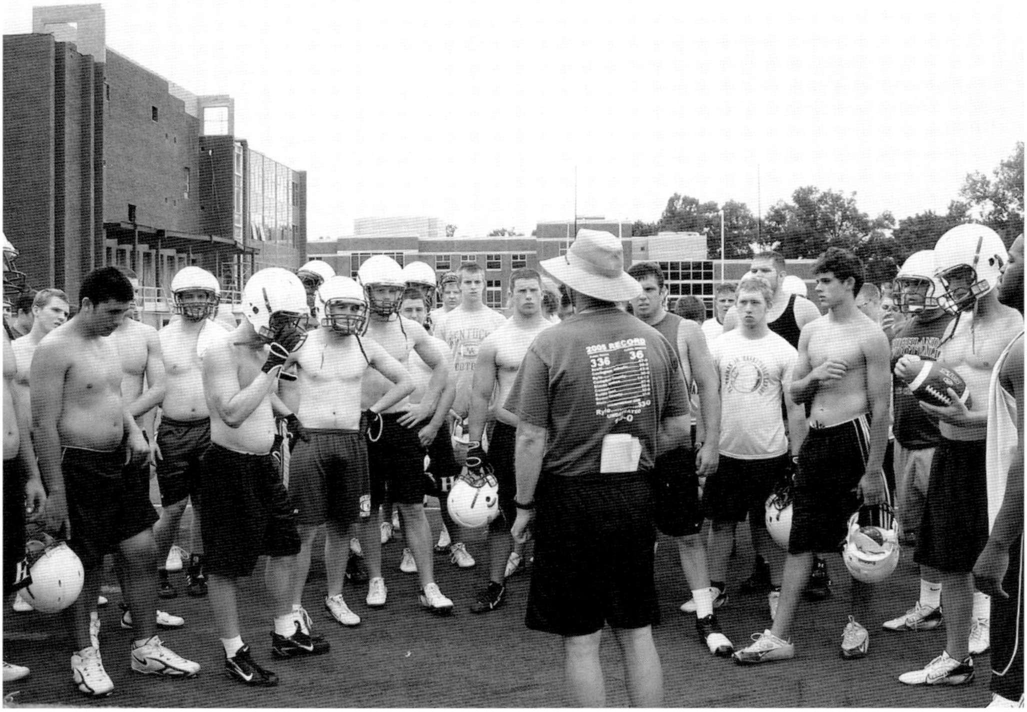

Coach Dale Mueller reviews the day's events with members of his team at the end of a 7-vs.-7 passing scrimmage.

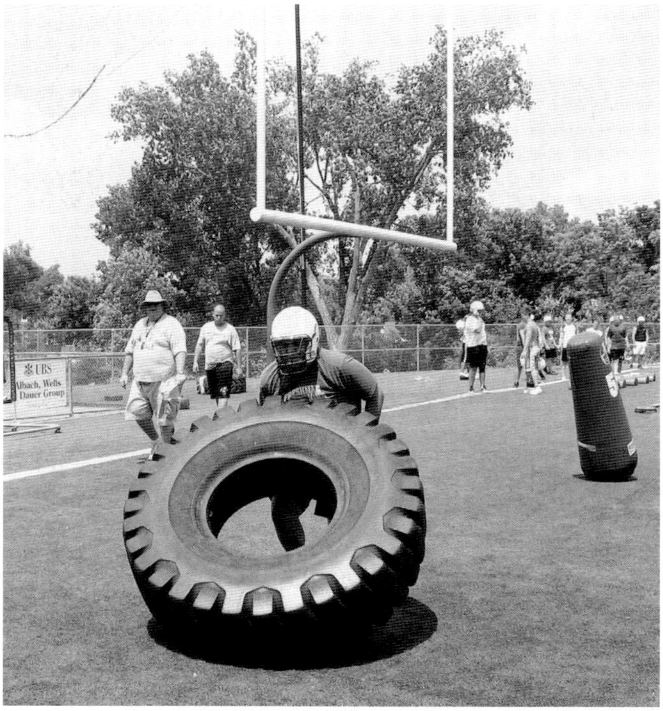

Defensive lineman Kody Rosenhagen flips a tire weighing hundreds of pounds under the watchful eye of coach Scott Turner. The linemen often do competitive drills while the quarterbacks, receivers, and running backs participate in 7-vs.-7 scrimmages with other teams. Coach Turner is the offensive line coach at Highlands and played football at Newport High School. He teaches science at the high school.

Clay Cecil (left) and Drew Simons (right) throw passes to youngsters attending the Highlands football camp in June. Kids play in the Fort Thomas Junior Football League before playing on the freshman team at Highlands.

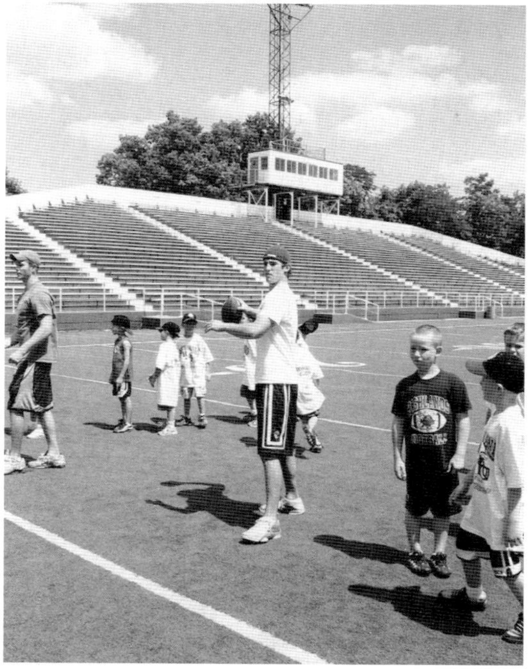

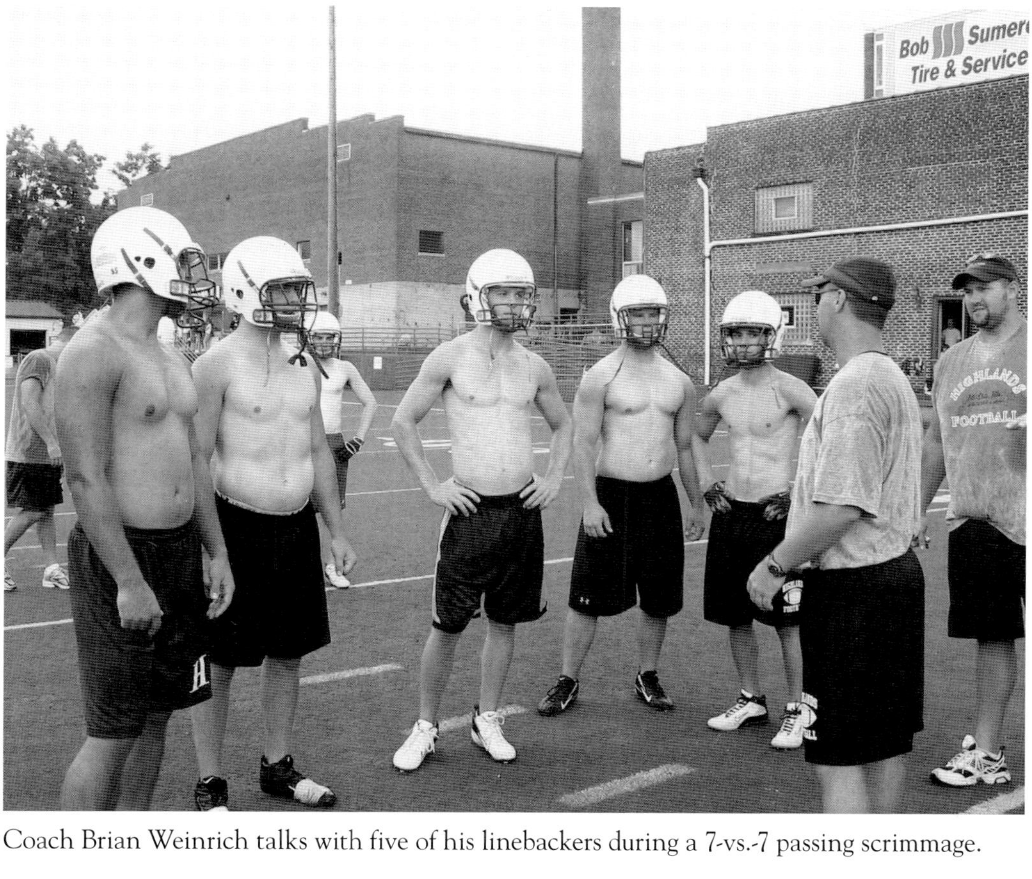

Coach Brian Weinrich talks with five of his linebackers during a 7-vs.-7 passing scrimmage.

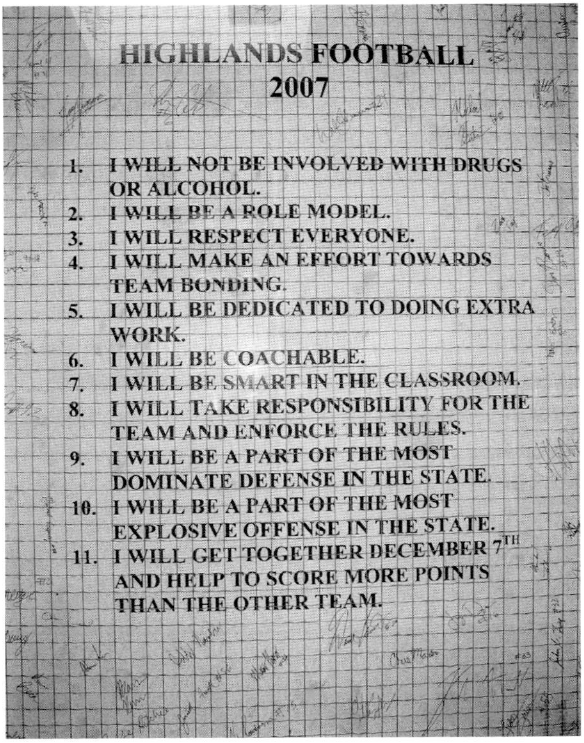

The players came up with a set of rules to follow during the 2007 football season. Each class elected a group of players to meet and come up with the rules that were approved in a team meeting. Each player signed a poster that was hung in the locker room and also received a smaller version of the poster to sign and take home.

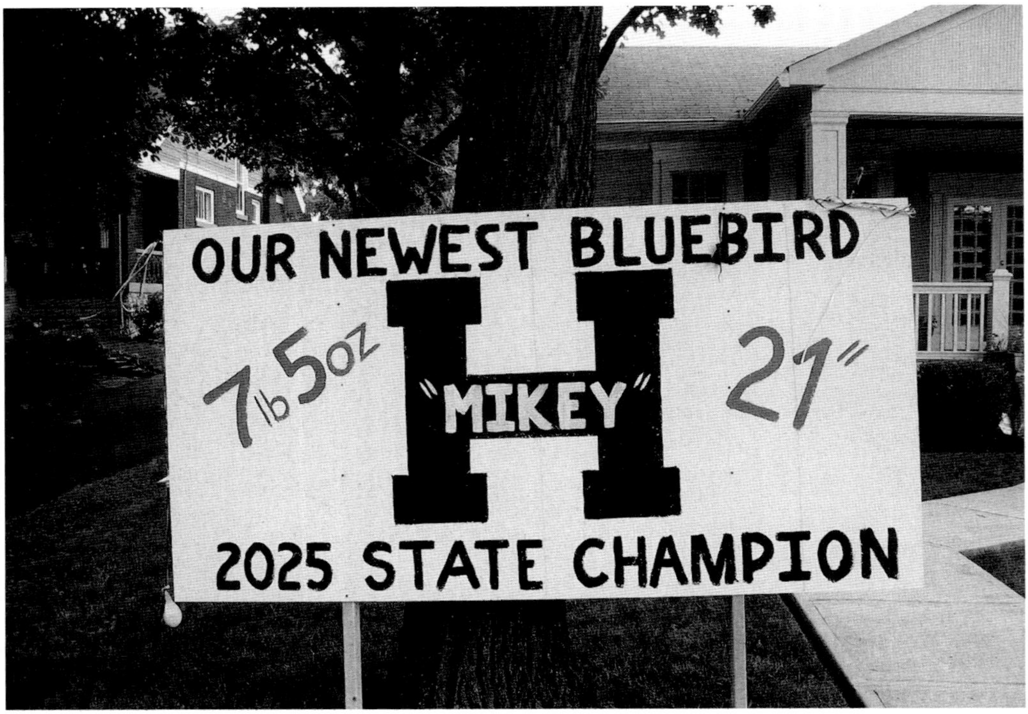

This sign was posted in the front yard of the home owned by Mick and Natalie Abner after the birth of their son Mikey.

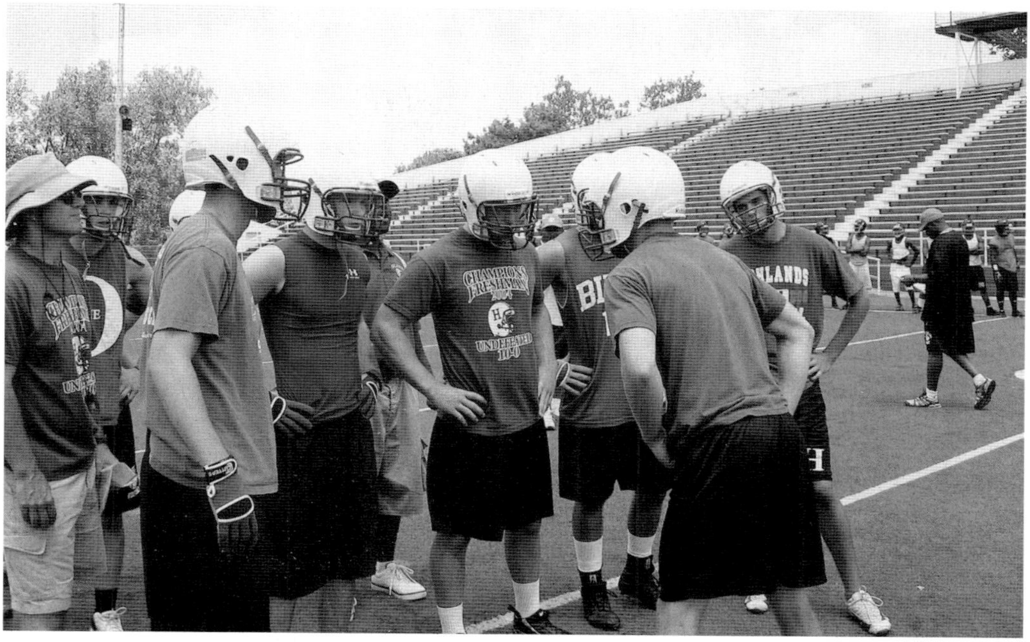

Quarterback Clay Cecil calls the play under the watchful eye of coach Mueller (left) during a 7-vs.-7 passing scrimmage against Cincinnati Withrow. These scrimmages were valuable because they helped develop passing and pass coverage skills. "You have to be prepared to pass the football even if you are predominately a running team," noted coach Mueller. "We work more on our passing game than our running game over the summer months."

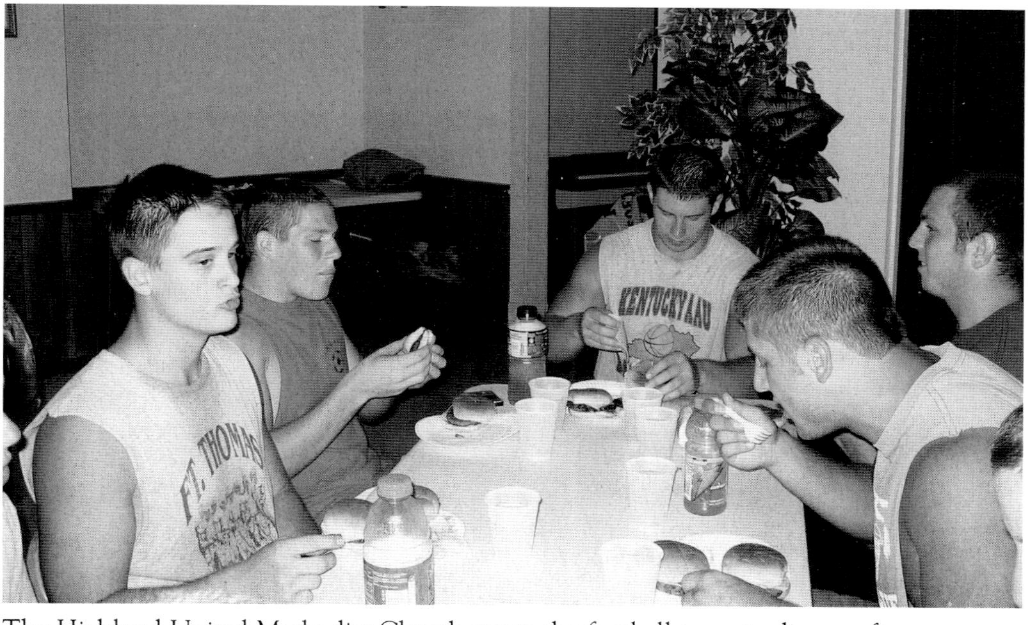

The Highland United Methodist Church treats the football team to dinner after a summer practice. The church is located across the street from the high school. Enjoying their meal from left to right are Adam Reis, Drew Bathiany, Ryan Ball, Luke Stein, and Zach Hurtt.

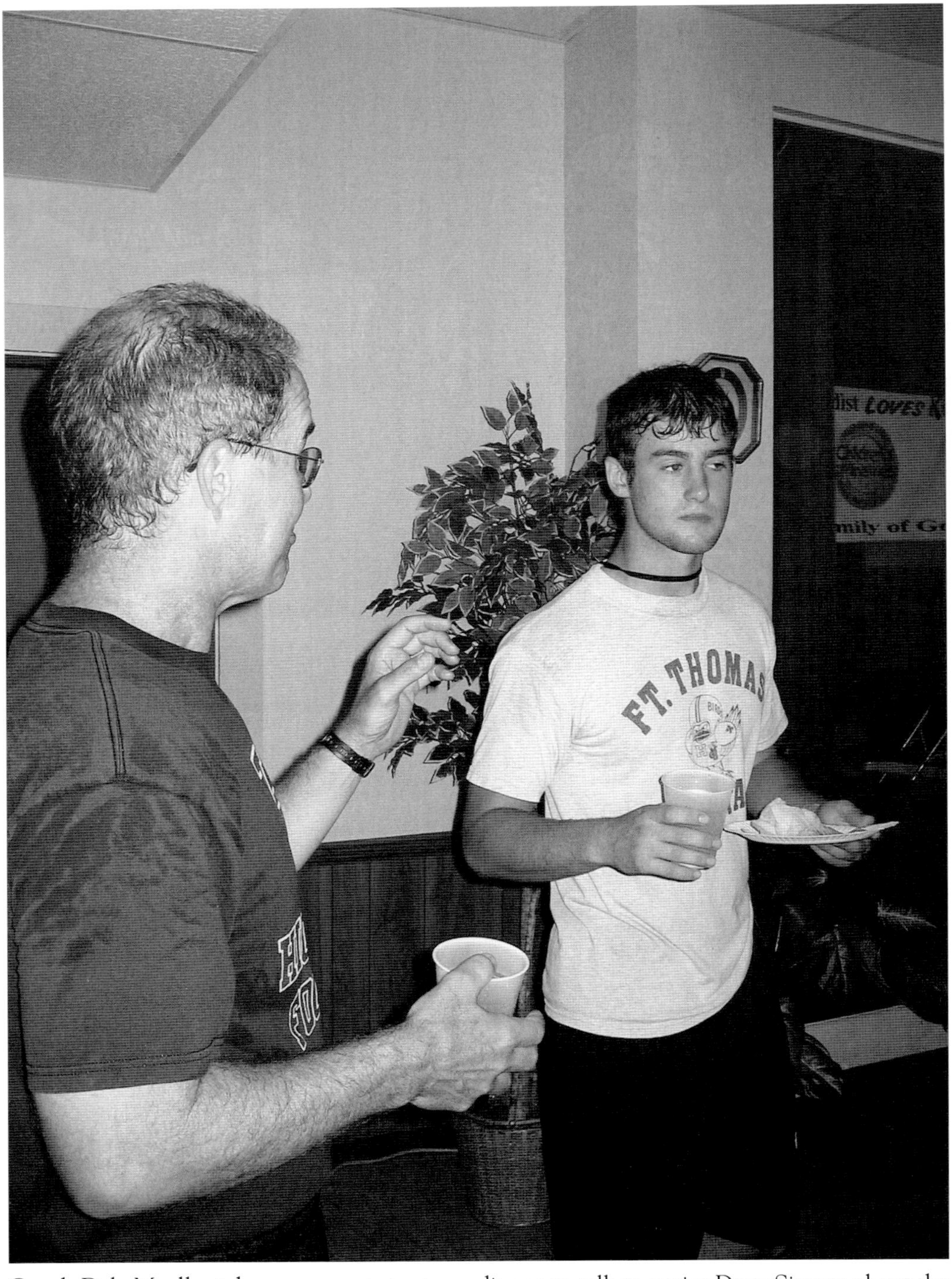

Coach Dale Mueller takes a moment at a team dinner to talk to senior Drew Simons about the possibility that he could see some action at wide receiver in the upcoming season. Simons was a starter for three seasons at outside linebacker.

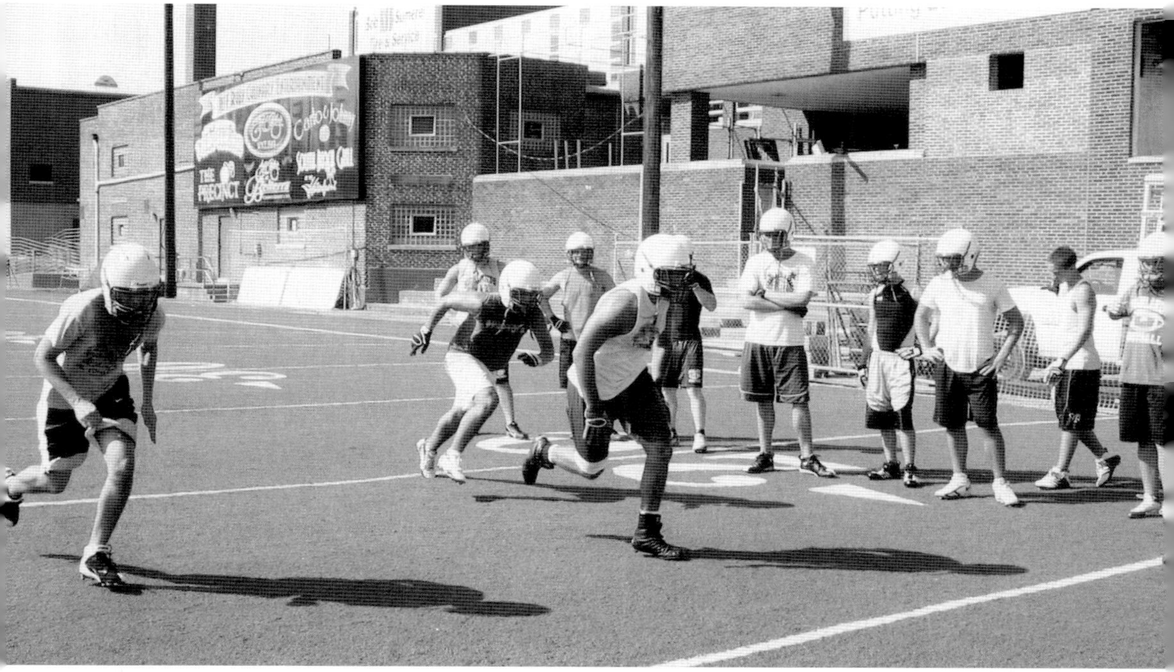

Jay Draper, Brandon Roller, and Trey Jurgens compete in a relay quickness drill at the end of a three-hour practice in August. The players worked out in extreme heat all summer. Coach Mueller usually practiced twice a day in late July and August. The first practice would begin at 7:00 a.m. and end at noon, and the second practice would run from 6:00 to 9:00 p.m. Practices often included lifting weights and watching film in the school.

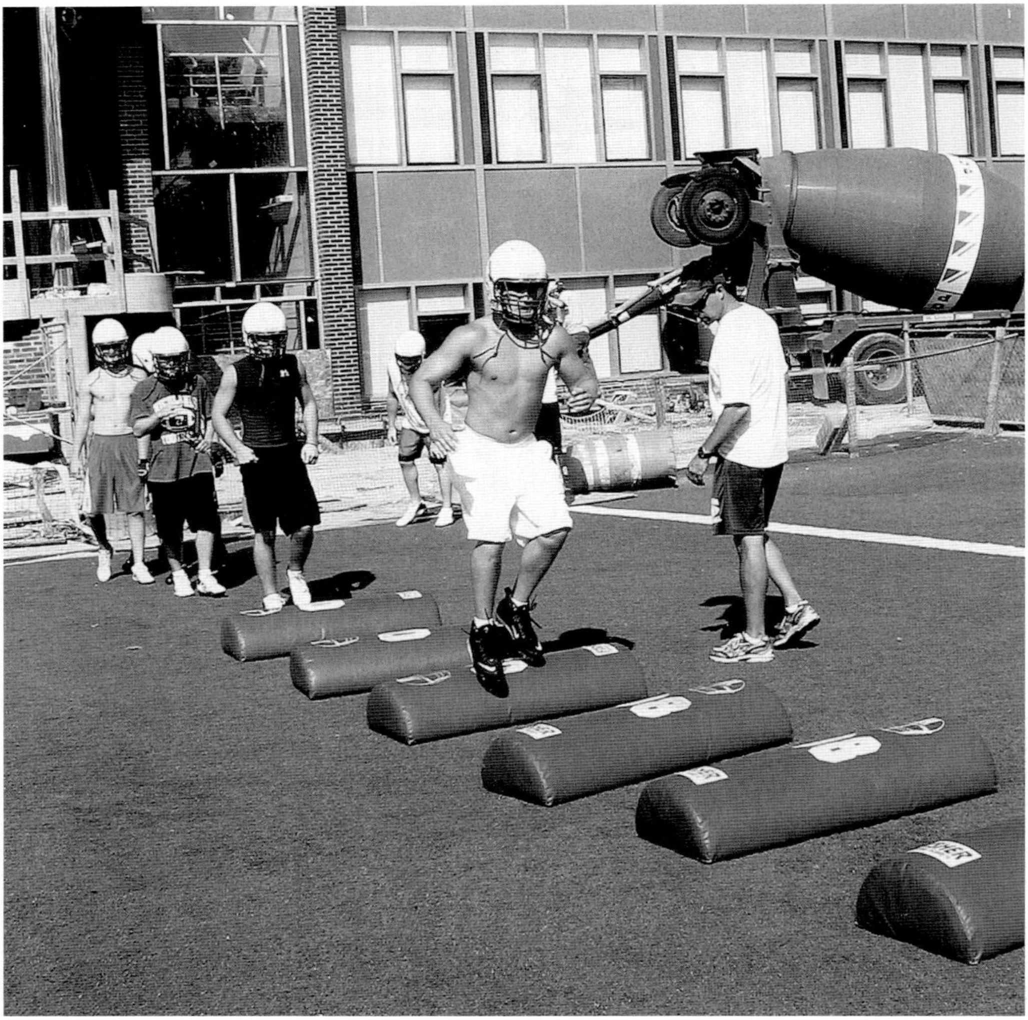

Coach Kevin Eichman supervises an agility drill during a summer practice session. Oliver Head, a junior, is jumping over the bags and junior Josh Conner (wearing a dark shirt) is about to begin the drill. Coach Eichman is a volunteer coach who works with the wide receivers and outside linebackers. He is a native of Kansas and played quarterback in high school. Coach Eichman owns a computer software business in Cincinnati.

5

The Regular Season

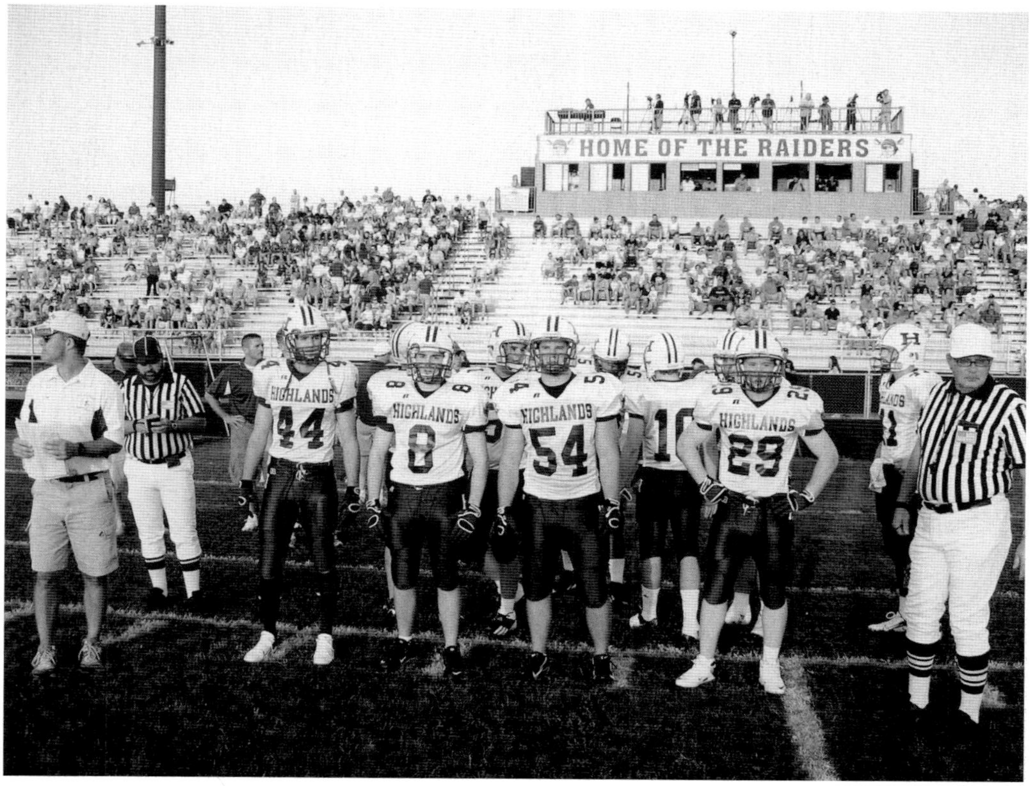

Highlands' senior captains and coach Dale Mueller (left) line up for the coin toss before the beginning of the season-opening game against Ryle High School. The captains, from left to right, are Drew Simons, Matt Reed, Ryan Ball, and Terry O'Brien. Ryle was the 2006 Class 4A Kentucky state runner-up, but Highlands had little trouble defeating the Raiders by a score of 49-21. The score was 28-0 at halftime. Junior running back Josh Conner rushed for 227 yards and five touchdowns on 19 carries for Highlands.

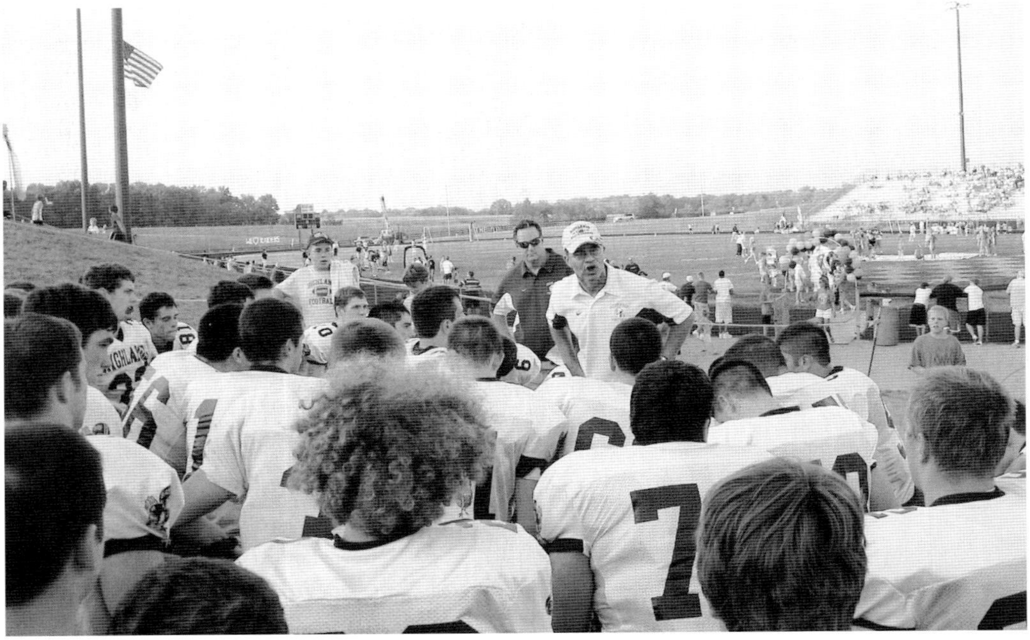

Coach Dale Mueller gives his pre-game talk to the team on the hillside outside the locker room at Ryle High School. He told the team that they had a chance to become one of the greatest teams in the history of Highlands High School. He also told them that they would have to earn that honor on the football field.

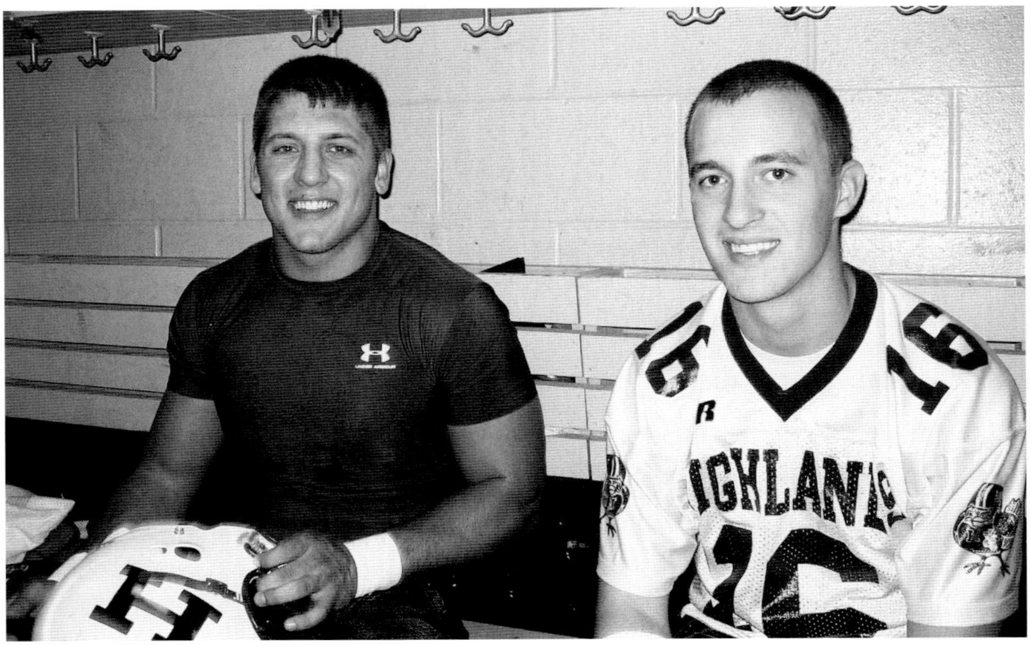

Seniors Luke Stein and Jay Draper relax in the locker room prior to the season opener against Ryle High School. Stein went on to become an All State linebacker with college offers during the season from Holy Cross and Gardner Webb. Draper started all season at wide receiver.

Coach Charlie Barr enjoys a laugh on the sidelines of a freshmen game early in the season. Coach Barr's team struggled to a 6-4 record this season after going undefeated in 2004, 2005, and 2006. Coach Barr has coached the Highlands freshman team for nearly 30 years and also scouts for the varsity team on Friday nights. He is excellent at preparing young players for the jump from the Fort Thomas Junior Football League to the varsity football team at Highlands.

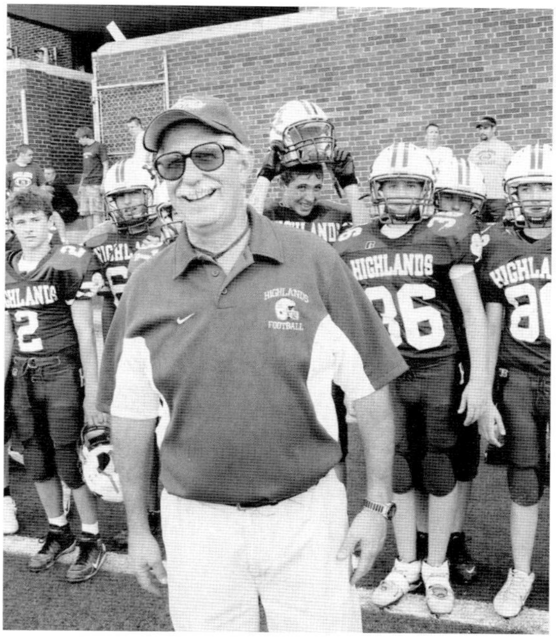

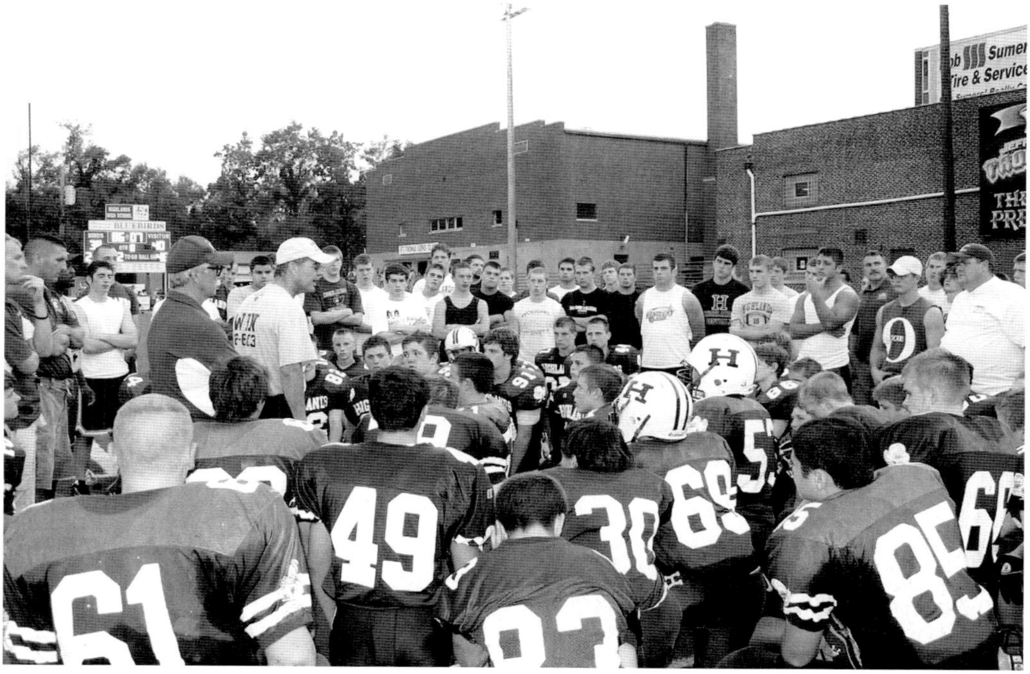

After the freshman football team lost its first game of the season and the first game since 2003, coach Mueller gathered his varsity players and talked to the freshman team on the field. Coach Mueller wasn't happy with their effort and told the players that they had to become more disciplined on and off the football field. He pointed out that they needed to pay better attention to their coaches and make every practice a great one. The freshman team went on to finish second in the Northern Kentucky playoffs.

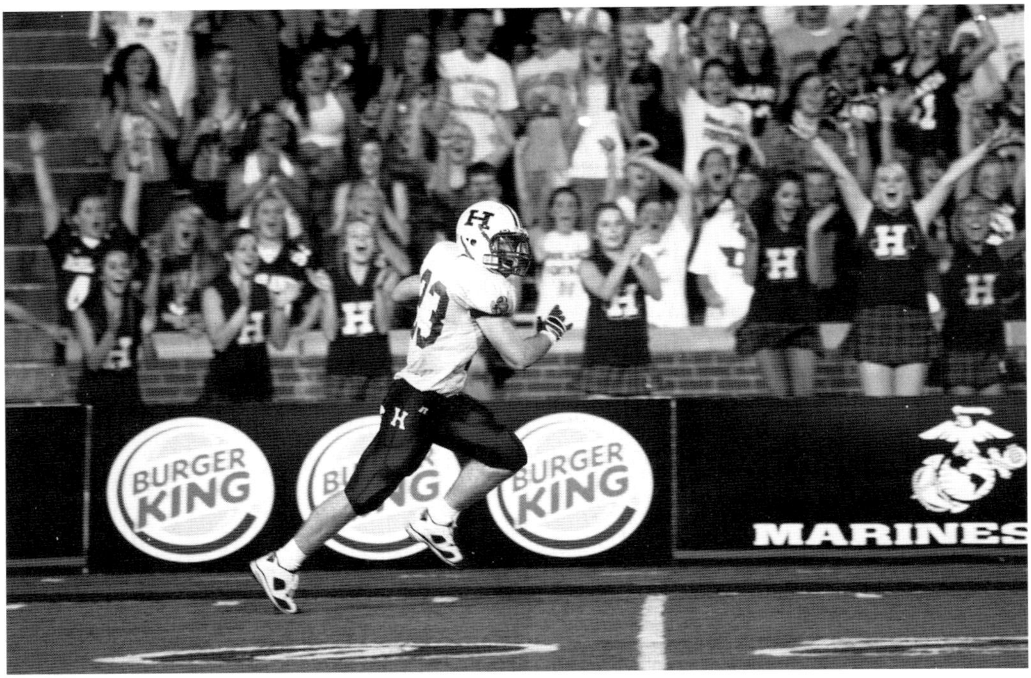

Josh Conner is on his way to a 51-yard touchdown after catching a game-winning pass from quarterback Tony Guidugli against Trotwood-Madison. Highlands won the game 24-20 in the Kirk Herbstreit Ohio-vs.-USA Challenge III at Nippert Stadium at the University of Cincinnati. The Bluebirds gained 313 total yards on the ground in the game. (Courtesy of BluegrassPreps.com.)

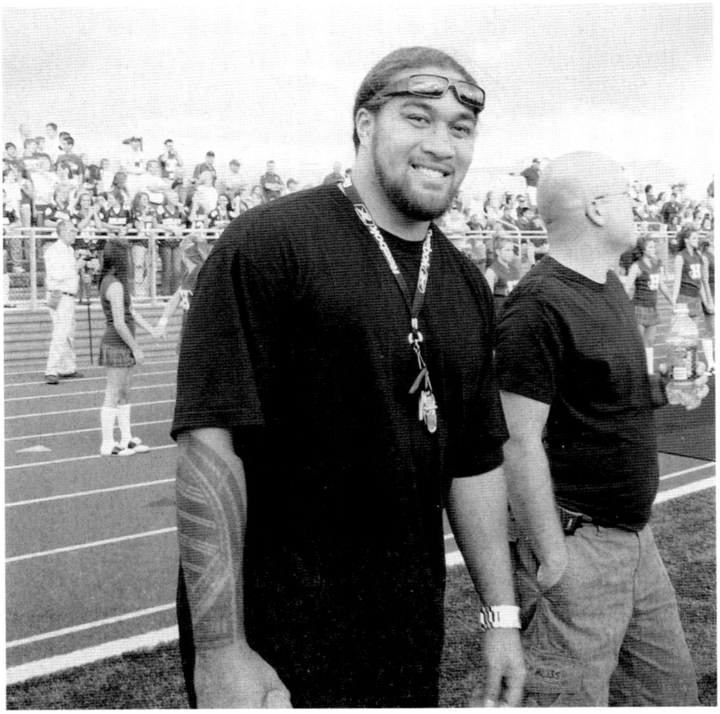

Domata Peko, starting defensive tackle for the Cincinnati Bengals, watched Highlands defeat Dixie Heights by a score of 44-14 in September. Peko's nephew Milton was a starting defensive lineman for Highlands in 2007.

Michael Buten is all smiles on the sidelines after catching an 85-yard touchdown pass thrown by Josh Conner in the victory over Dixie Heights.

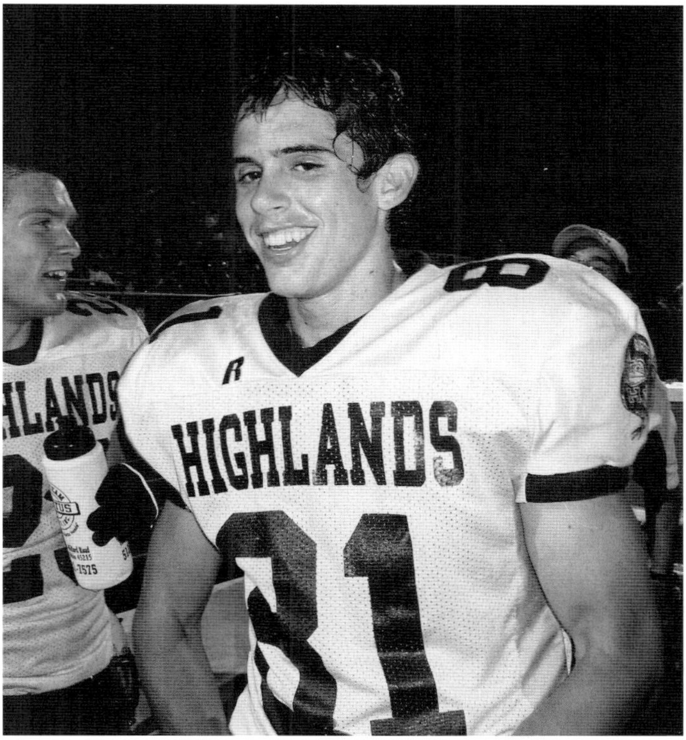

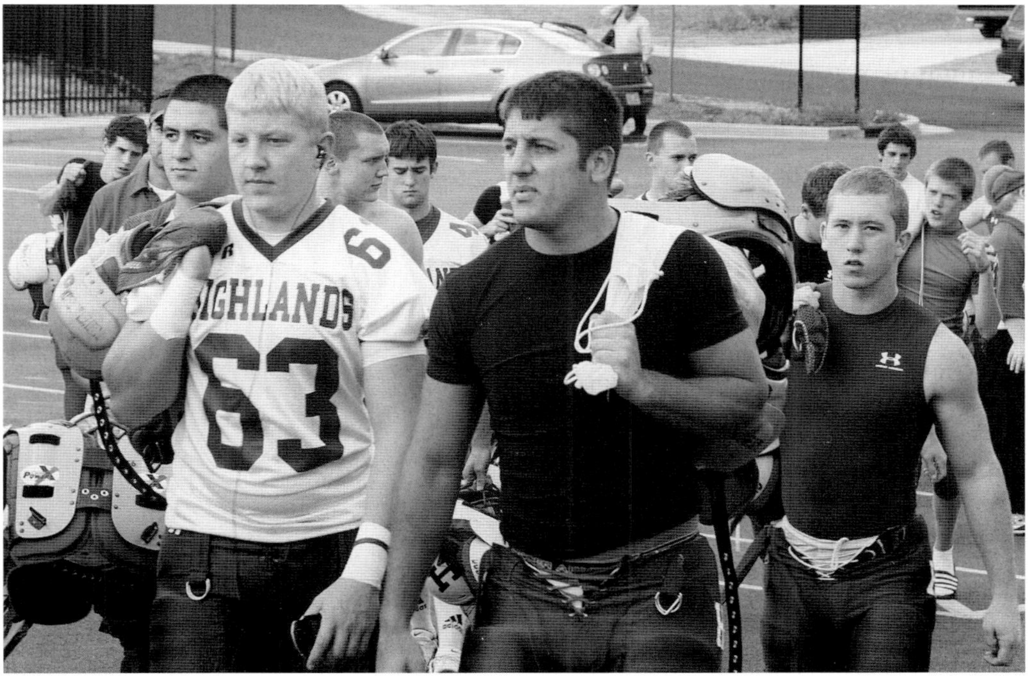

Highlands players arrive by bus for the game against Dixie Heights. Players closest to the camera are, from left to right, Jarred Frank, Adam Dempsey (No. 63), Luke Stein, and Terry O'Brien. (Courtesy of Ed Harber.)

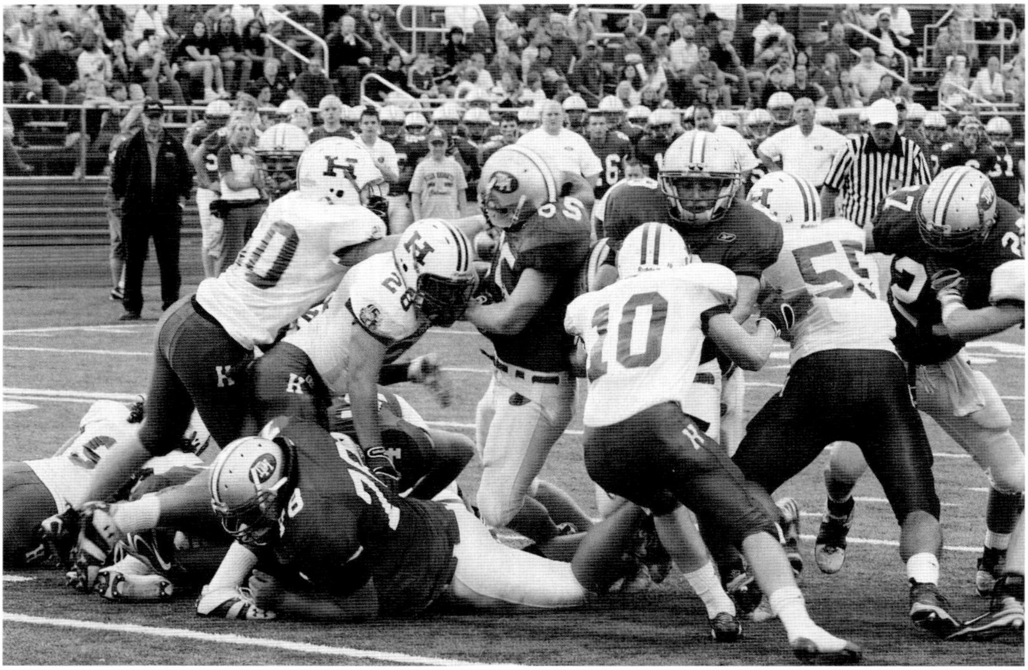

Highlands' defense swarms Dixie Heights en route to a 44-14 victory. Pictured from left to right are Joe Fitzgerald (No. 60), Michael Laber (No. 28), Drew Bathiany (No. 10), and Luke Stein (No. 55).

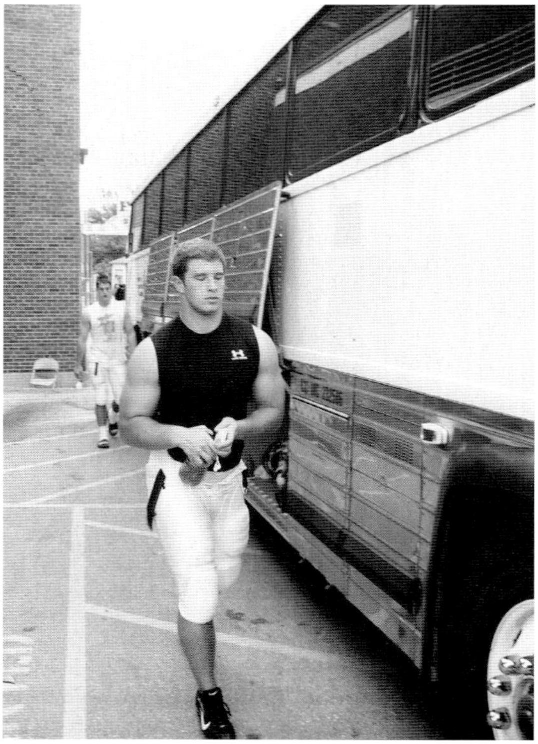

Ryan Ball and Adam Reis prepare to board the team bus to travel to Park Hills for the big match-up with rival Covington Catholic. Highlands has dominated competition between the two football powers, but in 2006, Covington Catholic beat Highlands twice and won the Class 3A state championship. Highlands' players had waited to play this game for nearly a year. Everything in practice is geared toward beating Covington Catholic. Even roll call during winter weight lifting reflects the intensity of the rivalry. When coach Dale Mueller calls a player's name in the weight room, the player's response is "Beat Colonels."

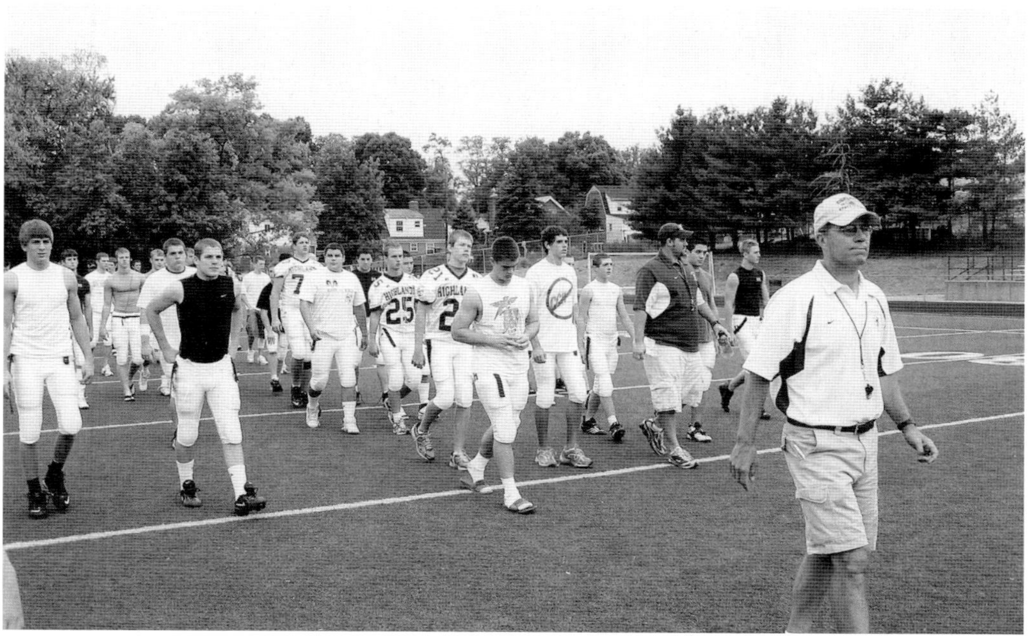

Coach Dale Mueller leads his team across Covington Catholic's field before pre-game warm-ups. Coach Mueller likes to get his team moving after taking a bus trip to an away game.

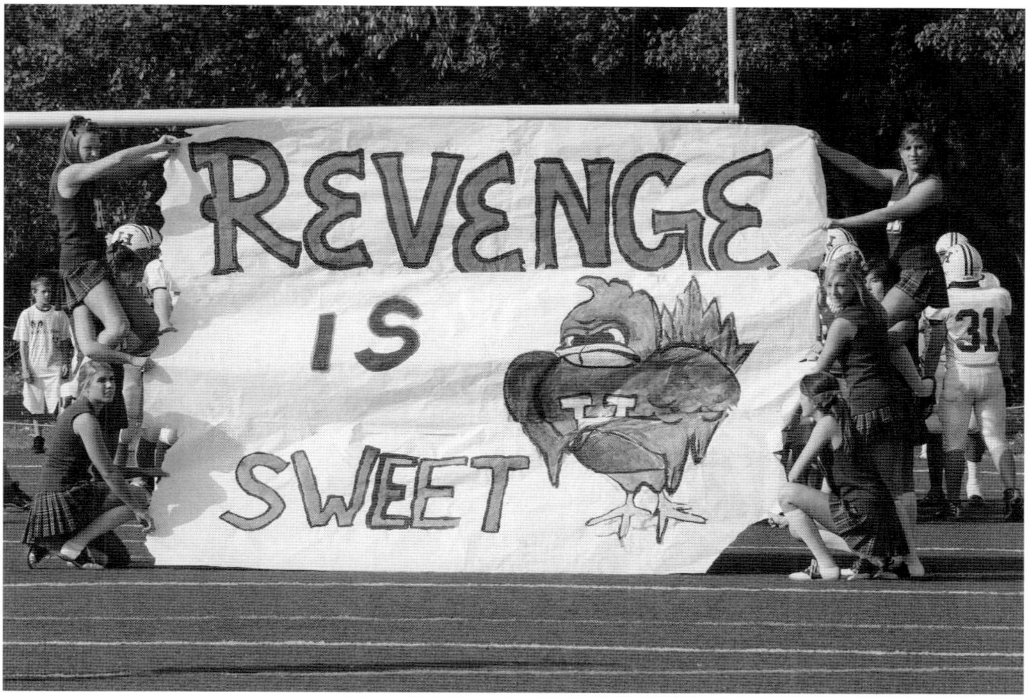

Highlands cheerleaders hold up a banner that says it all before the start of the Covington Catholic game that Highlands won by a score of 28-14. Highlands has won 17 of the last 21 contests between the two schools. A day later, the Highlands junior varsity team defeated Covington Catholic's junior varsity by a score of 53-21. (Courtesy of Ed Harber.)

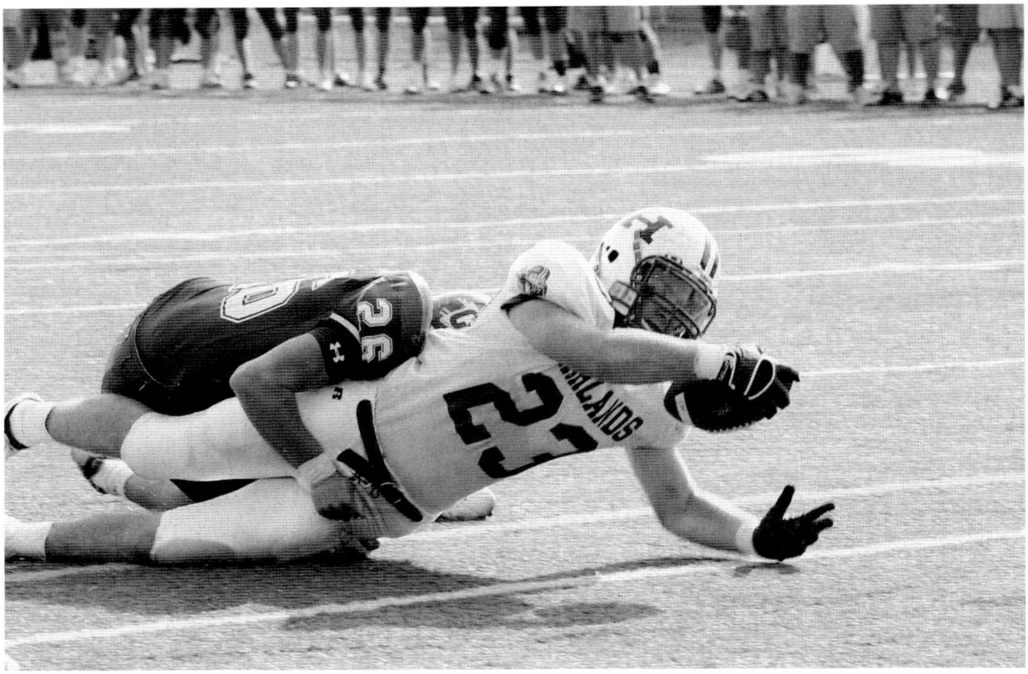

Josh Conner crosses the goal line for a Highlands touchdown in the regular season win over Covington Catholic. (Courtesy of Ed Harber.)

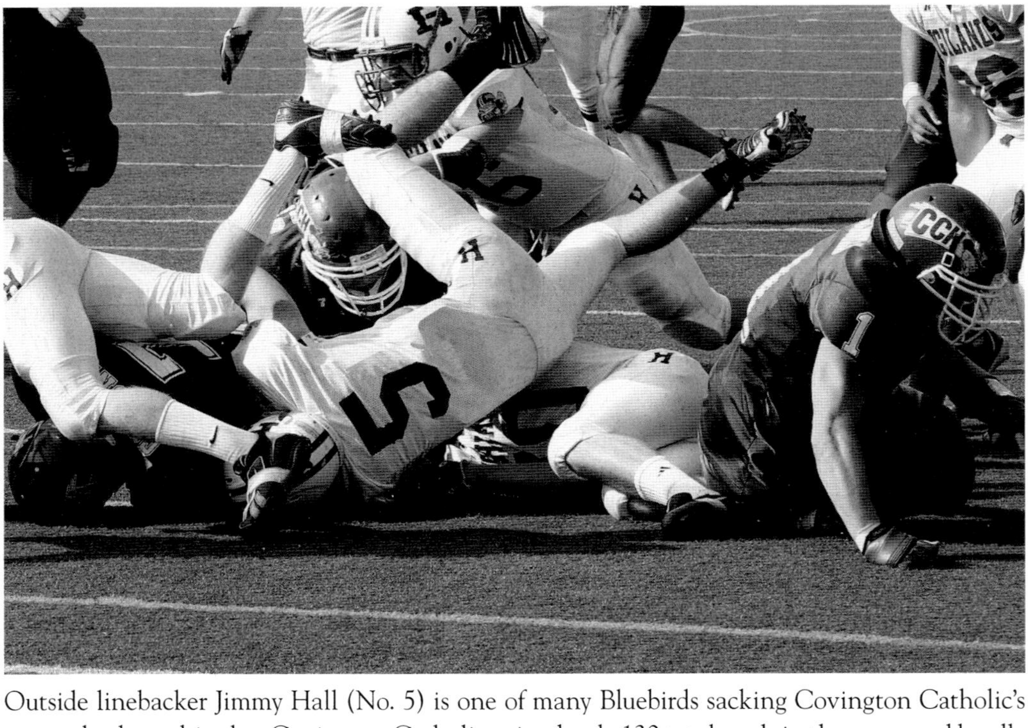

Outside linebacker Jimmy Hall (No. 5) is one of many Bluebirds sacking Covington Catholic's quarterback on this play. Covington Catholic gained only 130 total yards in the game and hardly touched the ball in the second half. (Courtesy of Ed Harber.)

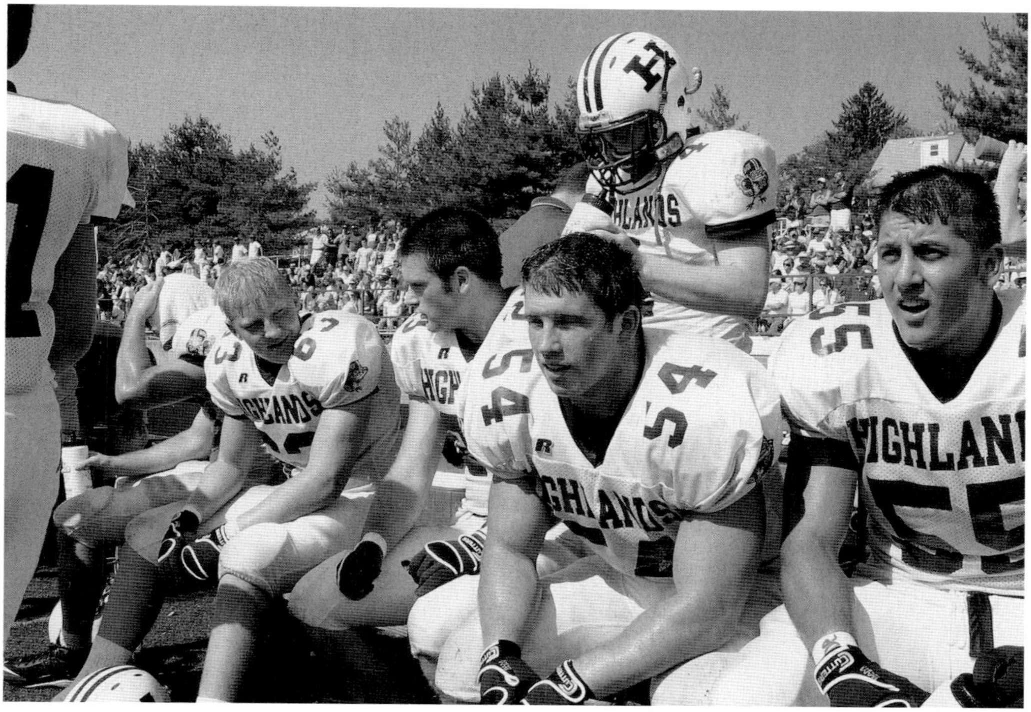

Highlands' offense takes a break on the sideline after scoring a touchdown in the game against Covington Catholic. Seated players are, from left to right, Adam Dempsey, Josh Conner, Ryan Ball, and Luke Stein. Quarterback Clay Cecil led the attack against Covington Catholic with 53 rushing yards and 124 passing yards.

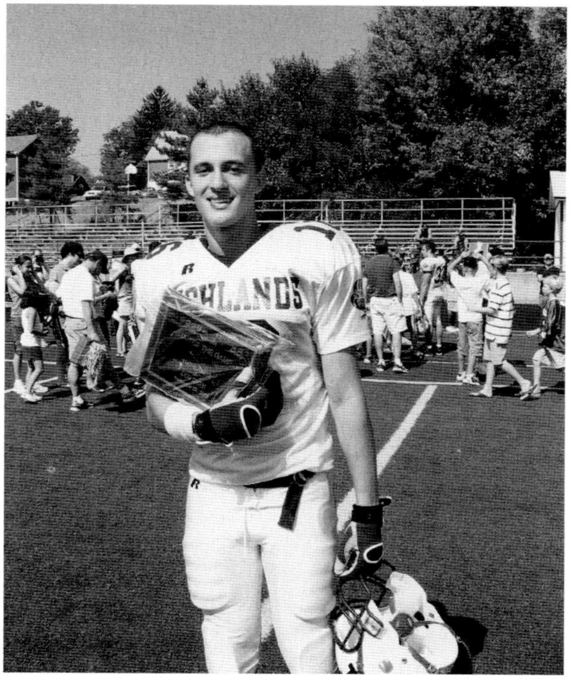

Wide receiver Jay Draper holds the Most Valuable Player trophy presented to him by a local radio station at the conclusion of the victory over Covington Catholic. Draper caught four passes for 116 yards against Covington Catholic.

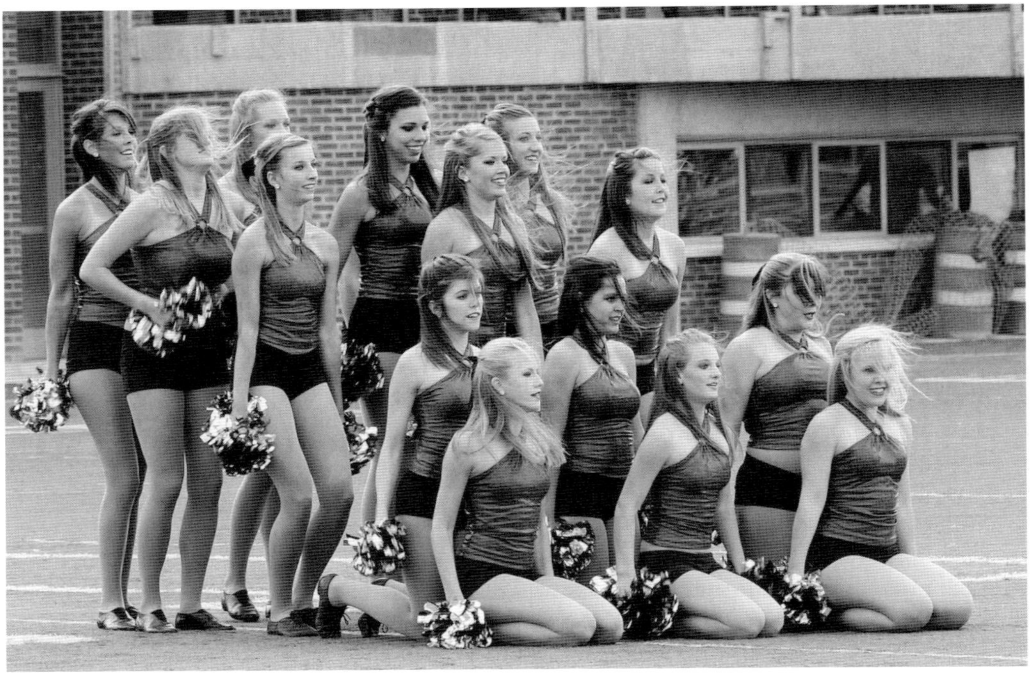

The Highlands dance team prepares to take the field for a performance at halftime of the home game against Covington Holmes. The dance team was organized a year ago and performs at football and basketball games. (Courtesy of Ed Harber.)

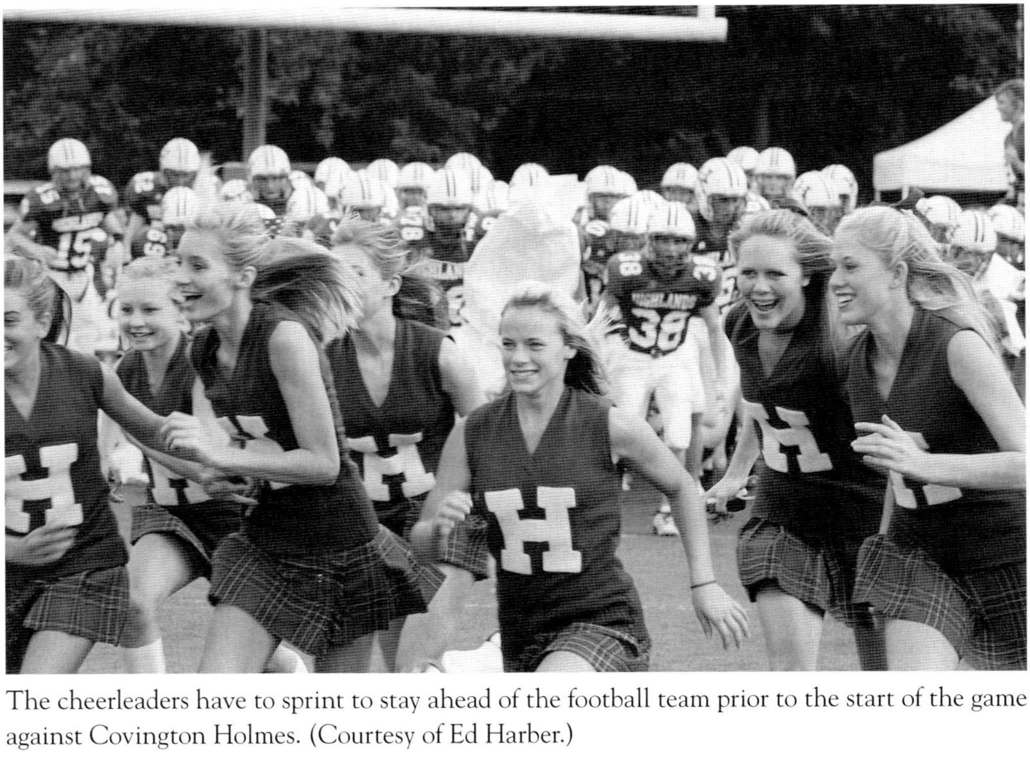

The cheerleaders have to sprint to stay ahead of the football team prior to the start of the game against Covington Holmes. (Courtesy of Ed Harber.)

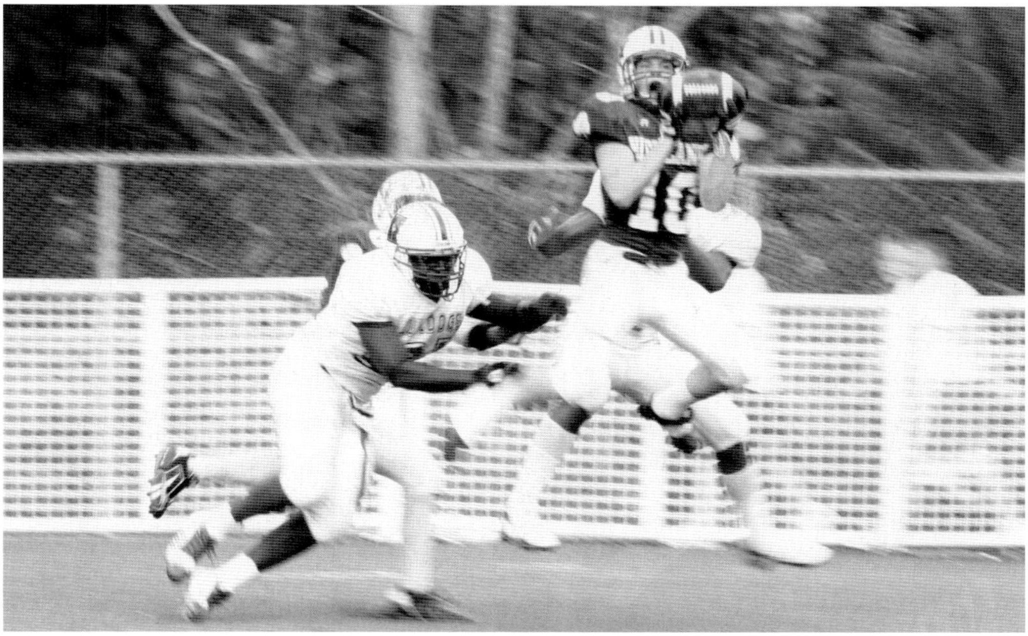

Senior defensive back Drew Bathiany comes up with a big interception against Covington Holmes. Highlands went on to defeat the Bulldogs by a score of 52-14. Steve Lickert, a former Highlands football player who went on to play for Georgetown College, is the coach at Covington Holmes. (Courtesy of Ed Harber.)

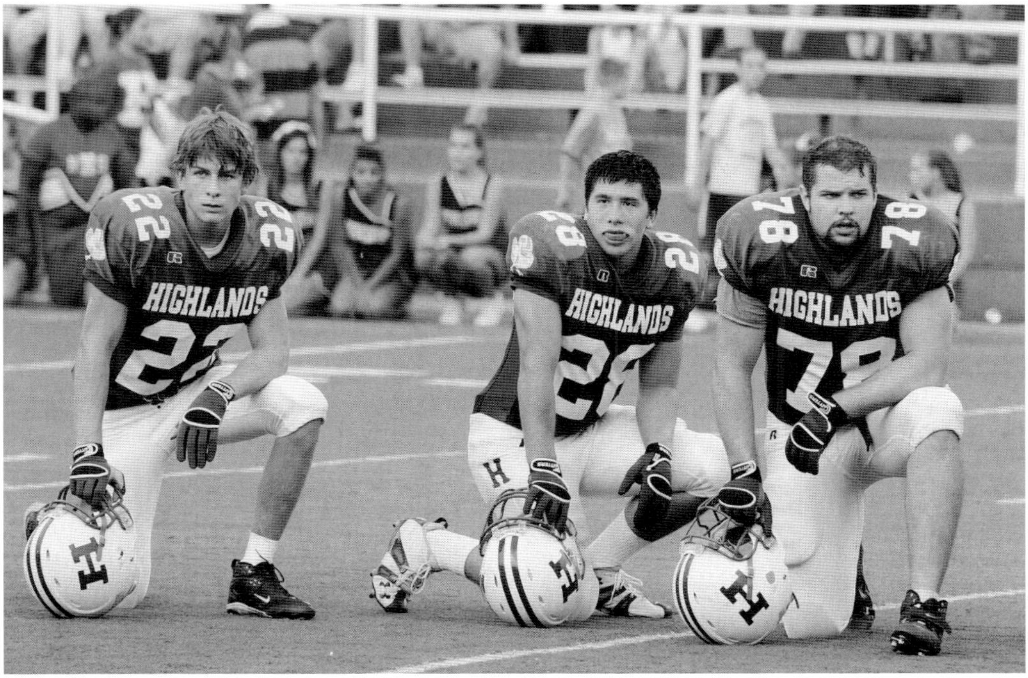

Austin Collinsworth (No. 22), Michael Laber (No. 28), and Alex Hempfling (No. 78) take a break before the Bluebirds kick an extra point against Covington Holmes. (Courtesy of Ed Harber.)

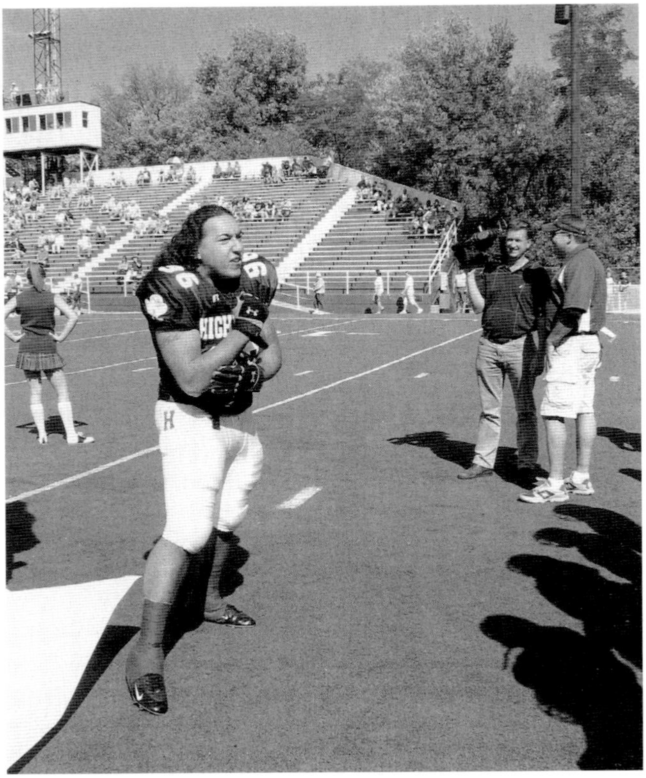

Milton Peko fired the team up before every game by doing a Samoan war chant. Peko is an American Samoan who moved to Fort Thomas from California in 2007. He believes American Samoans are such good football players because they have always been a warrior culture and have no wars to fight anymore. Instead young Samoan boys have turned to football. Peko was a force on the defensive line for Highlands all season.

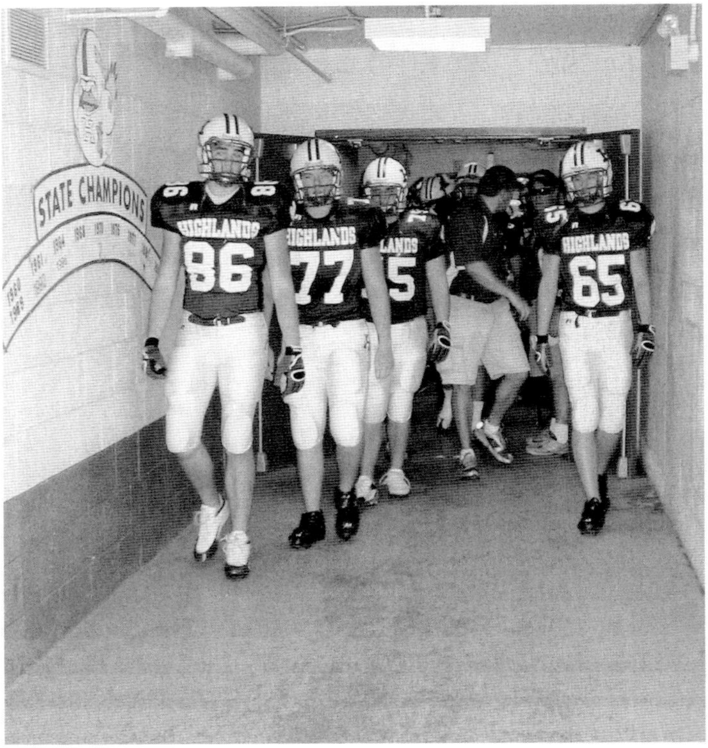

Players from Highlands start down the hallway from the locker room before the game against Hopkinsville. Players, from left to right, are sophomore Kyle Welz (No. 86), sophomore Tyler Combs (No. 77), junior Kody Rosenhagen (No. 75), and junior Nick Martin (No. 65). Highlands defeated Hopkinsville by a score of 42-8 behind the running of junior Josh Conner. Austin Collinsworth came up with two interceptions in the game and also returned a punt 63 yards for a touchdown.

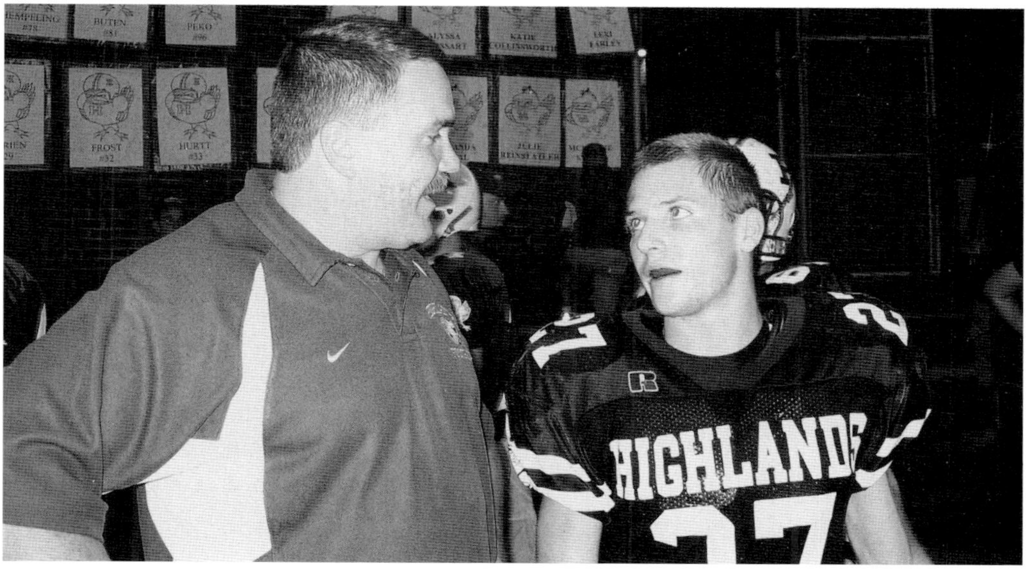

Assistant coach Mark Dill congratulates junior running back Clint Crawford after Crawford ran a kick-off back 93 yards for a touchdown against Scott High School. Highlands defeated Scott by a score of 58-0. Crawford scored four touchdowns in the game.

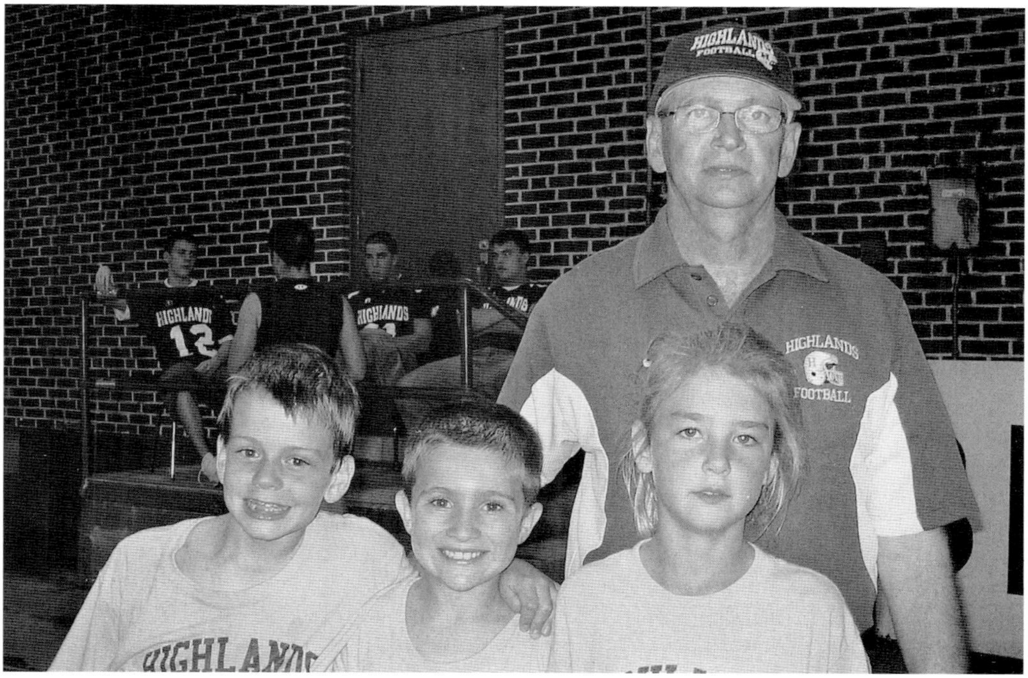

Assistant coach Ron Welch works with three of the young managers of the Highlands football team during the game against Scott High School. Coach Welch is a Vietnam War veteran who played football at Bellevue High School. He is a volunteer coach who does many of the jobs that are necessary to keep the program running smoothly each day. He is in charge of equipment and film exchange, and helps keep the locker room clean.

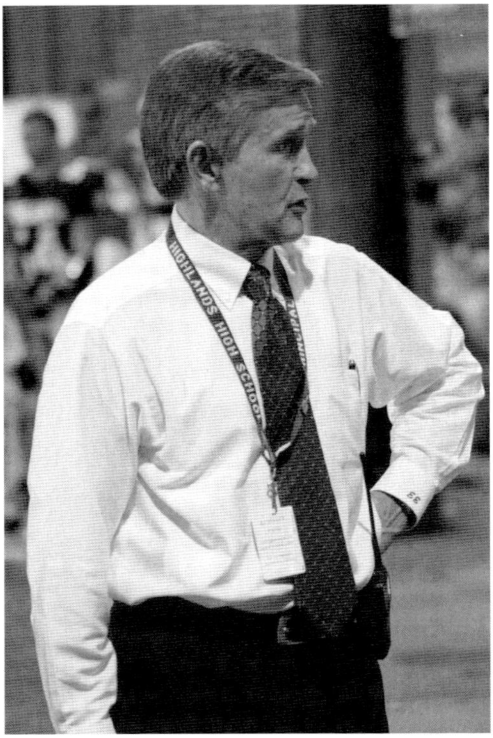

Highlands principal Elgin Emmons is a big supporter of the Highlands football program. (Courtesy of Ed Harber.)

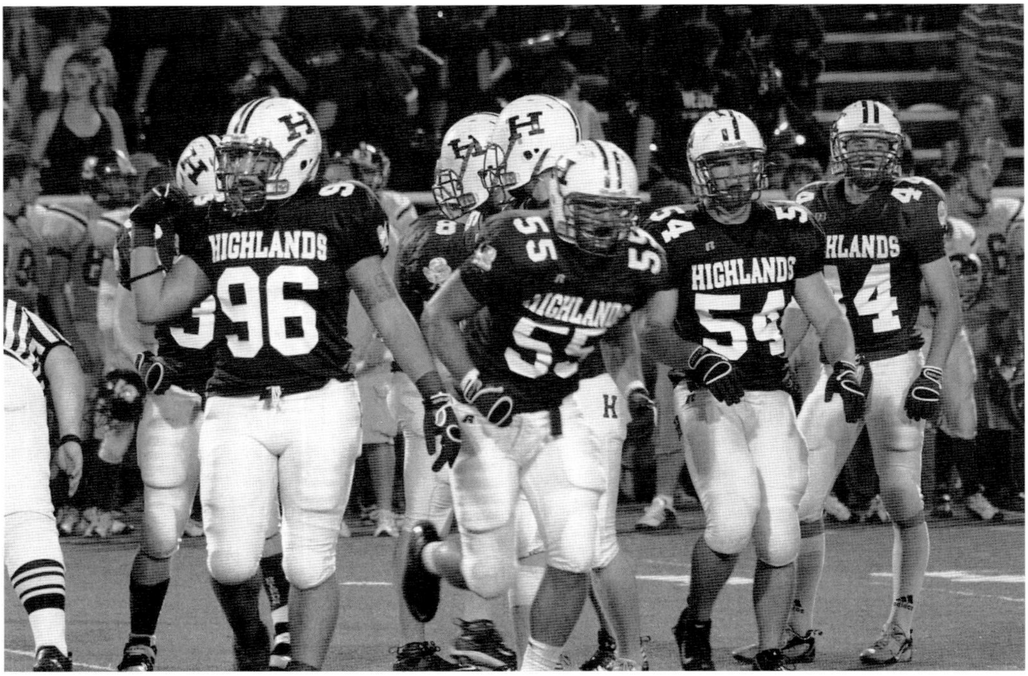

Highlands' defense prepares to leave the field after a big third down stop against Scott High School. Players, from left to right, are Milton Peko (No. 96), Luke Stein (No. 55), Ryan Ball (No. 54), and Drew Simons (No. 44). (Courtesy of Ed Harber.)

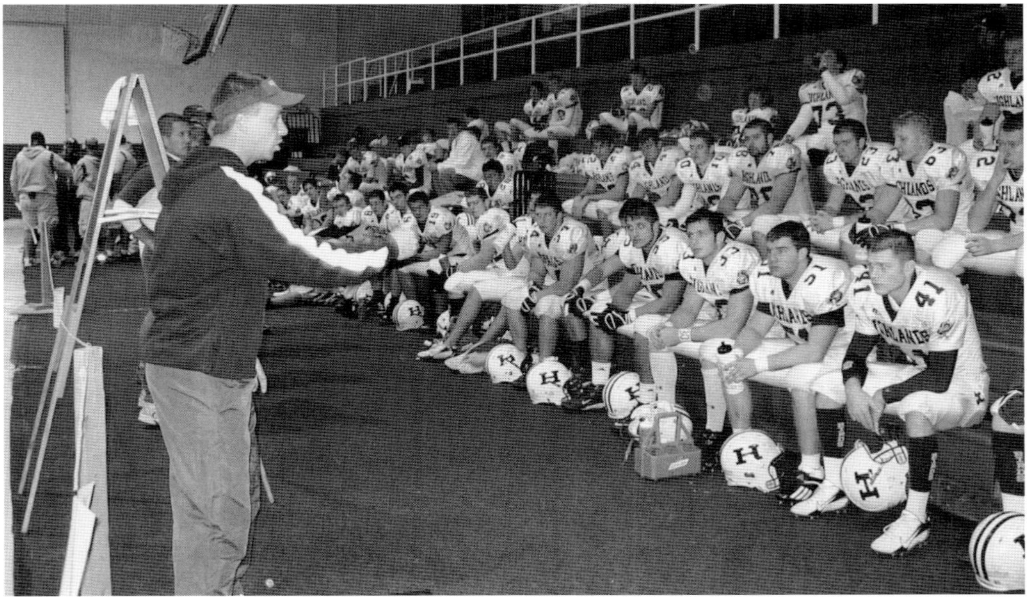

Defensive coordinator Brian Weinrich goes over last minute instructions with the defense in the gym at Lexington Catholic. Highlands struggled in the first quarter against Lexington Catholic before getting untracked and winning by a score of 32-9. Lexington Catholic played eight men in the box on defense and man-to-man coverage on Highlands three receivers. "Things we thought would work, didn't," said Coach Mueller. "We made adjustments to get outside quicker and that helped us take control of the game." Highlands finished the game with 263 yards gained on the ground. Lexington Catholic went on to win the Kentucky Class 4A state championship.

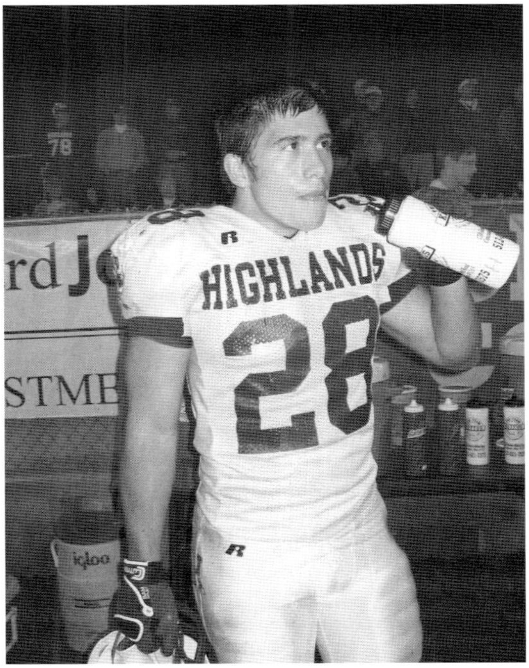

Junior linebacker Michael Laber had a big game against Lexington Catholic.

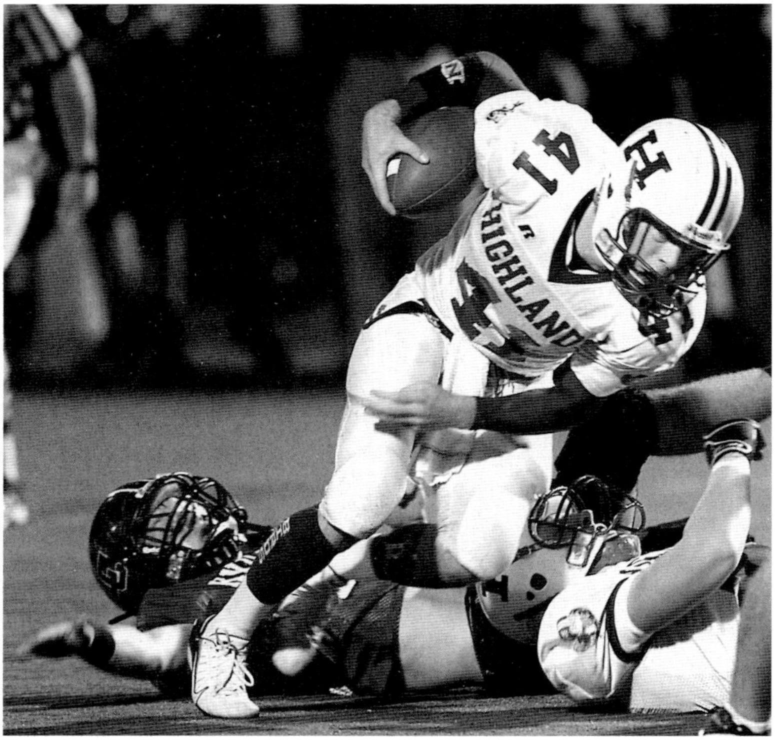

Quarterback Clay Cecil breaks a tackle and gains a few extra yards against Lexington Catholic. (Courtesy of Pablo Alcala.)

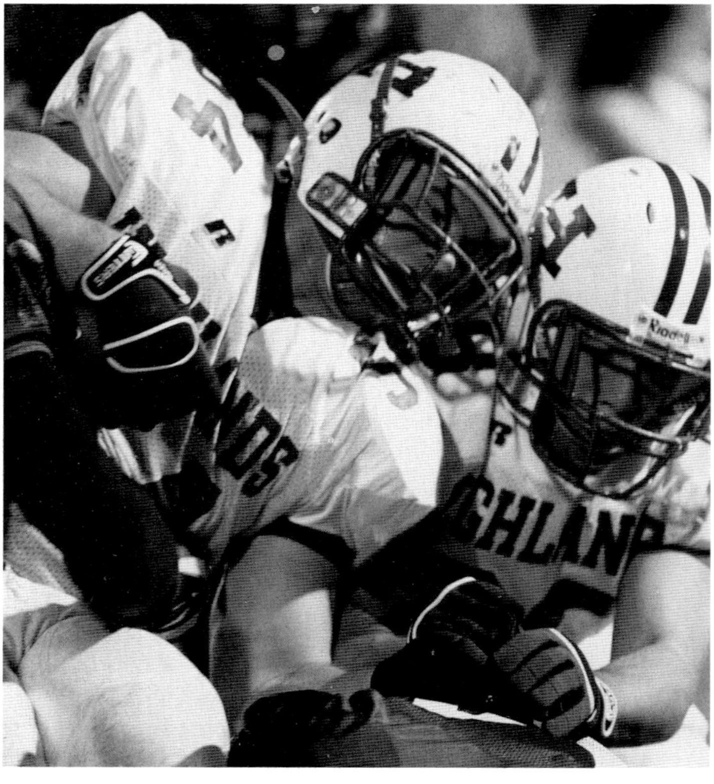

Ryan Ball gains tough yardage on a punt return against Lexington Catholic. (Courtesy of Pablo Alcala.)

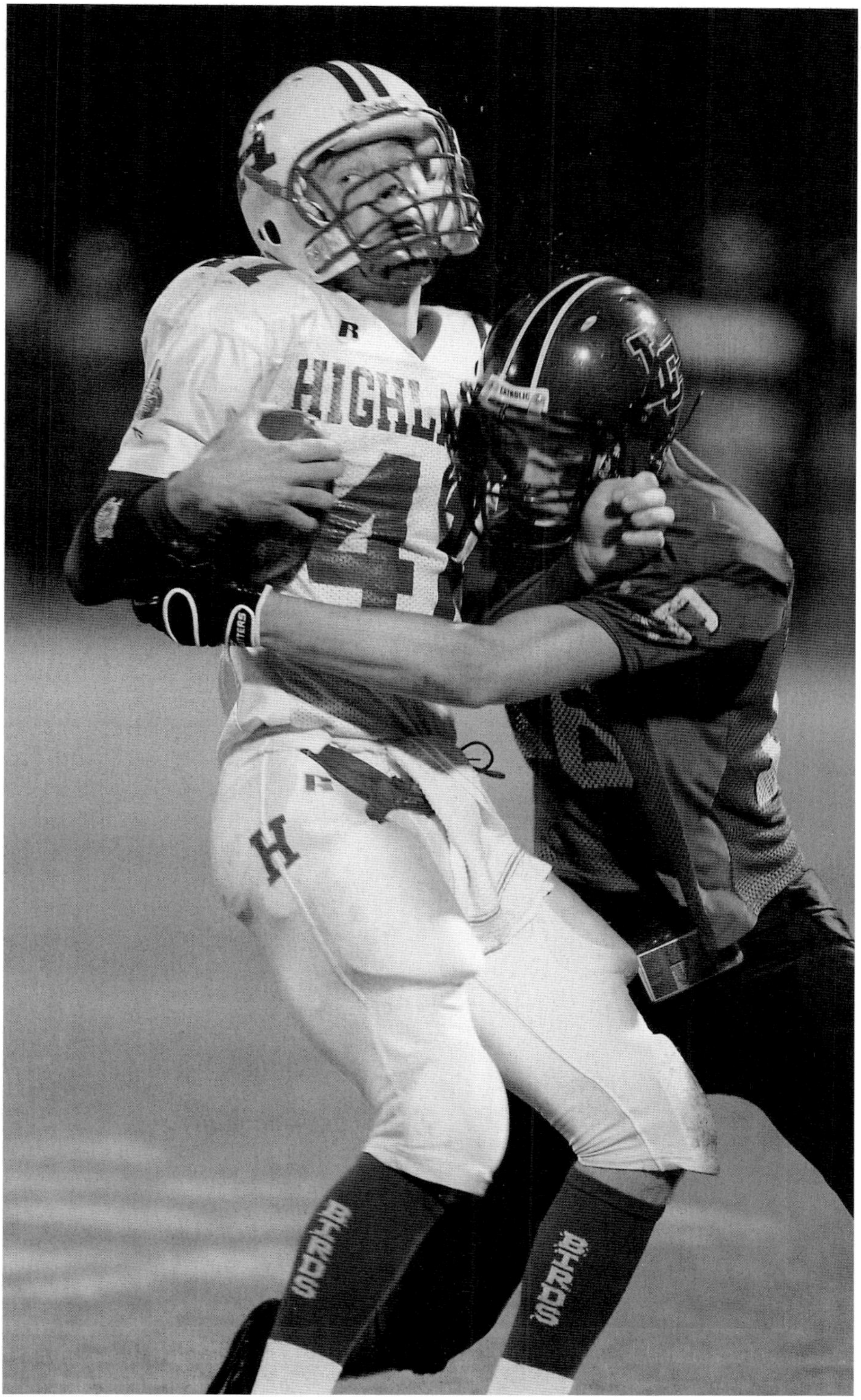

Clay Cecil is hit and dropped for a loss behind the line of scrimmage at Lexington Catholic. (Courtesy of Pablo Alcala.)

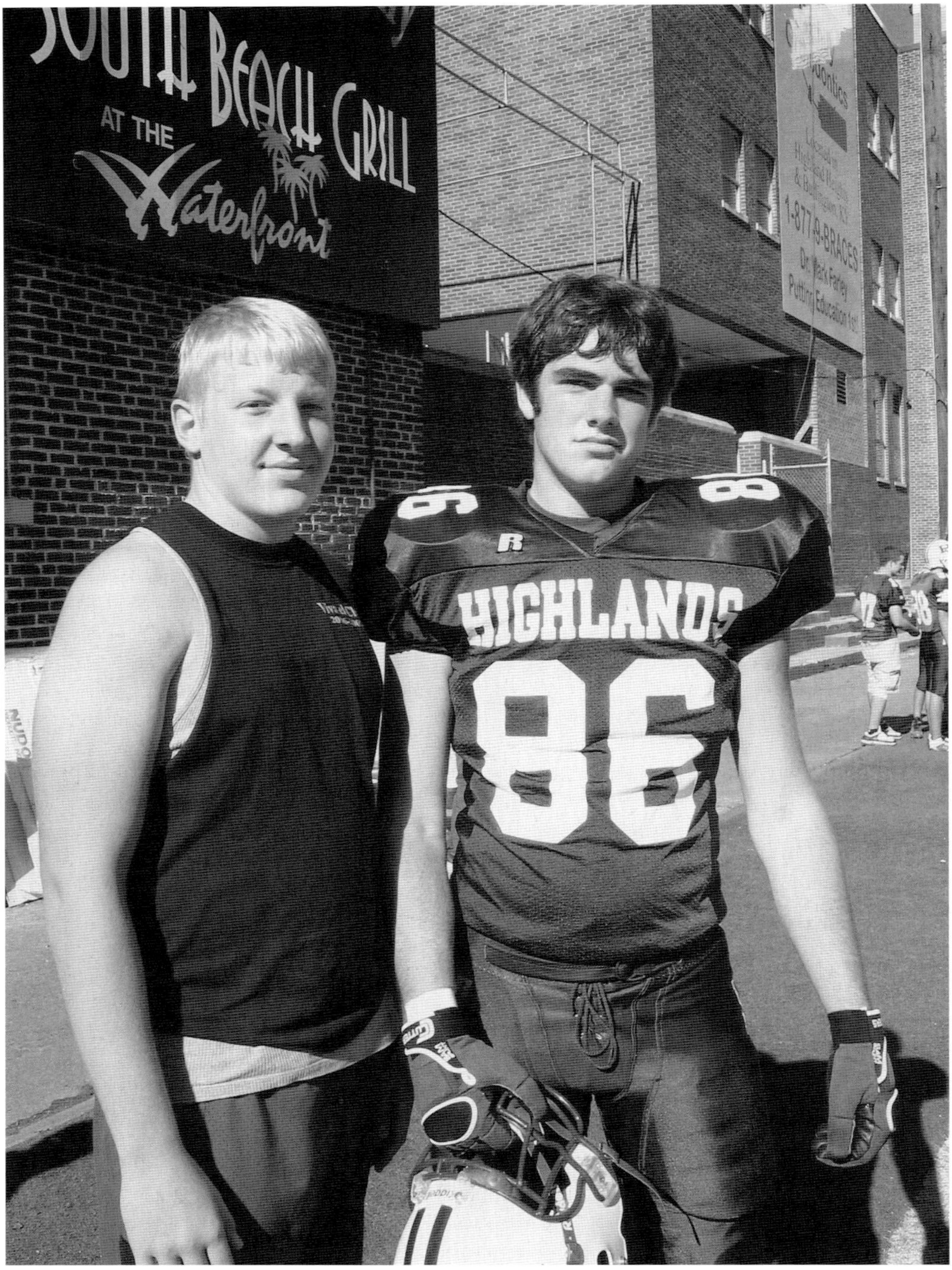

Offensive tackle Adam Dempsey (left) talks with tight end/outside linebacker Kyle Welz before the junior varsity game against Lexington Catholic. Highlands defeated Lexington Catholic by a score of 48-14. The junior varsity team finished the season with a 9-1 record.

6

The State Playoffs

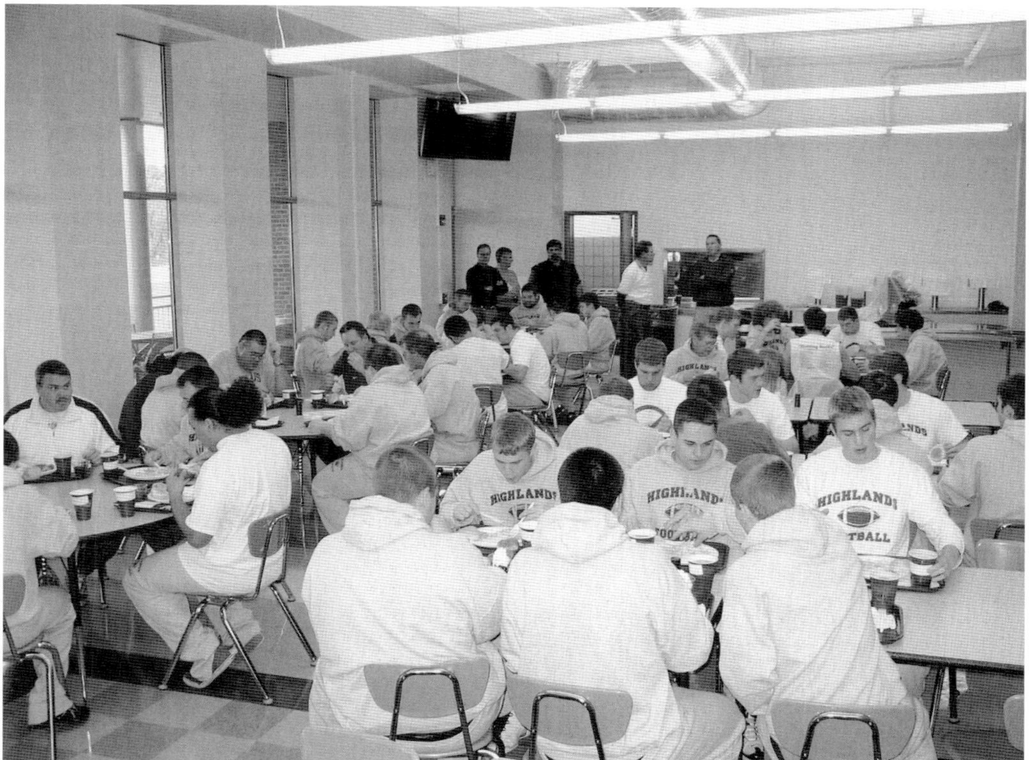

After victories over Madison Central and Louisville Central to finish the regular season with a 10-0 record, Highlands defeated Scott High School in the first round of the district tournament by a score of 50-0. That set up a rematch with rival Covington Catholic for the district championship in Fort Thomas on November 16, 2007. Players and coaches met in the cafeteria after school for a pre-game meal prior to the Covington Catholic game. The meal was prepared and served by parents of the players.

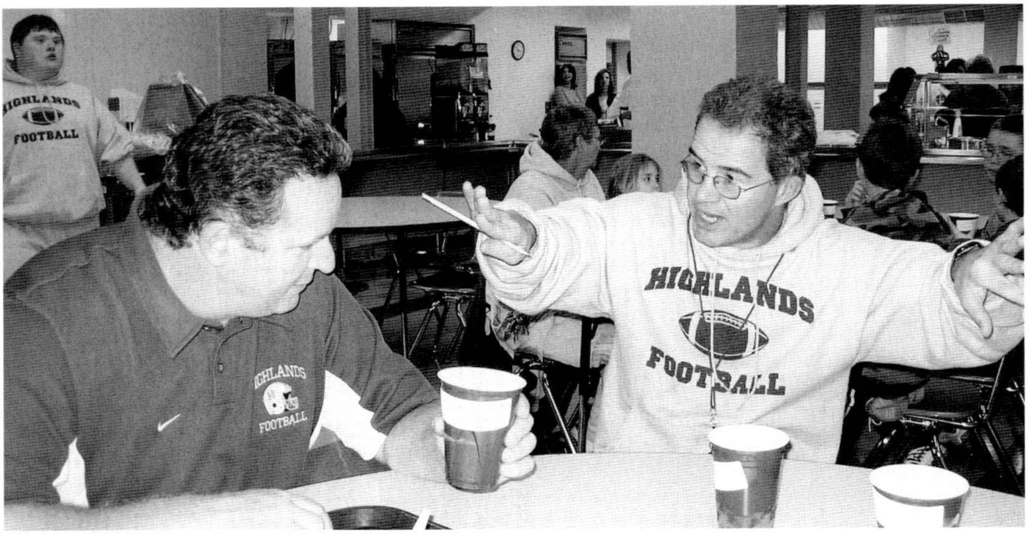

Highlands head coach Dale Mueller (right) talks football with assistant coach Robert Vilardo during the pre-game meal prior to the Covington Catholic game. Coach Vilardo serves as the assistant offensive coordinator and quarterback coach at Highlands. He is a graduate of Withrow High School and coached with Dale Mueller at Withrow and Sycamore High Schools. A volunteer coach at Highlands, Vilardo also served as head football coach at Milford High School in Cincinnati.

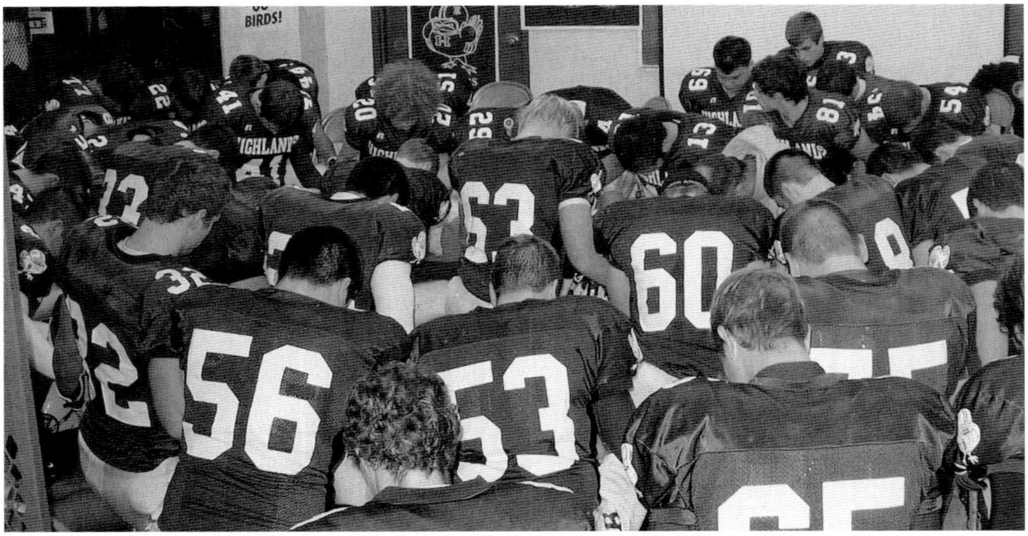

The players and coaching staff take time for a moment of silence before each football game. This photograph was taken in the locker room before the start of the district championship game against Covington Catholic. After the moment of silence, coach Mueller told his players that they had to go to work to beat Covington Catholic. He told his players that they were a "workingman's team" and that he wanted them to use that work ethic to defeat Covington Catholic. "Football is probably the best way for a high school student to grow up and become a man, and now it's time to go to work," he said.

Drew Simons delivered some major hits on defense for Highlands in the district championship game against Covington Catholic. Highlands dominated the game and won by a score of 40-0. The defense held Covington Catholic to just 157 yards while the offense had no trouble running the ball against the Colonel defense. Coach Mueller countered Covington Catholic's speed on defense by running the ball right up the gut and eliminating plays that required a fake handoff before handing the ball off to the intended running back. Quicker plays gave Covington Catholic less time to react on defense. The score was 21-0 at the half, and Highlands scored 16 quick points in the third quarter to put the game away. The Bluebirds added a field goal late in the game to wrap up the scoring.

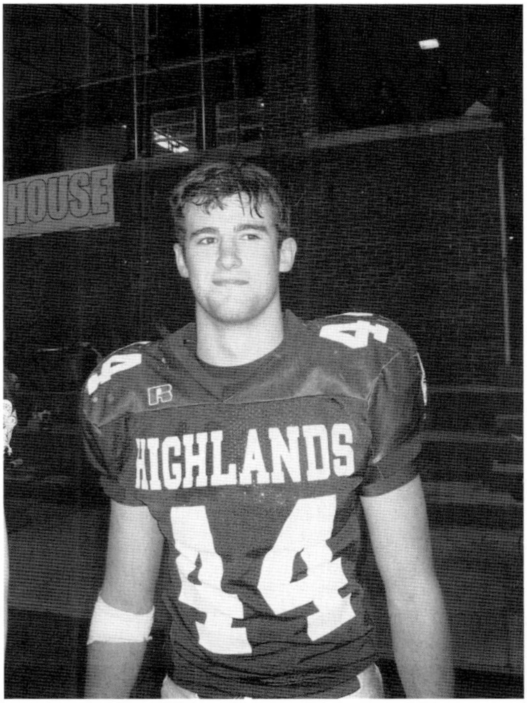

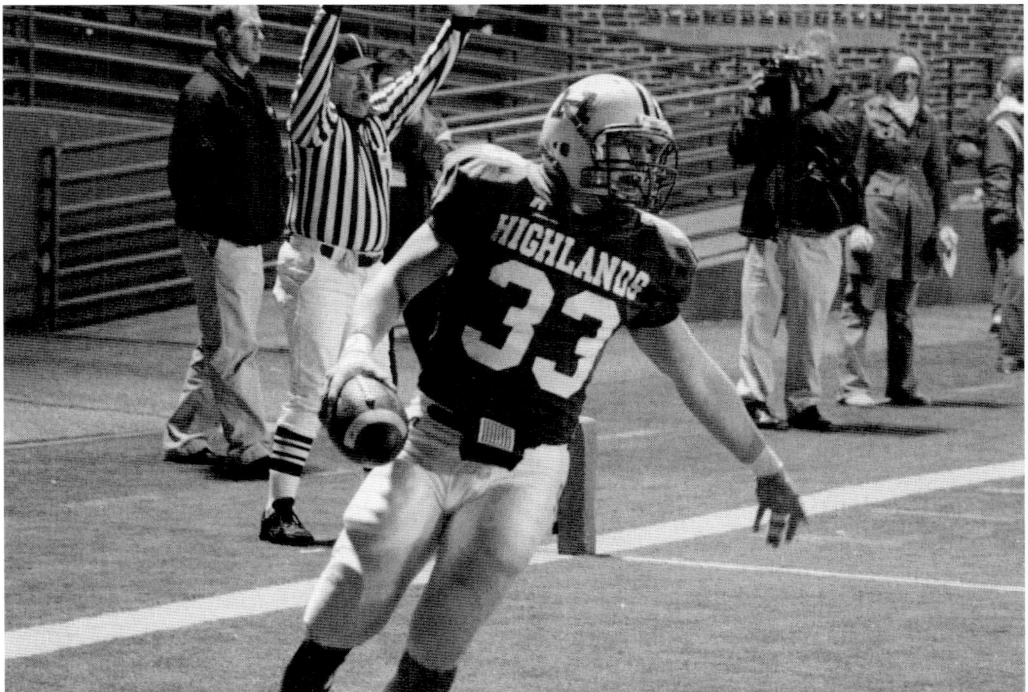

Highlands' senior running back Zach Hurtt scores on a 22-yard run in the first half against Covington Catholic in the district championship game. He would score on another 22-yard run in the second half of the game. (Courtesy of Ed Harber.)

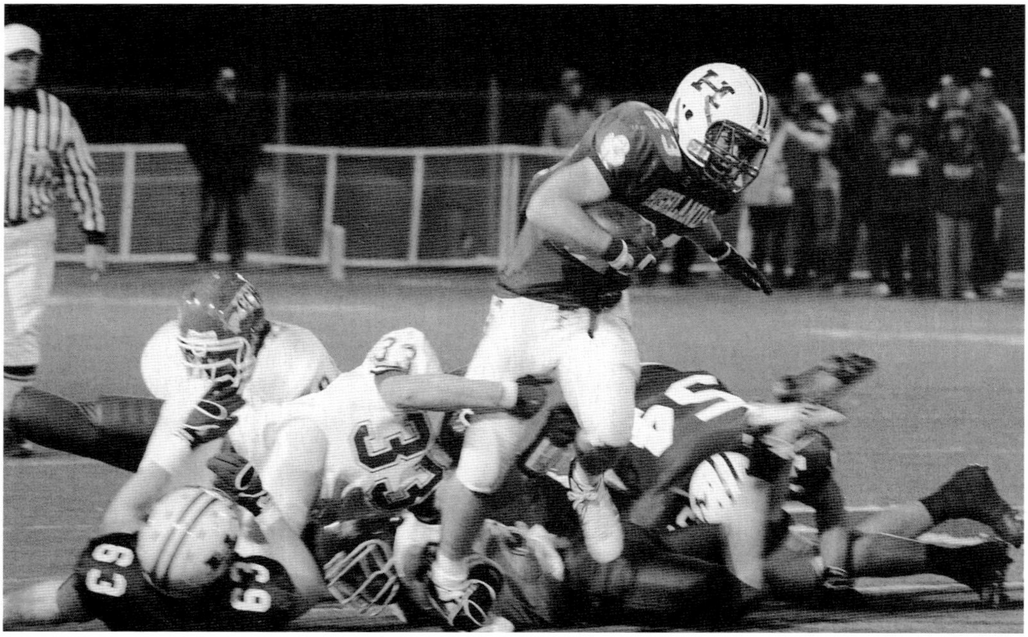

Josh Conner breaks a tackle and picks up a first down against Covington Catholic. Conner scored two touchdowns against the Colonels, including a 72-yard kickoff return. (Courtesy of Ed Harber.)

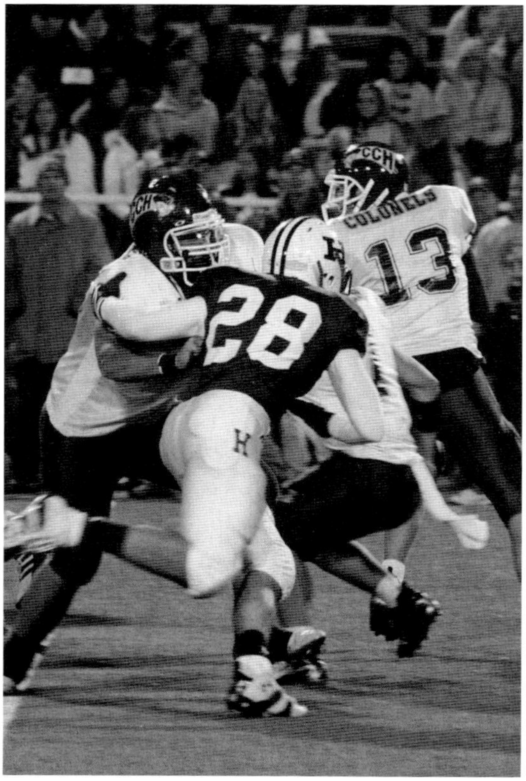

Junior Michael Laber (No. 28) applies pressure on Covington Catholic's quarterback in the 40-0 Highlands victory. (Courtesy of Ed Harber.)

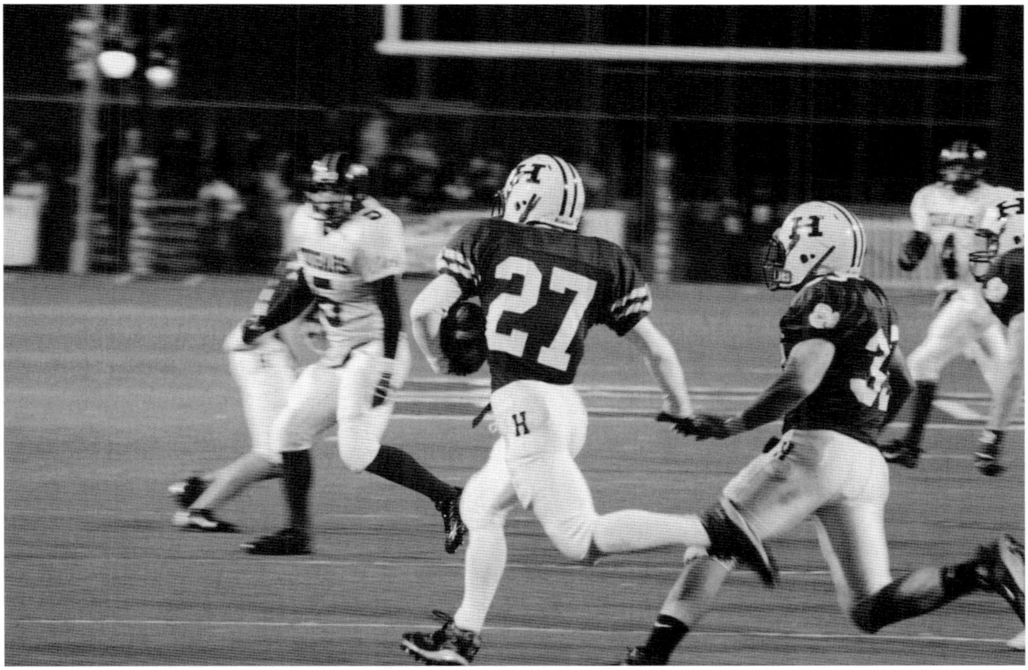

Junior running back Clint Crawford found plenty of running room in Highlands' 52-12 victory over Letcher County Central in the regional championship game. (Courtesy of Ed Harber.)

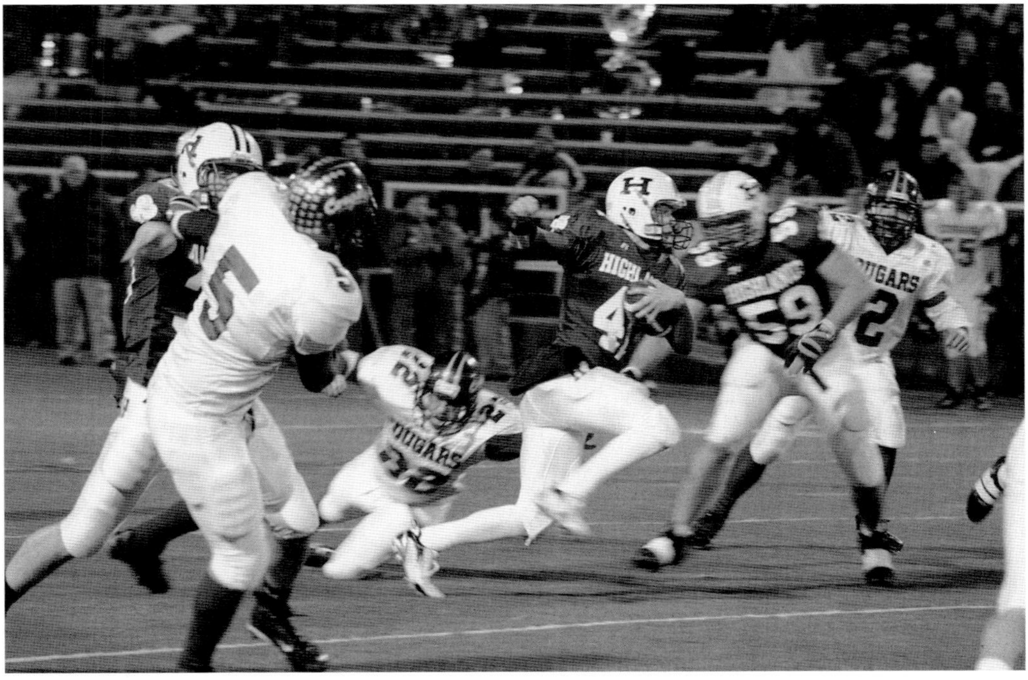

Quarterback Clay Cecil bursts through a big hole on a quarterback draw against Letcher County Central. Cecil scored a touchdown and threw a touchdown pass to wide receiver Jay Draper as Highlands gained 360 total yards for the game. (Courtesy of Ed Harber.)

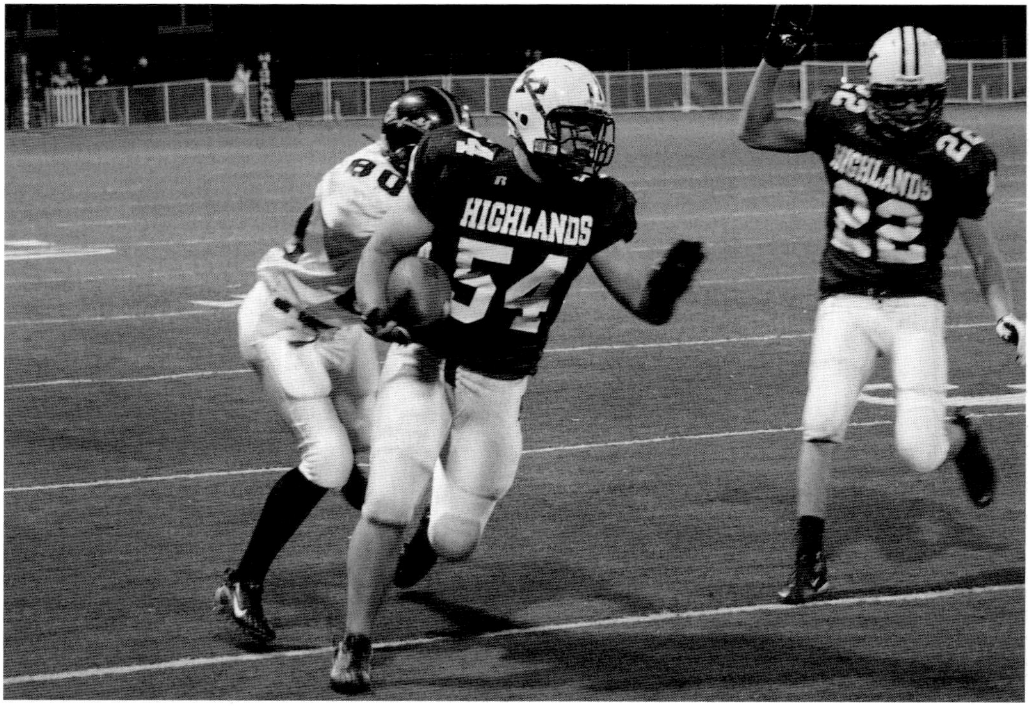

Ryan Ball (No. 54) returns a punt against Letcher County Central. Austin Collinsworth (No. 22) is also in this photograph. Ball and Collinsworth returned punts for Highlands all season. Ball was unique because he was an offensive lineman as well as a punt-return specialist. (Courtesy of Ed Harber.)

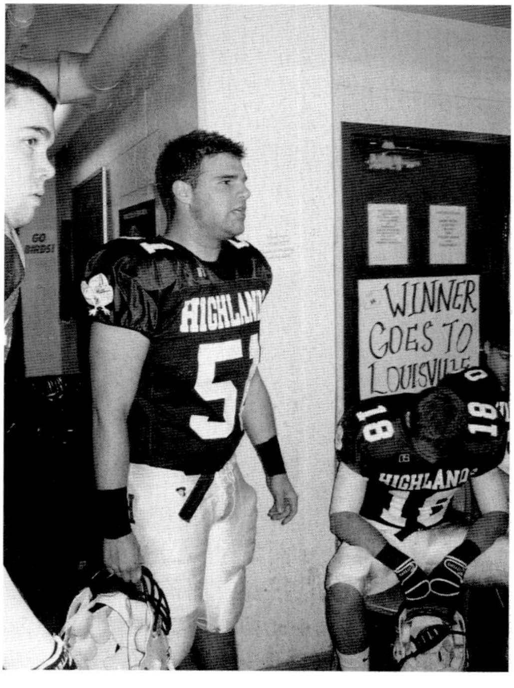

Senior center Brady Dowling addresses the team in the locker room prior to taking the field for the state semifinal game against Lincoln County. Dowling reminded each of the seniors that this would be their last game on their home field. He urged each of them to play their best game of the season.

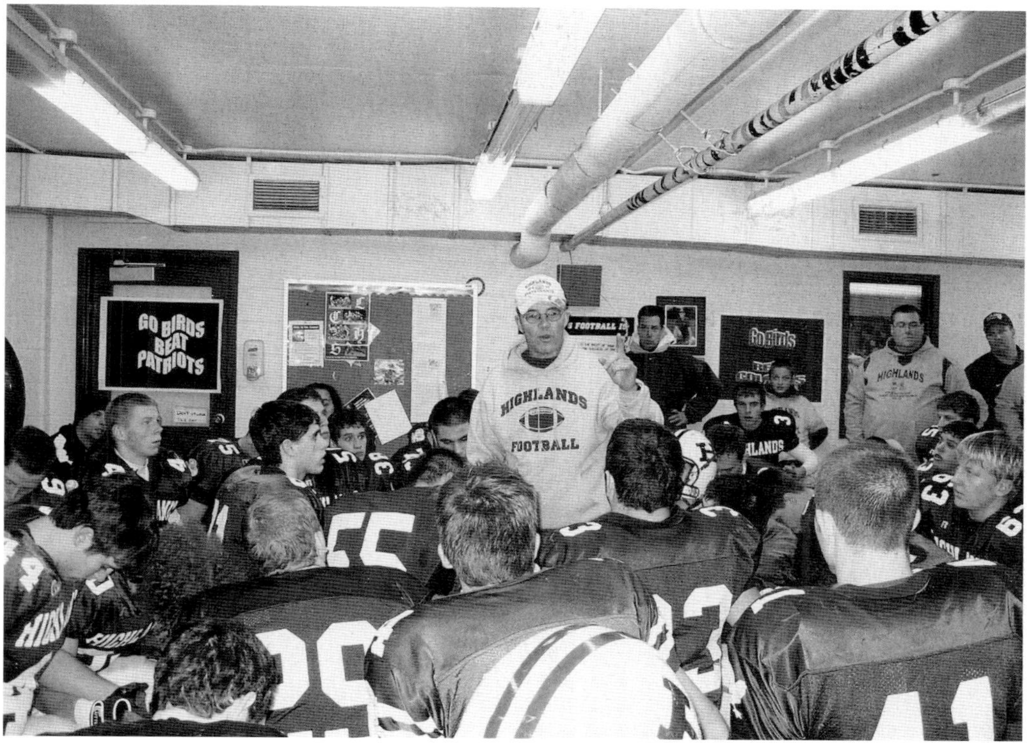

Coach Dale Mueller addresses the team in the locker room after the players listened to Brady Dowling. Coach Mueller told the players to stay focused and play hard on every down.

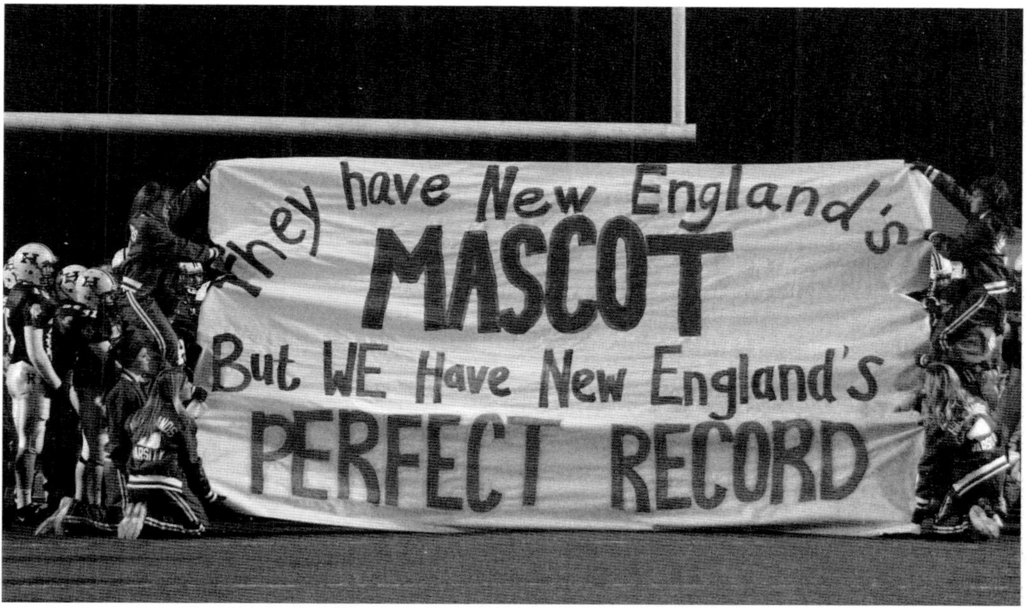

The cheerleaders' banner for the game against Lincoln County makes a reference to Lincoln County's mascot name, the Patriots. Highlands entered the game with a perfect 14-0 record. (Courtesy of Ed Harber.)

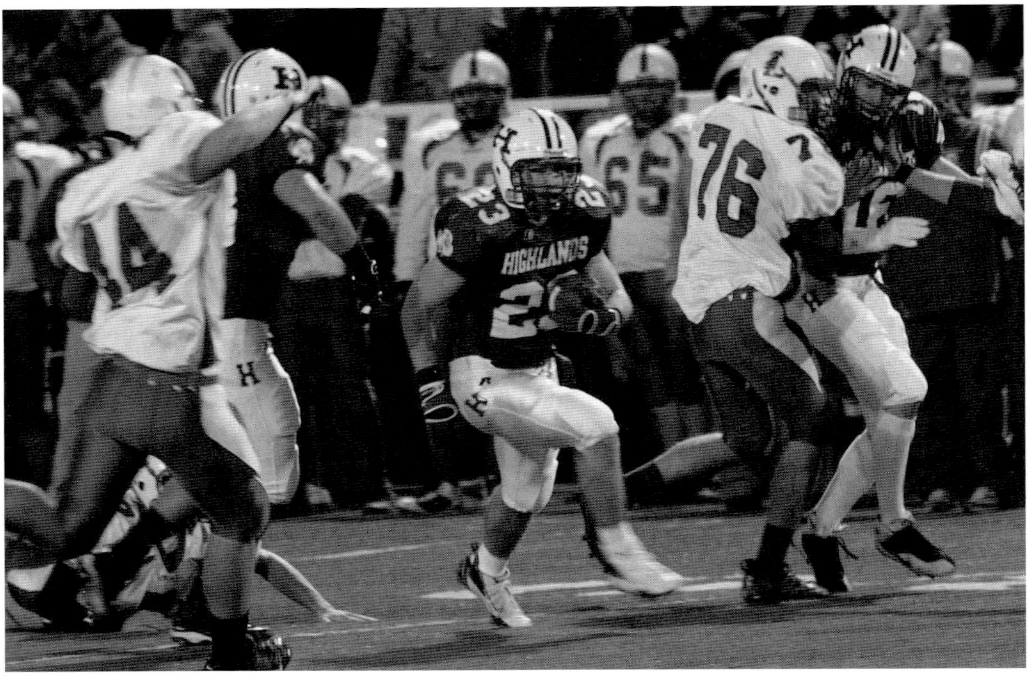

Josh Conner runs up the middle through a hole wide enough for a truck against Lincoln County. Highlands led by a score of 49-0 at the half, and the second and third team players were on the field for the entire second half except for one series played by the first team defense. (Courtesy of Ed Harber.)

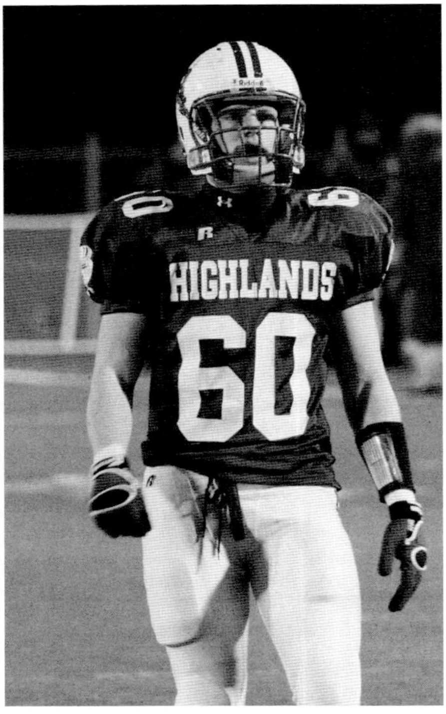

Highlands coach Dale Mueller called middle linebacker Joe Fitzgerald the "heart and soul" of the team. (Courtesy of Ed Harber.)

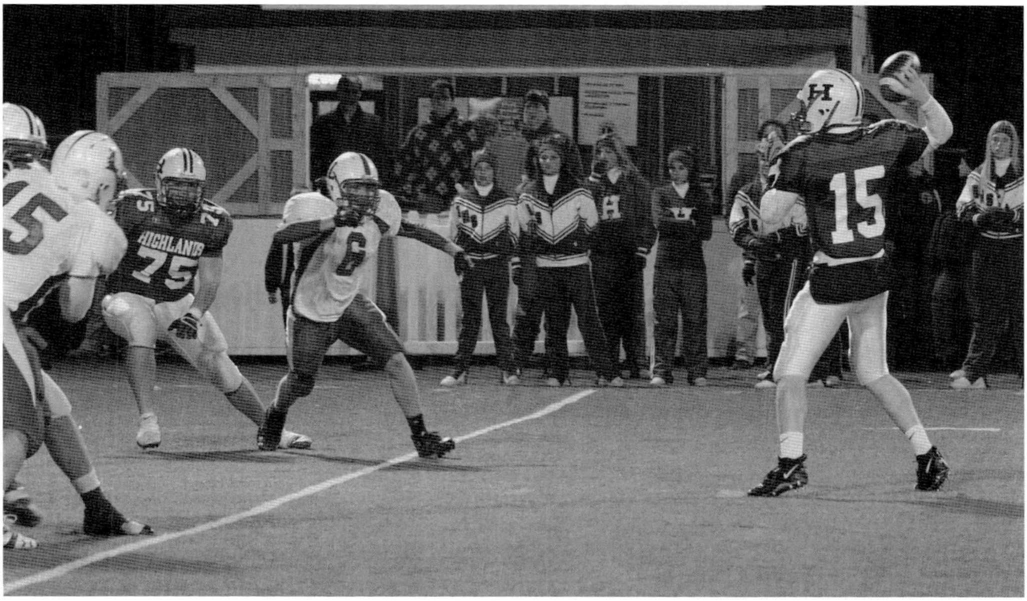

Quarterback Tony Guidugli prepares to throw a screen pass to Oliver Head in the second half against Lincoln County. Offensive tackle Kody Rosenhagen (No. 75) is letting his man get through the line to set up the screen. (Courtesy of Ed Harber.)

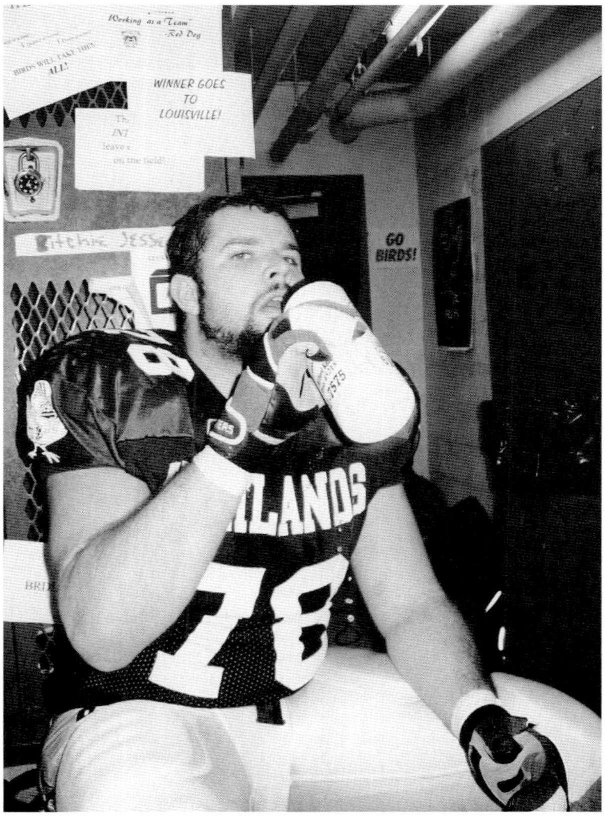

Offensive tackle Alex Hempfling rests up in the locker room at halftime against Lincoln County. Hempfling will play college football at Union College.

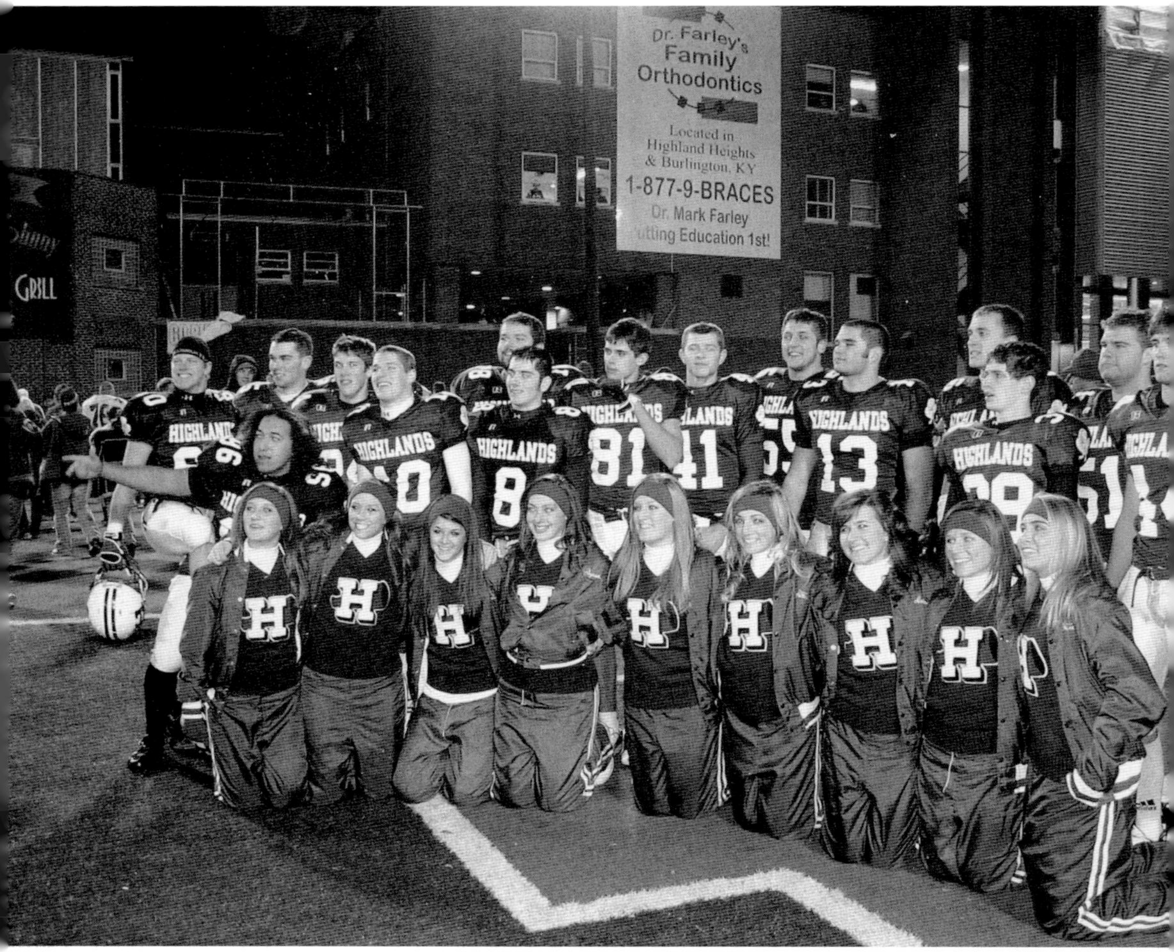

Highlands' cheerleaders and many of the seniors on the football team celebrate their 49-21 victory over Lincoln County in the Class 5A state semifinals. The Bluebirds advanced to the state championship game in Louisville against Bowling Green. Players, from left to right, are Joe Fitzgerald, Jimmy Hall, Milton Peko, Will Coleman, Drew Bathiany, Alex Hempfling, Matt Reed, Michael Buten, Clay Cecil, Luke Stein, Trey Jurgens, Jay Draper, Jeremy Hickman, Brady Dowling, and Drew Simons.

7

Looking Back

Highlands' Greatest Players

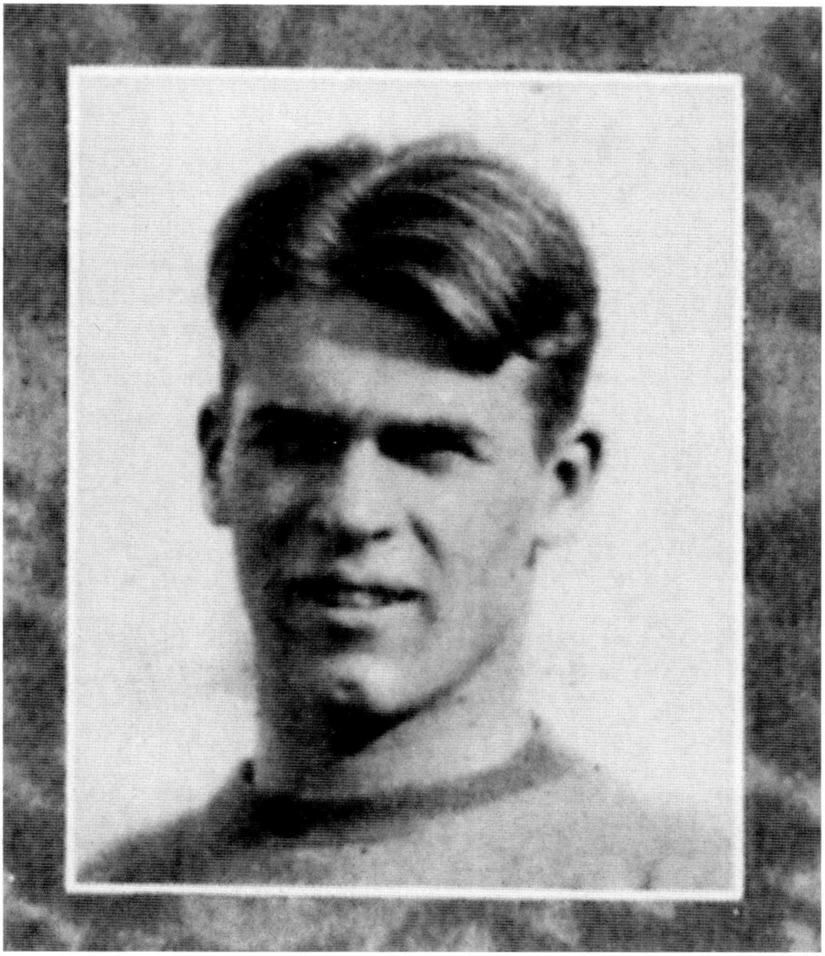

John Kellogg was a running back and punter on the 1925 Highlands football team. He was captain of the football, basketball, and baseball teams at Highlands. After earning All Cincinnati in football, Kellogg played running back in college at the University of Kentucky. He was also a member of the baseball team there.

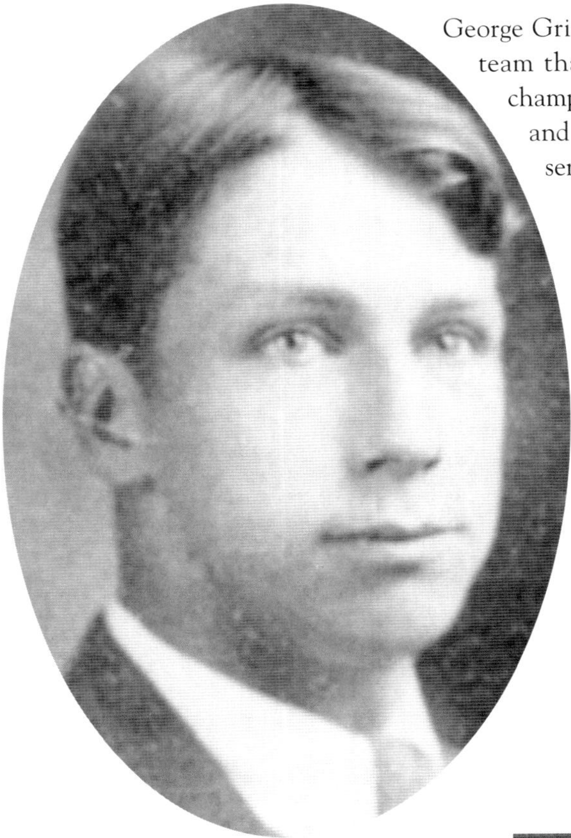

George Grimm was a guard on the 1926 Highlands team that won the Greater Cincinnati Class B championship. Grimm was also the team's kicker and earned All Greater Cincinnati honors his senior year.

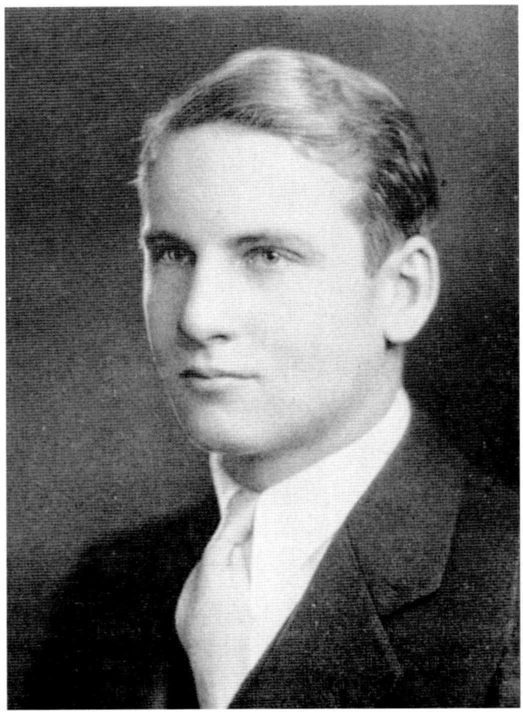

Bob Stegeman was a four-year starter at end and played on the 1926 and 1929 Greater Cincinnati Class B championship teams at Highlands. Stegeman was named All Cincinnati and All Southern, and was captain of the Kentucky All Star Team.

John Hosking played fullback on the undefeated 1930 Highlands team that won the Greater Cincinnati championship. The team was ranked No. 1 in Kentucky at the conclusion of the season, but there was no state playoff system at the time. Hosking was named All Greater Cincinnati, All State, and All Southern. He went on to start at guard for Ohio State and the University of Cincinnati. He was also the Ohio State and University of Cincinnati heavy weight boxing champion and a catcher for the Toledo Mud Hens.

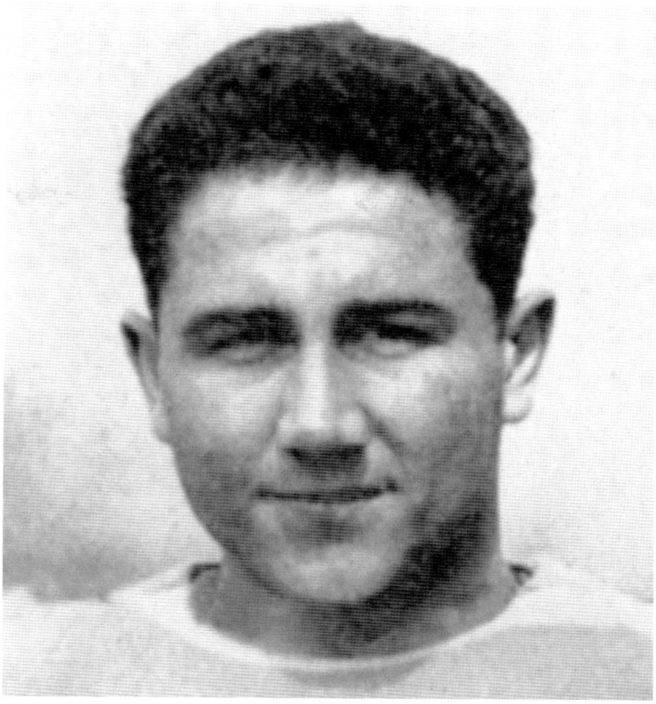

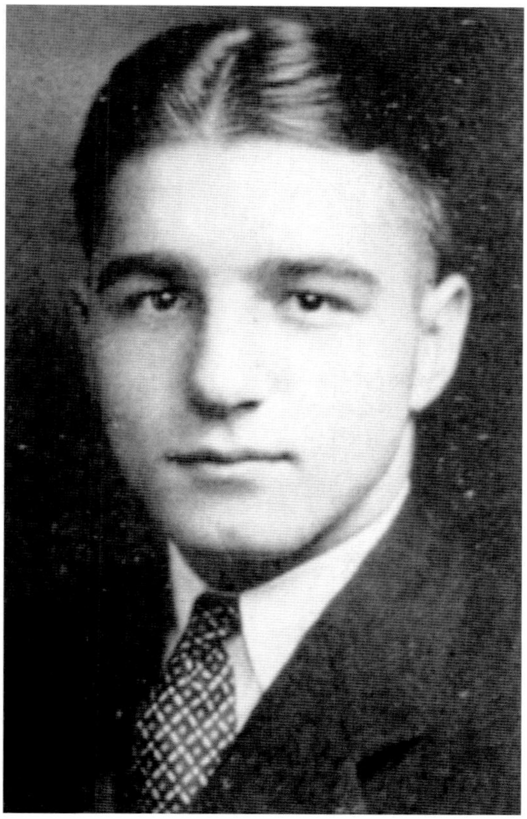

Frank Burdick was a four-year starter at end and played on the 1926 and 1929 Greater Cincinnati Class B championship teams at Highlands. He was captain of the team, All Greater Cincinnati and Second Team All State. Burdick was awarded 13 athletic letters at Highlands for football, basketball, baseball, and track. He played halfback for the University of Cincinnati.

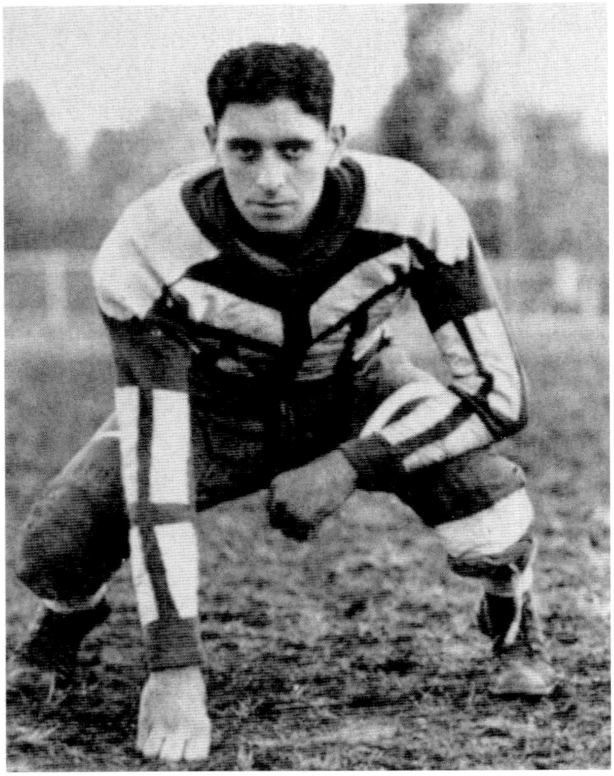

Rick Picola played guard on offense and defense for the 1937 conference champions. He was All Conference, All Northern Kentucky, and All State his senior year.

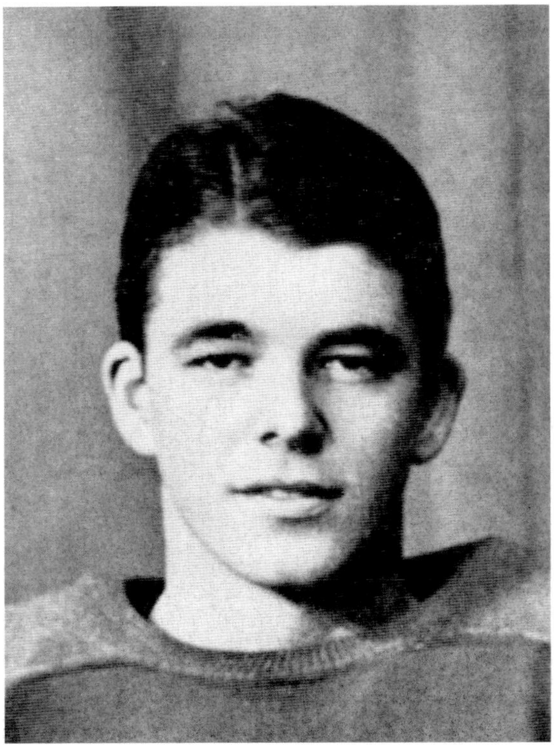

Bruce Ross was the quarterback of the 1937 conference champions and Northern Kentucky champions at Highlands. Ross was named All Conference and All Northern Kentucky his senior year. Ross would later serve as mayor of Fort Thomas for a number of years.

Jack Casner was a tackle on the 1937 and 1938 conference championship teams at Highlands. He was named All Conference, All Northern Kentucky, and Third Team All State. Casner started at guard for the University of Kentucky.

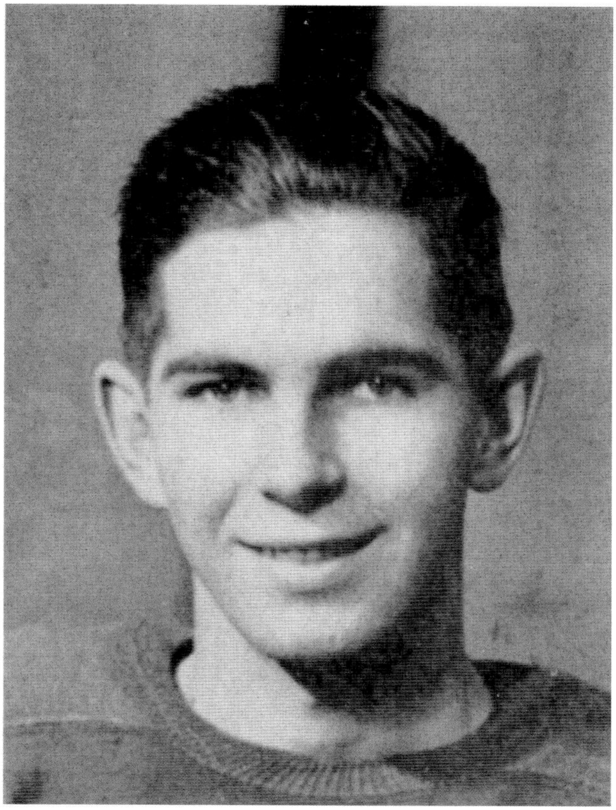

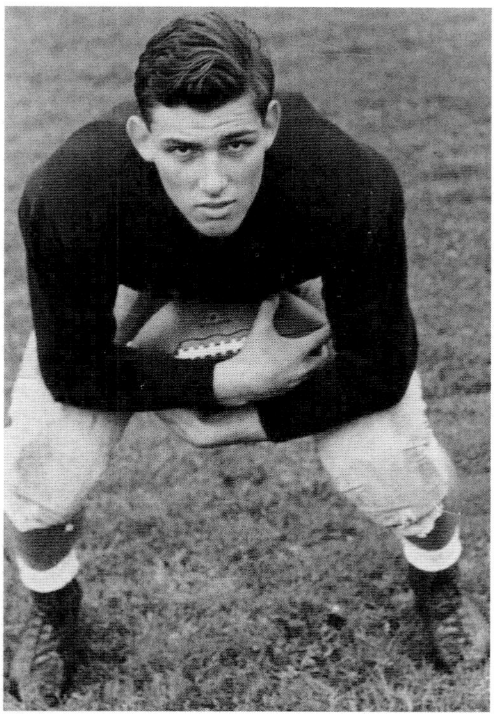

Bud Pogue was a fullback on the 1937 Highlands team that won the Little Six Conference championship. Pogue was named All Conference, All Northern Kentucky, and Honorable Mention All State. He played on the basketball team at Dartmouth and participated in two NCAA tournaments. (Courtesy of Hank Pogue.)

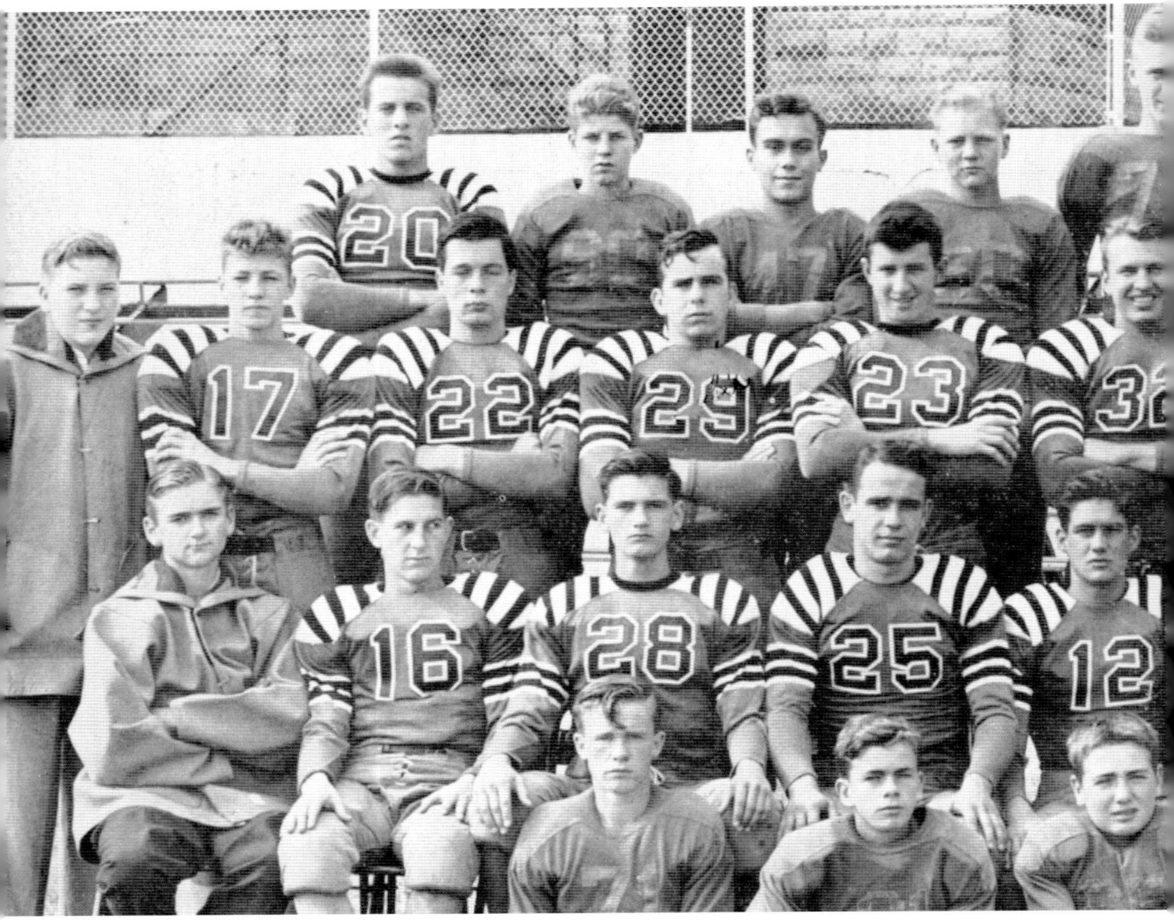

This photograph of members of the 1941 Highlands football team includes four of the best players from that decade. George Mogge (No. 28) played guard on the 1941 Highlands team that won the conference championship. Mogge also started at guard for Eastern Kentucky University. He was a career pilot and the back-up pilot for President Eisenhower. Jim Howe (No. 17) was a running back on the 1943 Highlands team that finished as No. 1 in the state before Kentucky had a playoff system. Howe was a member of the All Conference and All State teams. He went on to start at halfback for the University of Kentucky. Jim Schweitzer (No. 32) played tackle on the 1941 Highlands team that captured a conference championship. He went on to play service football in the U.S. Navy. Jack Cook (No. 20) was a three-year starter from 1939–1941 at Highlands. Cook was named to the All Conference team, All State team, and participated in the East-West Shrine Game. Cook played guard for a year at the University of Kentucky.

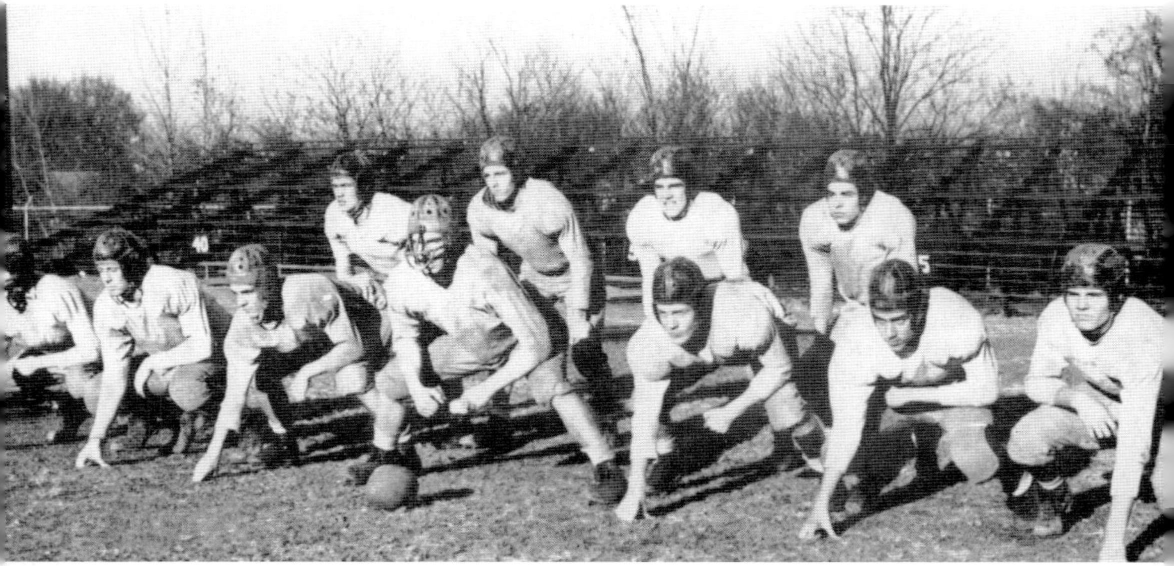

This is a photograph of the starting offense in 1942 when Highlands captured the Northern Kentucky Athletic Conference championship. A lineman and a running back rank as all-time greats at Highlands. Don Reder (third from left on the line) was a guard on the 1942 team and the 1943 Highlands team that finished as No. 1 in the state before Kentucky had a playoff system. Reder was named All Conference, All Northern Kentucky, and All State his senior year. Richard Kruer (second from the right in the second row) was a running back on the 1941 and 1942 Highlands teams that won conference championships. Kruer was named All Conference, All Northern Kentucky, and was a member of the Shriner's All State team. He rushed for an average of 96 yards a game in 1942.

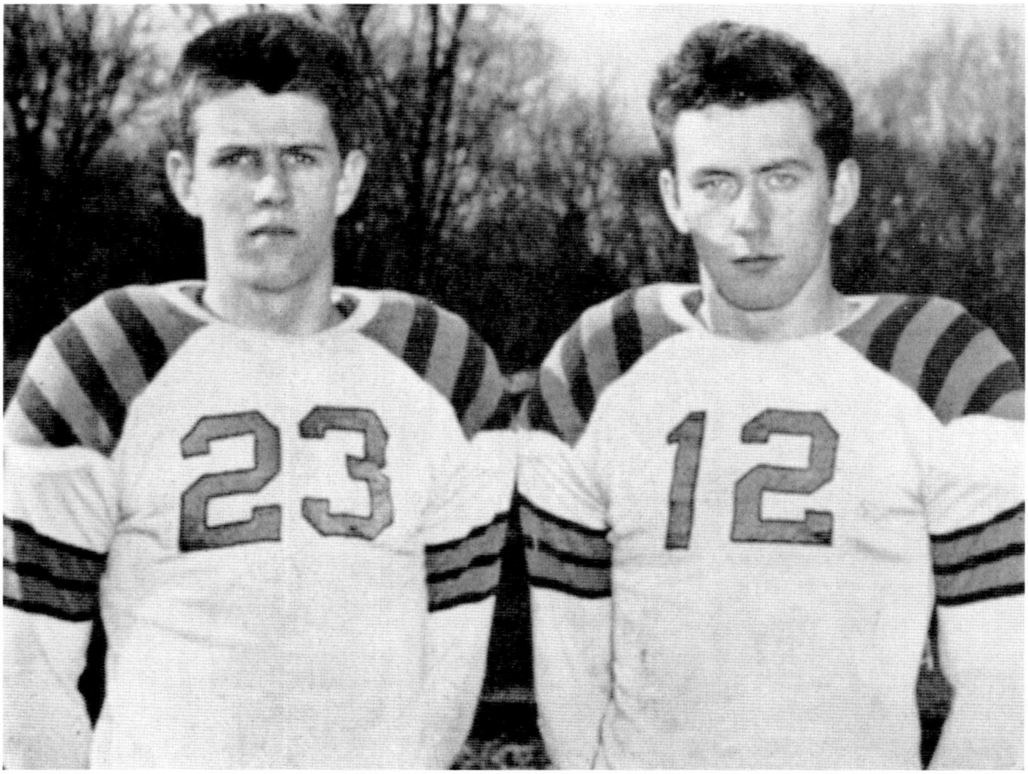

Jerry Cecil (No. 12) was an end and tackle on the 1939 and 1940 Highlands football teams. He made the All Conference team and Honorable Mention All State. Cecil played at Miami University for a season.

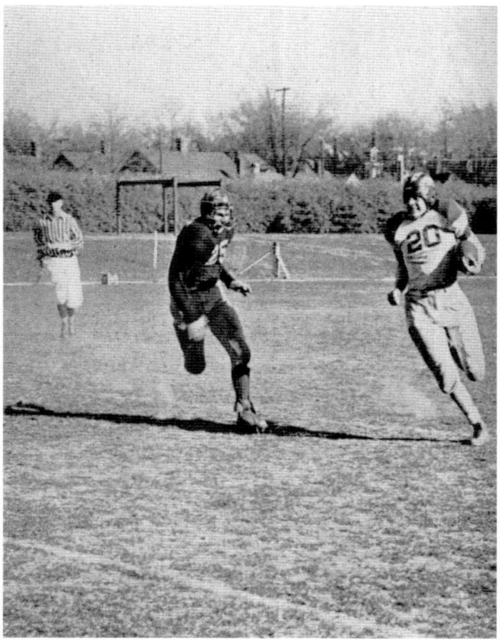

Bob Luecke was a wingback on the 1943 mythical state championship team and the 1944 conference championship team at Highlands. In this photograph, Luecke is picking up big yardage against Ashland in the post-season state championship game played at Stoll Field on the campus of the University of Kentucky. Luecke made All Conference, All Northern Kentucky, and Honorable Mention All State. Luecke went on to play halfback at Ohio University. He taught at Highlands and coached the basketball and track teams for many years.

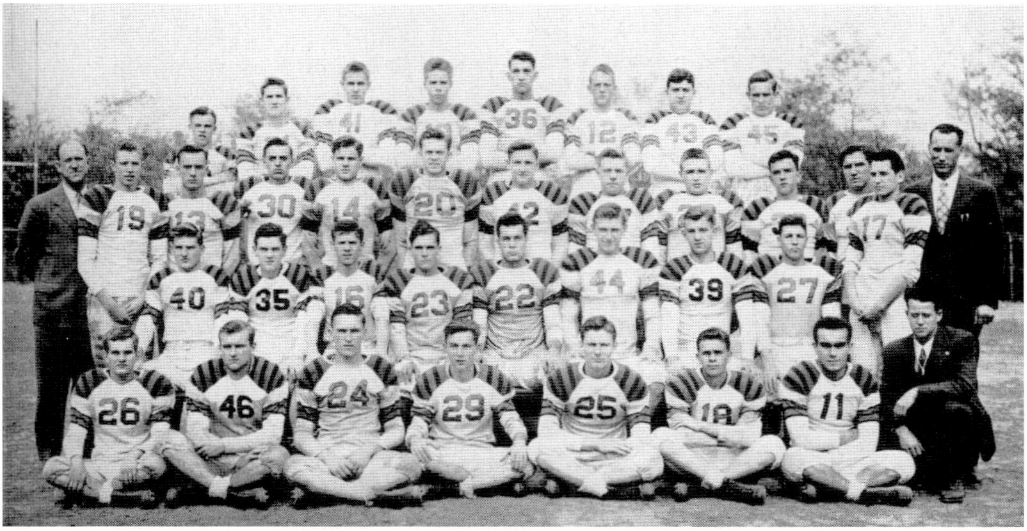

Homer Rice was the quarterback and safety on the 1943 Highlands team that won the mythical state championship and the 1944 team that won the conference championship. Rice (No. 17) can be seen in this team photograph standing on the right next to coach Judge Waddell. Rice was the leading scorer in the conference and was named to the All Conference and All State teams. He played quarterback at Centre College and was a member of the Little All American Team. He went on to be head coach at Highlands, the University of Cincinnati, Rice, and the Cincinnati Bengals. Rice was also director of athletics at University of North Carolina and Georgia Tech.

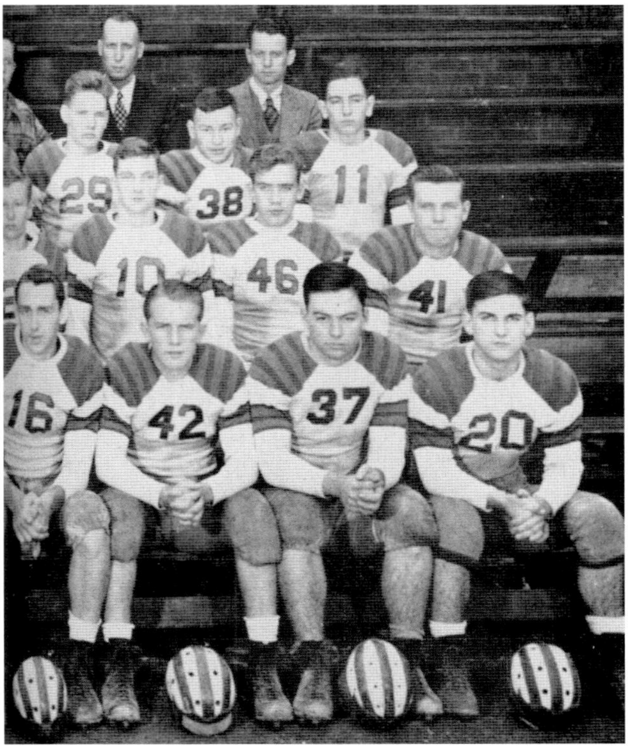

J. C. McFarland (No. 41 in the second row of this 1945 team photograph) played guard for Highlands from 1944 to 1946. McFarland was named All Conference and Second Team All State. He played football for the University of Cincinnati and Eastern Kentucky University.

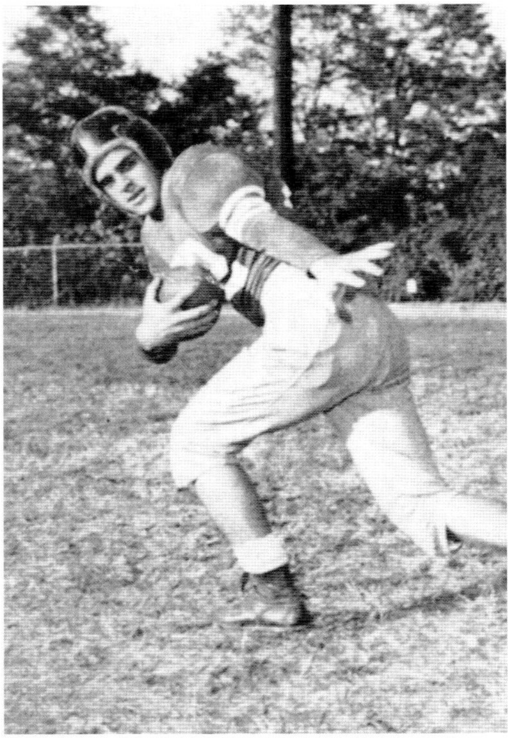

Duke Schneider was a running back and a four-year starter at Highlands from 1945 to 1949. He was awarded 12 athletic letters for football, basketball, baseball, and track. Schneider earned All Conference, All Greater Cincinnati, and All State honors.

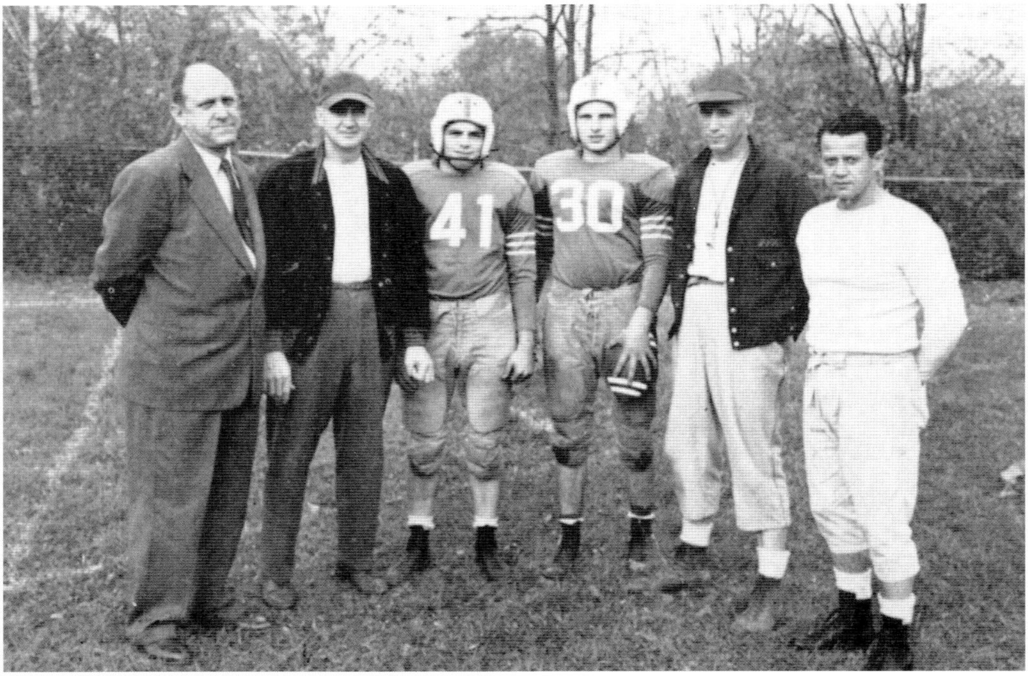

Pete Thress (No. 30) was a three-year starter at center and played on the 1950 Highlands team that finished second in the state and the 1951 team that finished the season with a 9-1 record. Thress made All Conference and All State as a senior.

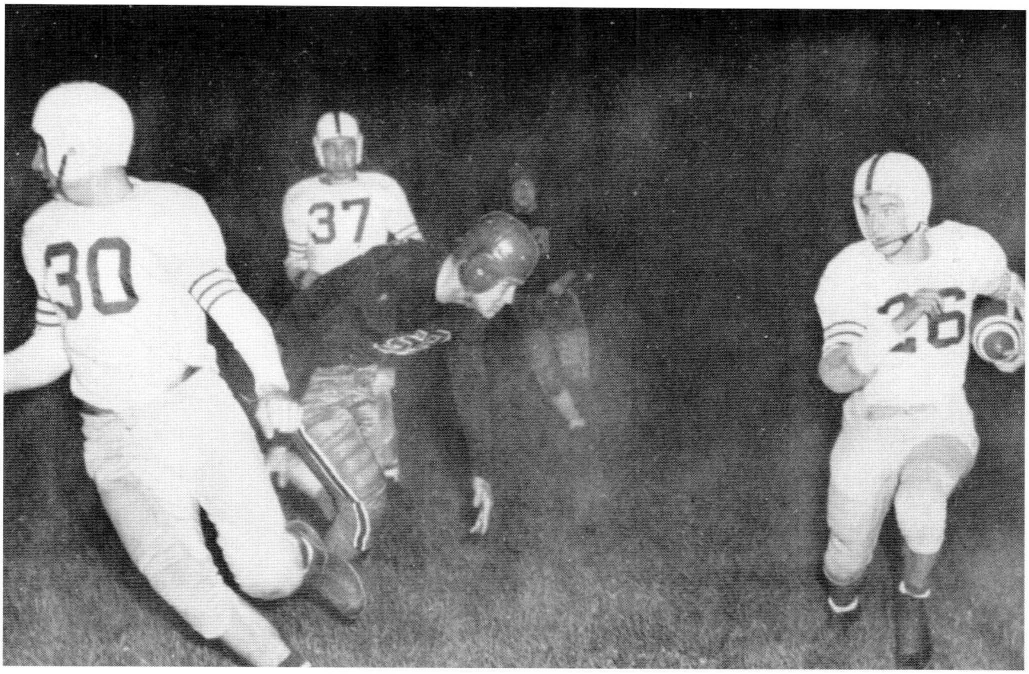

Tom Rohrer (No. 26) looks for a block from Pete Thress (No. 30) in this run around left end in a 1950 game. Rohrer was a running back who started in 1950 and in 1951 when Highlands finished second in the conference with a 9-1 record. Rohrer was named to a number of All Star teams, including All Conference, All State, and *Collier's* Magazine All American Team. He led the conference in scoring and went on to play halfback at Notre Dame University.

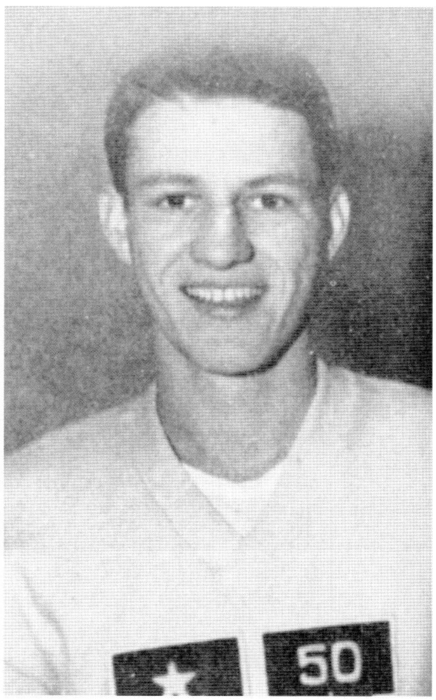

Bob Curtice was an end on the 1950 Highlands team that finished the season with a 12-1 record. He was named All Conference, All Greater Cincinnati, and First Team All State. Curtice played end at Purdue University for a season.

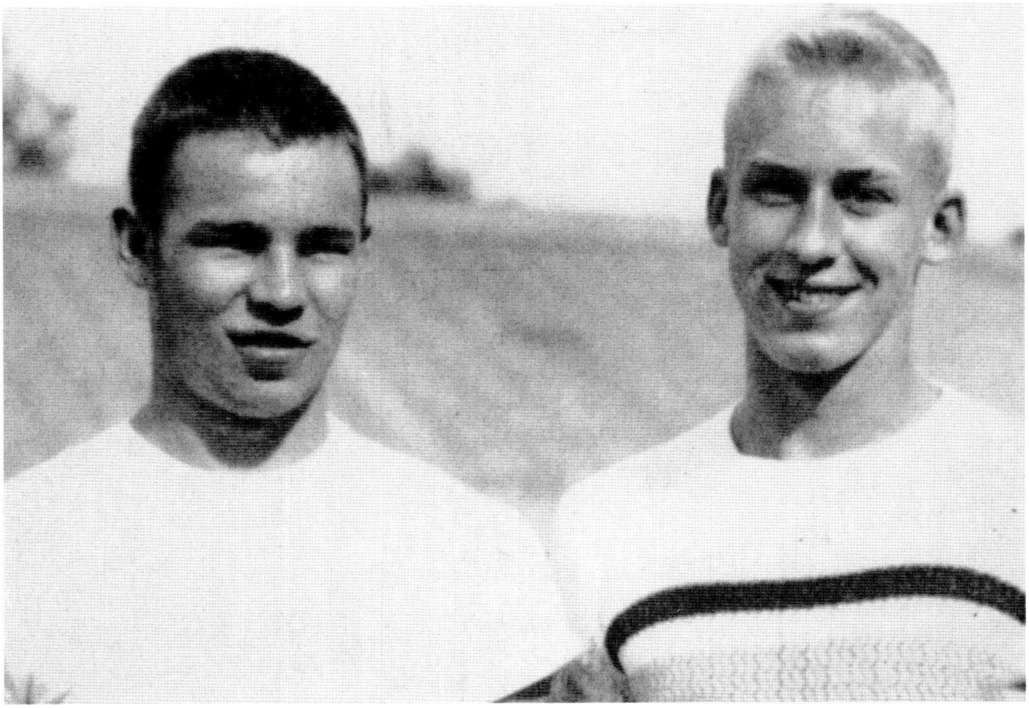

Ted Finneseth (right) was a running back and team captain on the 1951 and 1952 Highlands teams that finished with an overall record of 21-2. Finneseth was All Conference and Honorable Mention All State, and played for the U.S. Army and the University of Cincinnati.

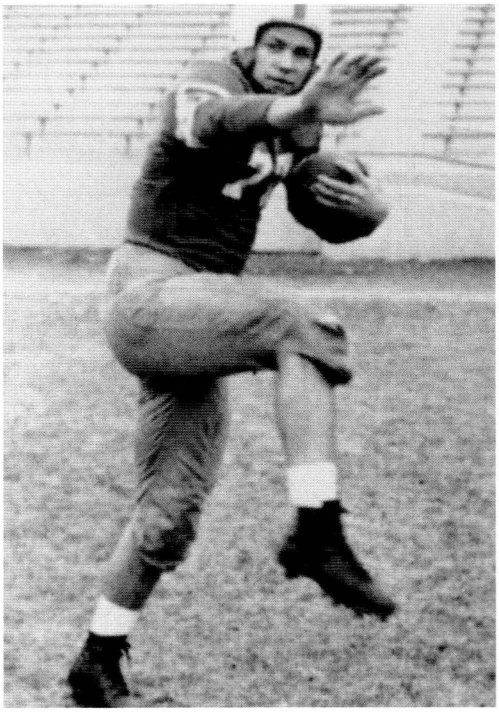

Ray Mosley was a running back and defensive back for Highlands from 1951 to 1953. He earned All Conference and Honorable Mention All State recognition. Mosley played for two years at the University of Kentucky.

Denny McAtee (right) was a defensive back, wide receiver, and punt returner on the 1956 and 1957 Highlands teams, which compiled an overall 19-2 record. McAtee was named All Conference and Honorable Mention All State. He played split end and cornerback at Western Kentucky University.

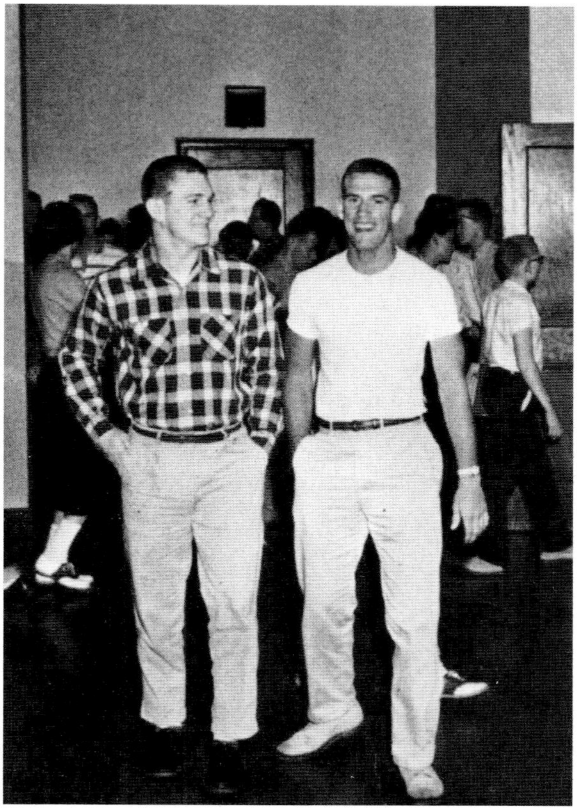

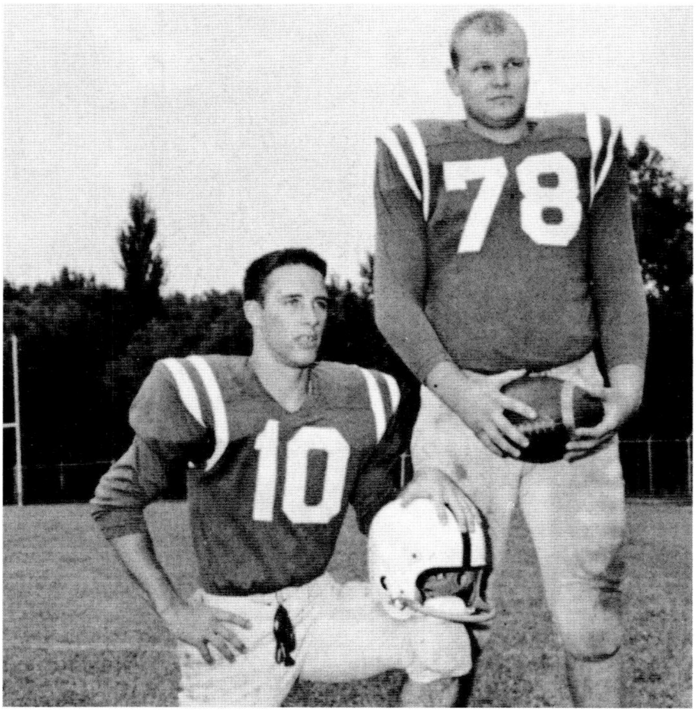

Tackle Paul Finneseth (No. 78) and quarterback Richie Emmons (No. 10) were the captains of the 1958 football team at Highlands. They started on the 1957 and 1958 teams that compiled an overall 20-1-1 record. Finneseth earned All Conference and Honorable Mention All State honors. He played tackle and guard at Western Kentucky University. Emmons was a great running quarterback and earned All Conference and All State honors.

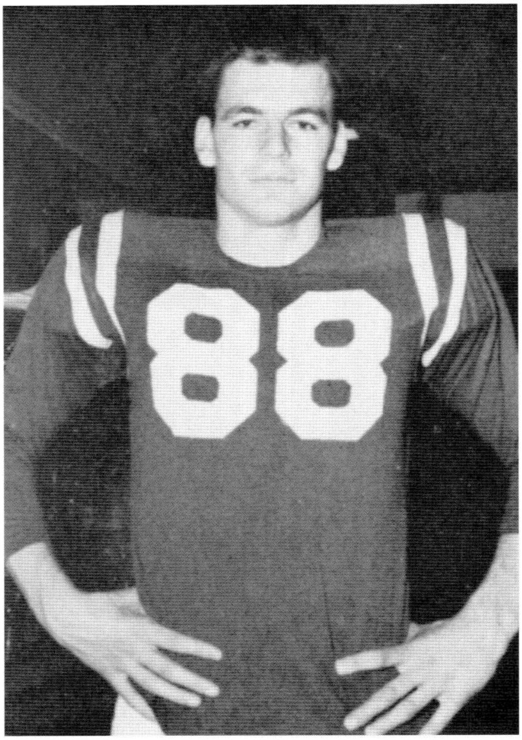

Dave Hudepohl was a defensive end and wide receiver on the 1957 mythical state championship team and the 1958 team at Highlands. Hudepohl went on to play defensive end and wide receiver at Harvard University, where he was All Ivy League, All East, and Honorable Mention All American.

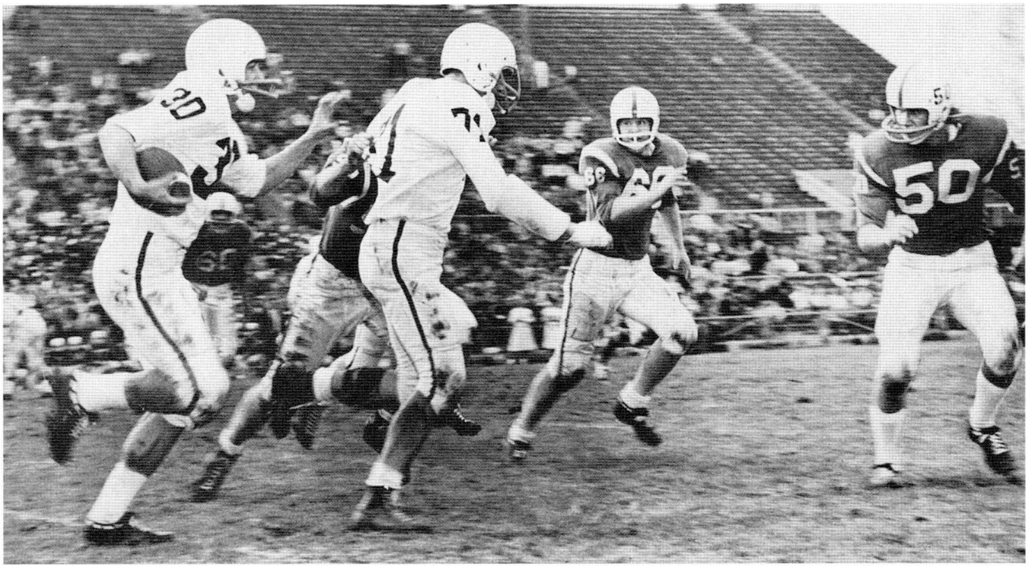

Jim Burt (No. 30) heads up the right side of the field in Highlands' 21-13 victory over Lexington Lafayette in the Kentucky Class 2A state championship game in Lexington in 1960. Burt was a tailback and defensive back, and was named to the All Conference and All State teams. He played running back and defensive back for Western Kentucky University where he was an All American and a member of the All Ohio Valley Conference All Star Team. Burt was drafted by the Los Angeles Rams but chose to attend medical school instead.

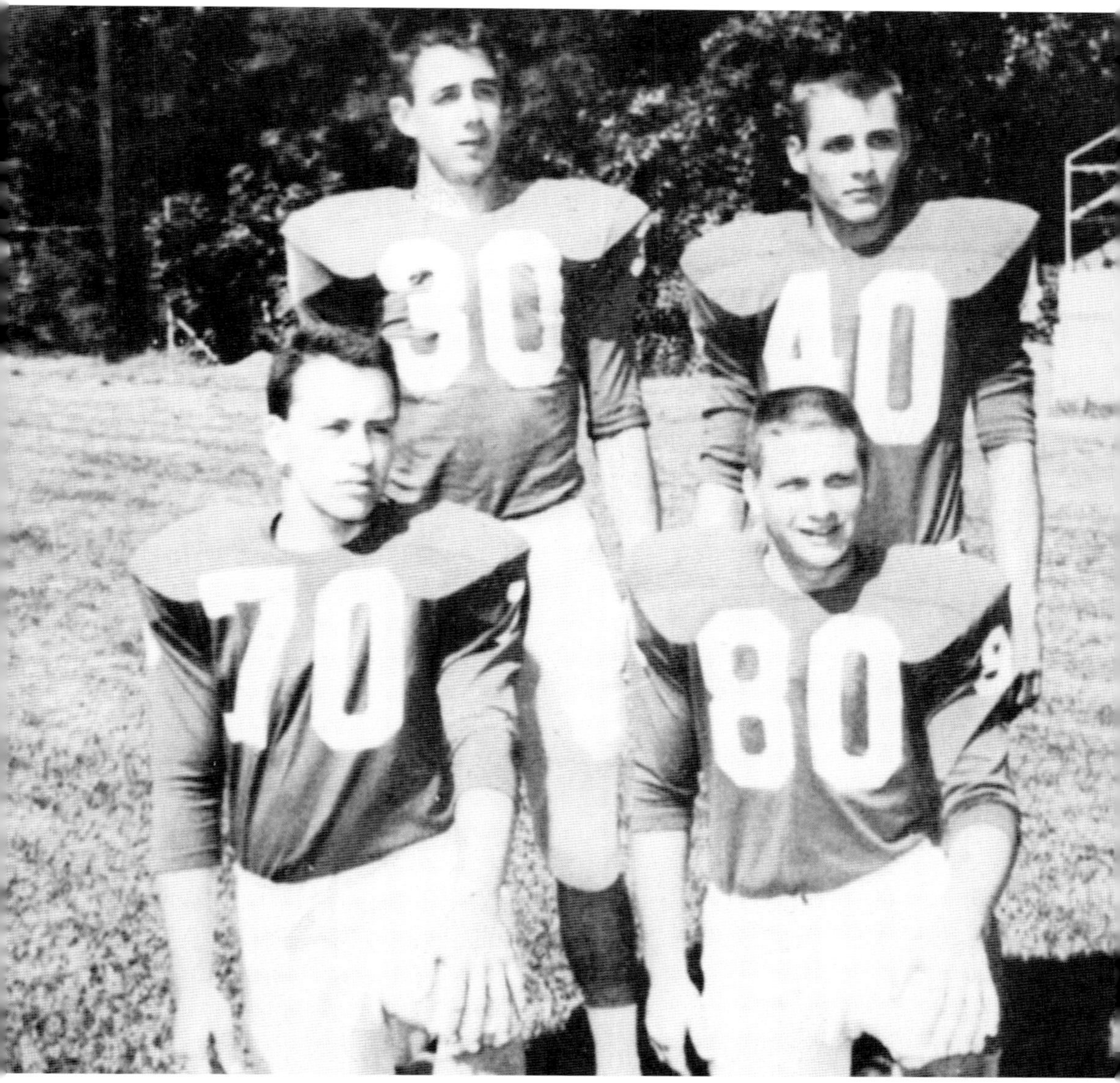

The captains of the 1960 Highlands football team that won the Class 2A state championship were as follows: (kneeling) Alan Berry and Bob Steinhauser; (standing) Jim Burt and John Burt. Burt (No. 40) was a fullback and linebacker on the Highlands teams that finished second in the state in 1959 and captured the state championship in 1960. He earned numerous All Conference and All State honors at Highlands. Burt went on to play fullback at Western Kentucky University. Bob Steinhauser was an All Conference and All State offensive and defensive end on the 1959 and 1960 Highlands teams. He played safety at the University of Cincinnati and was a member of the All Missouri Valley Conference All Star Team. Alan Berry played offensive and defensive tackle for Highlands and was named to a number of All Conference and All State teams. Berry played college football at Duke University.

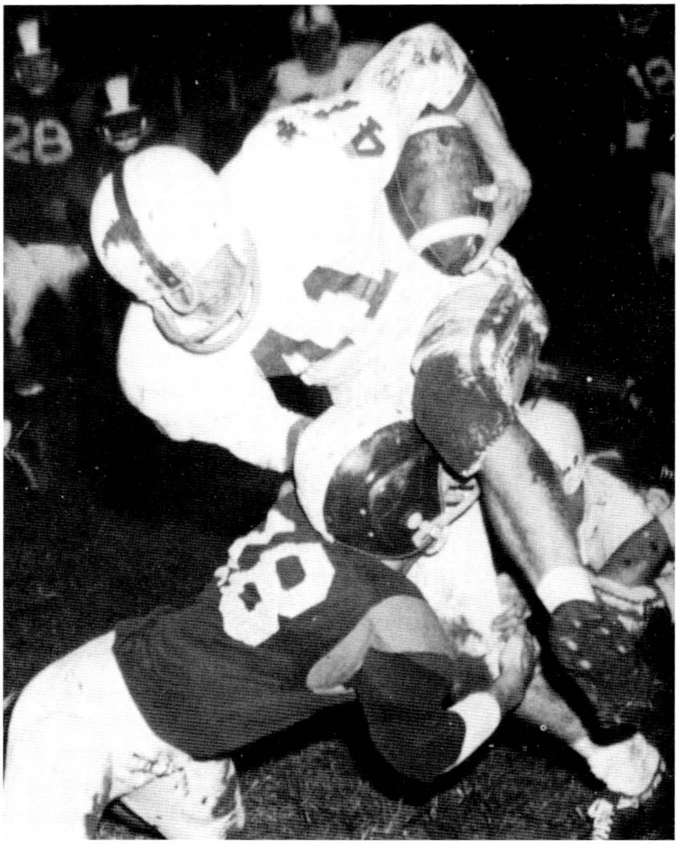

Mike McGraw (No. 41) punishes a Hazard defender in the 1961 state semifinal game won by Highlands by a score of 34-0. McGraw was a fullback and linebacker on the Highlands team that went undefeated and captured the Class 2A state championship. McGraw made All Conference and Second Team All State. He went on to start at running back and linebacker at the University of Kentucky. McGraw held the University of Kentucky record for most tackles in a season and was named to the All Southeastern Conference Team. He played running back in the National Football League for the Baltimore Colts.

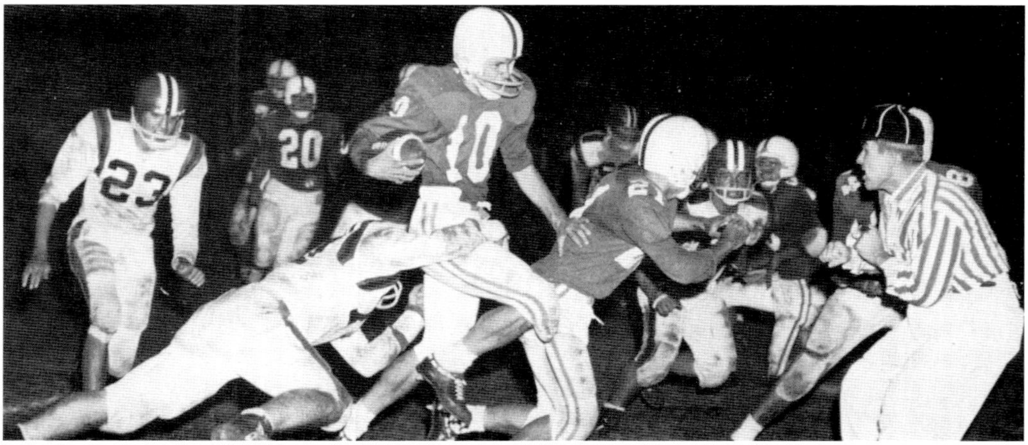

Roger Walz breaks a tackle in a 26-12 victory over Newport during the 1961 season. Walz was the quarterback on teams from Highlands that went undefeated and won state championships in 1960 and 1961. He won All Conference and Second Team All State honors. Walz completed 156 of 281 passes for 3,826 yards and 38 touchdowns in his high school career. He went on to play quarterback for the University of Cincinnati and University of Kentucky.

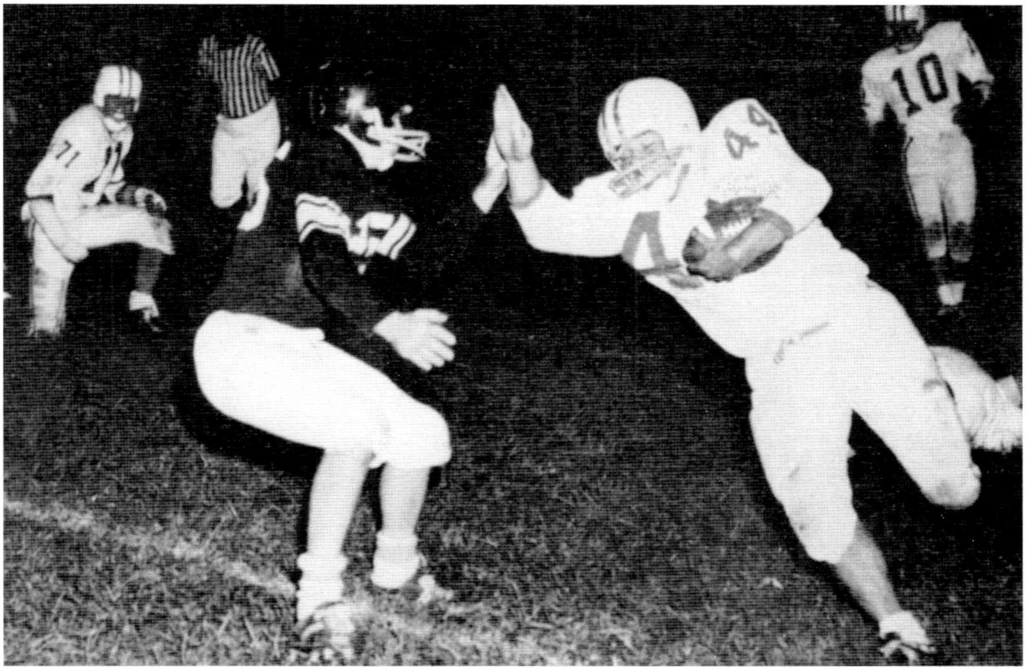

Mike Lawson turns the corner for a big gain against Bellevue in 1962. Lawson played fullback and down lineman for Highlands from 1961 to 1963 and earned All Conference and All State honors. He went on to play for Cameron State College in Oklahoma, the No. 1–ranked junior college in the nation at the time. Lawson was named a Third Team Junior College All American and played semi-pro football for eight seasons.

Chuck Kyle (No. 71) and Mike Roth (No. 87) led Highlands to an undefeated season and Class 2A state championship in 1964. Kyle was a tackle and down lineman who was a high school All American his senior year. He played nose guard at Purdue University and was named to the All Big Ten Team and All American Team. Kyle was drafted by the Dallas Cowboys and played two seasons with the Saskatchewan Rough Riders in the Canadian Football League. Mike Roth played end and linebacker, and was named All Conference and Honorable Mention All State. He played college football at Indiana University.

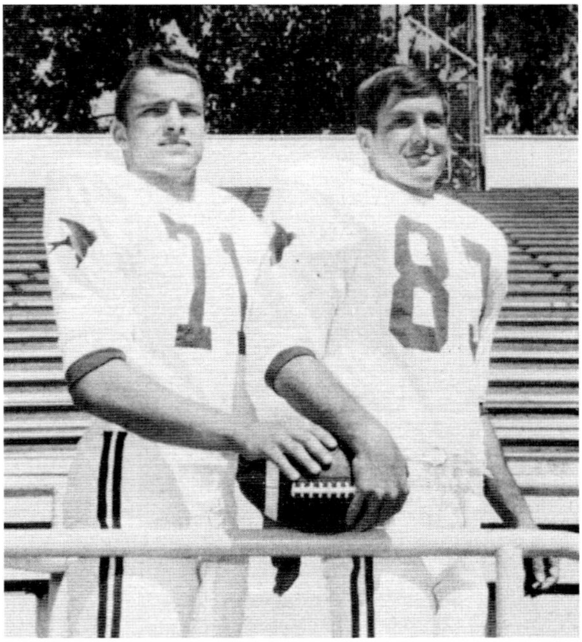

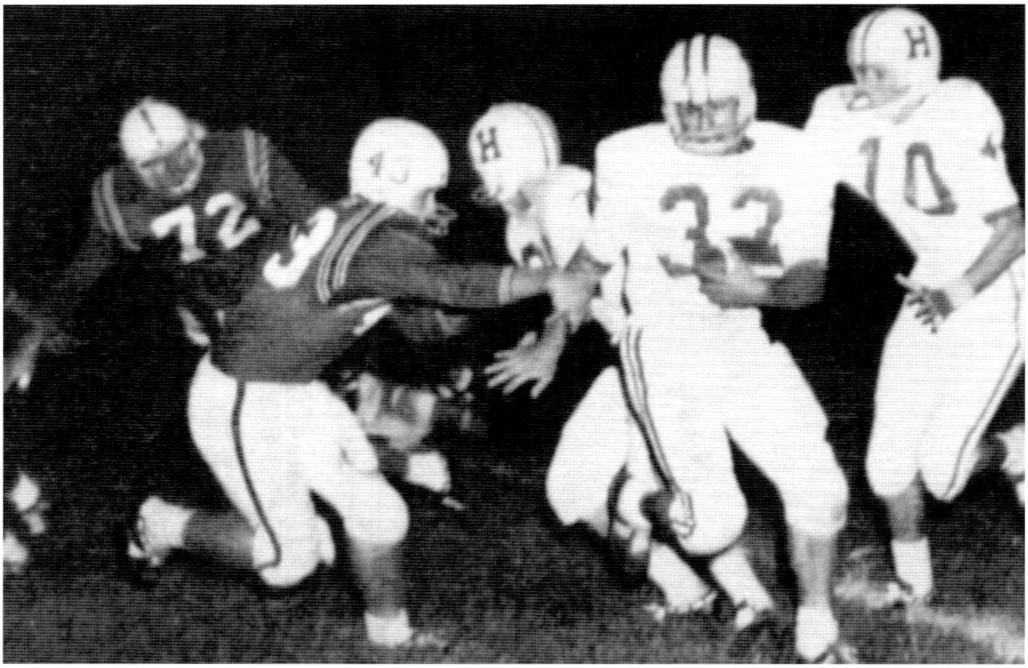

Jim "Effie" Vorhees takes a handoff from quarterback Cam Coffman and uses his speed to break open in Highlands' regular season 20-7 victory over Lexington Lafayette. A running back, Vorhees was the state's leading scorer while leading Highlands to a state championship in 1964. He was named First Team All State and went on to start at the fullback position at Western Kentucky University.

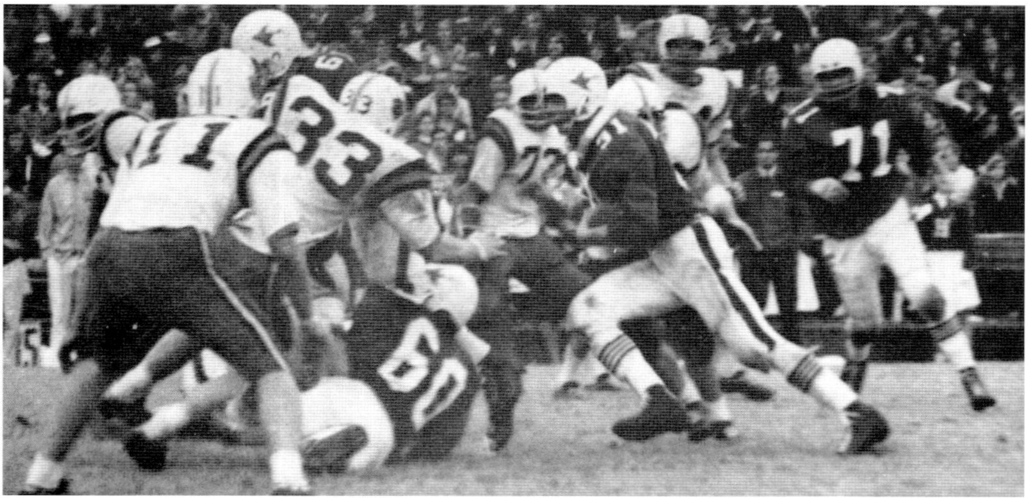

Hank Pogue (No. 31) carries the ball up the middle in the 1966 Class 2A state championship game where Highlands lost to Hopkinsville. Pogue played tailback and was named All Conference, All State, All South, and Third Team All American his senior year. Pogue was also the leading scorer in the state in 1966. He went on to start three years at fullback at Indiana University and received Indiana's Best Offensive Back award in 1969 and 1970.

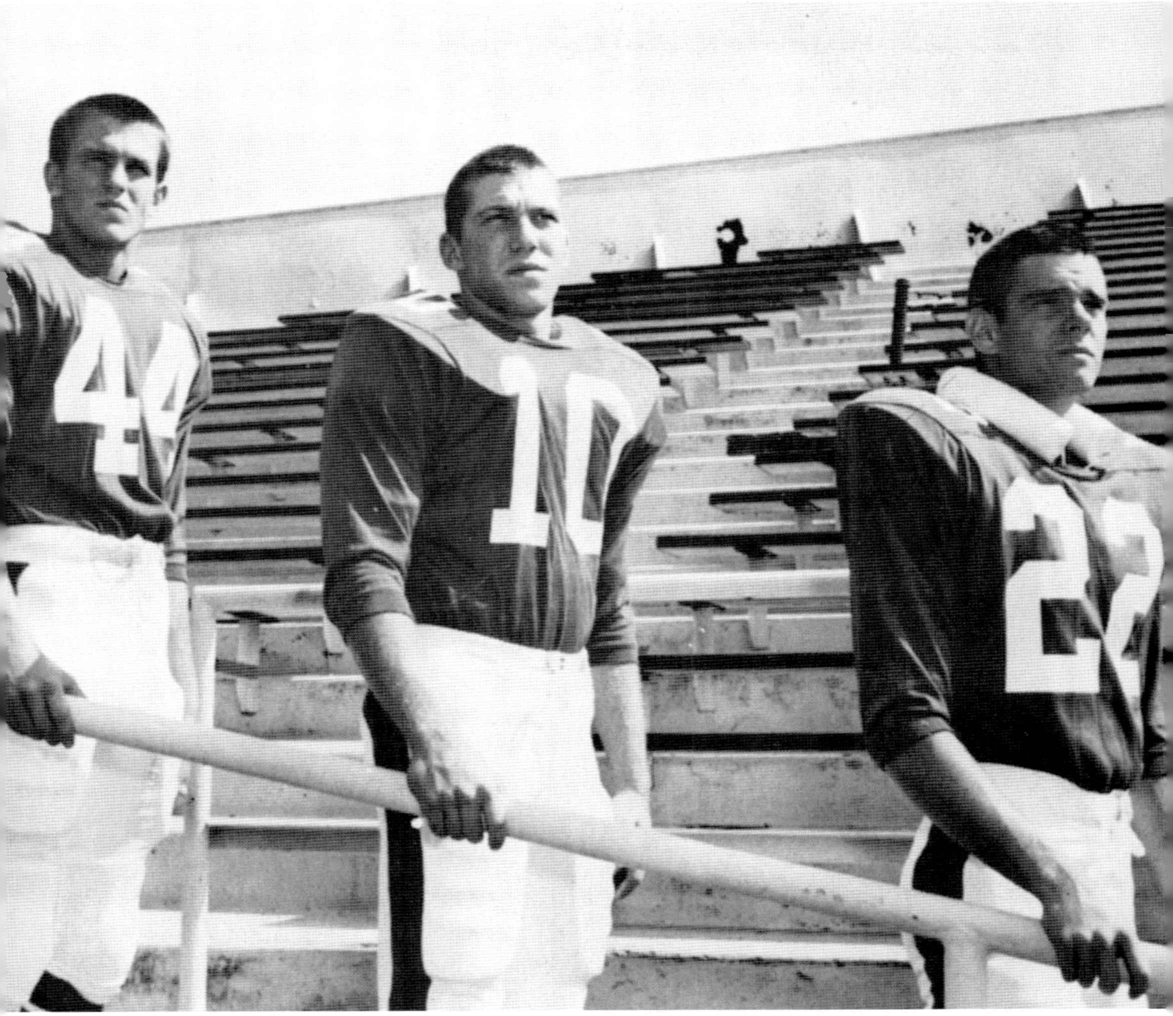

Captains of the 1968 Highlands football team that went 13-0 and easily won the Class 2A state championship, from left to right, are Rick Hoffman, Tim Racke, and Clem Fennell. Hoffman was a tailback and defensive back, and rushed for 1,800 yards in 1968. He was named All Conference, All State, and Honorable Mention All American. Hoffman played tailback and was a kickoff return specialist at Indiana University. Tim Racke played quarterback and defensive back for the 1968 state champions, and was an All Conference and All State player at Highlands. He played defensive back at Purdue University where he was named to the All Big Ten Defensive Team and All Big Ten Academic Team. Clem Fennell played wingback and defensive back on the 1968 state championship team. Fennell was also the team's punter, and one of his punts against Lexington Bryan Station in the playoffs sailed 80 yards into the end zone. Fennell was a four-year letterman as a punter and wide receiver at the University of Cincinnati.

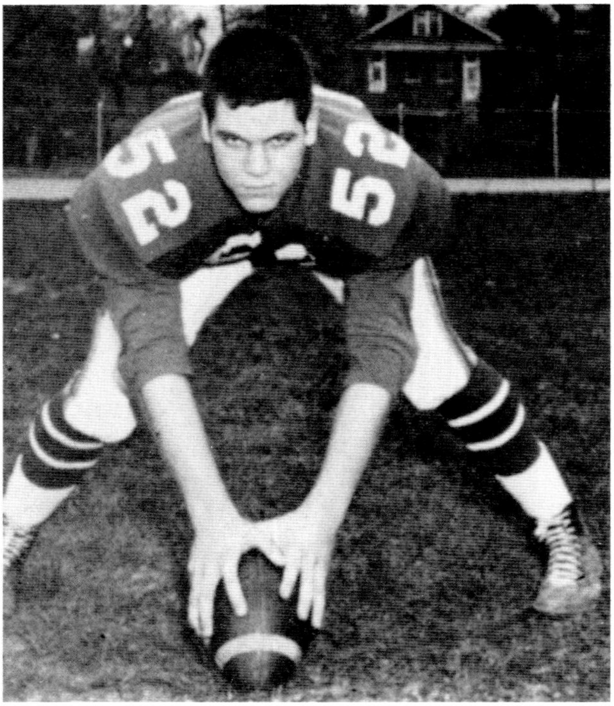

Jim Waite played center on the undefeated 1968 Highlands team. Waite, a National Merit Scholar, made Honorable Mention All Conference and All State his senior year. He played center on the Cornell University team that won the Ivy League championship in 1971. Waite was honored his senior year as a Cornell National Scholar. His son, Michael, is an assistant coach at Highlands.

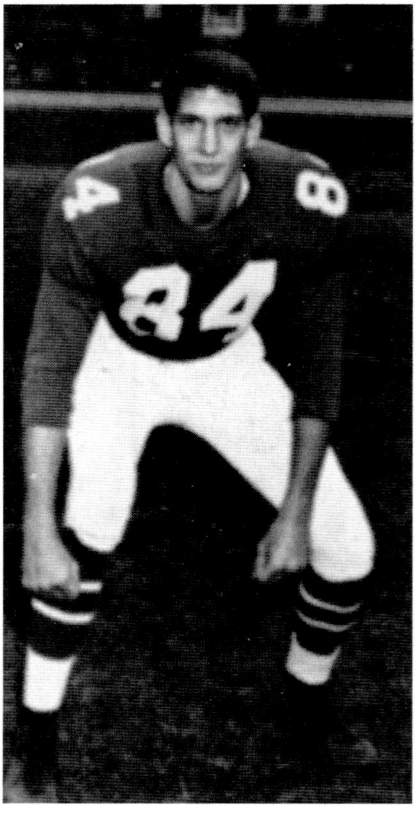

Greg Oetjen was a defensive end and offensive tackle on the 1968 state championship team. He was named Best Offensive Lineman, All Conference, and Second Team All State. Oetjen played defensive end at the University of Cincinnati and won the *Sports Illustrated* Defensive Player of the Week award for his play against Colorado in 1972.

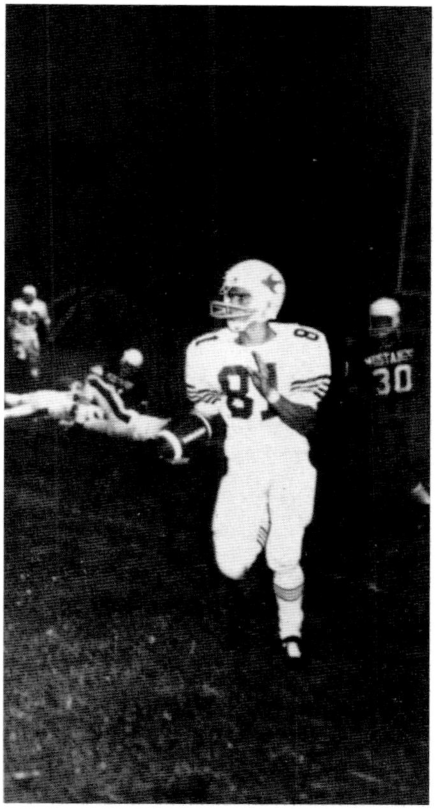

Steve Graves heads for the end zone against Western Hills in 1968 after catching a pass from quarterback Tim Racke. Graves played split-end on the 1968 team and was named Honorable Mention All Conference. He used his quickness and great hands as a wide receiver to play in a semi-pro league for a number of years.

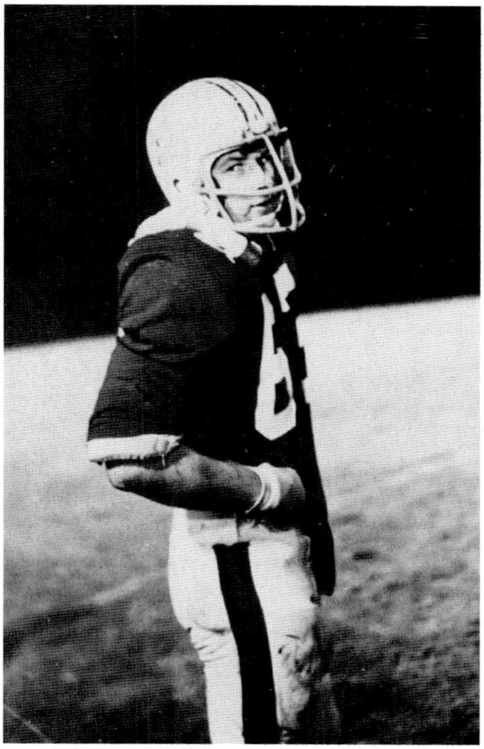

Bill Roller was a middle linebacker and offensive guard on the 1970 team that went undefeated and captured the Class 2A state championship. Roller made All Conference and First Team All State at linebacker and Second Team All State at offensive guard. He was the key to stopping future University of Kentucky great Sonny Collins when Highlands defeated Madisonville in the state championship game. Roller played semi-pro football for 10 years.

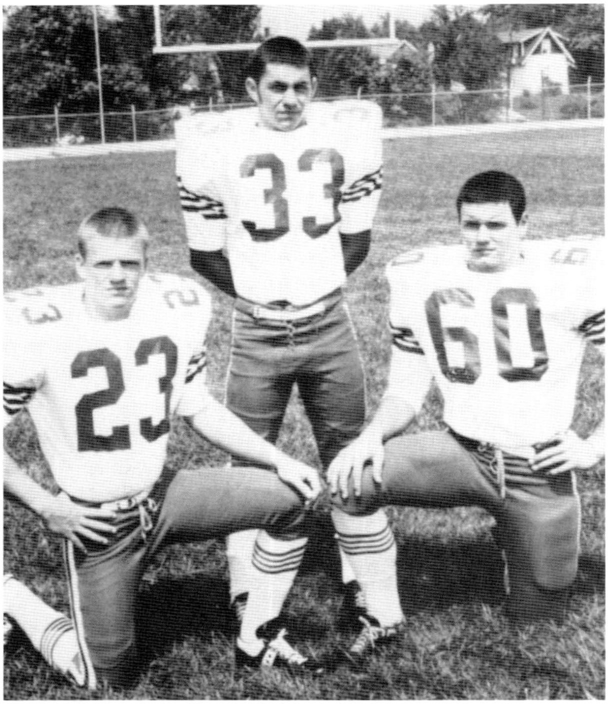

The captions of the 1970 state champion team were outstanding football players. They are pictured from left to right as follows: Dave Freer (No. 23), Dan Schneider (No. 33) and Rick Grover (No. 60). Freer was an All State tailback and played at Eastern Kentucky University; Schneider was an All State wingback and defensive back who played defensive back for a year at Morehead State University; and Grover was an All State, All Southern, and All American offensive guard who played one year at linebacker for the University of Cincinnati. Craig Leftin was another top senior on the 1970 team. Leftin was an All State offensive tackle and defensive end.

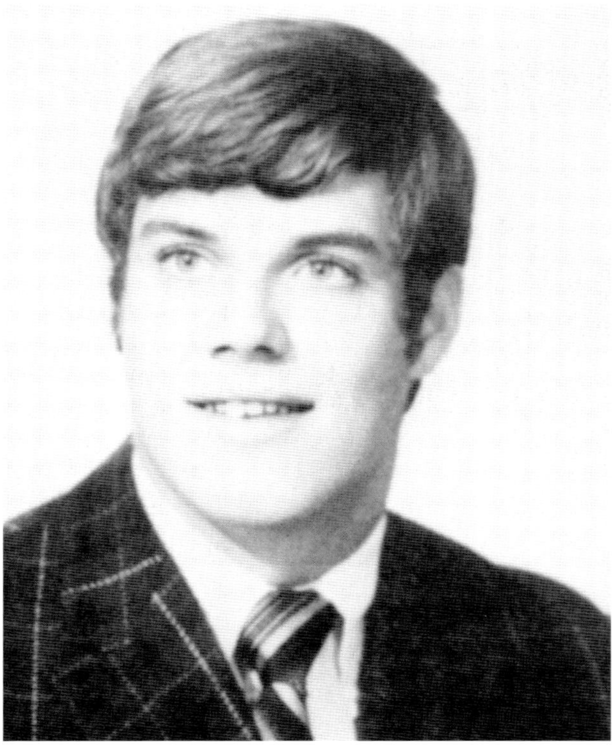

Bert Bathiany was quarterback and a defensive back on the Highlands team that went undefeated and won a state championship in 1970. Bathiany made All Conference and All State, and played in the Kentucky East-West All Star Game. He played defensive back at Denison University and was also a member of the lacrosse team.

Danny Long was an All State and All American end at Highlands, and played on the 1970 team that won a Class 2A state championship. Long played football at the University of Kentucky until a knee injury ended his career.

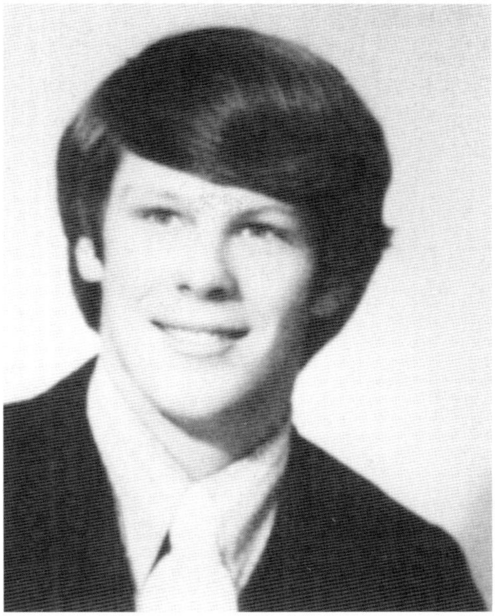

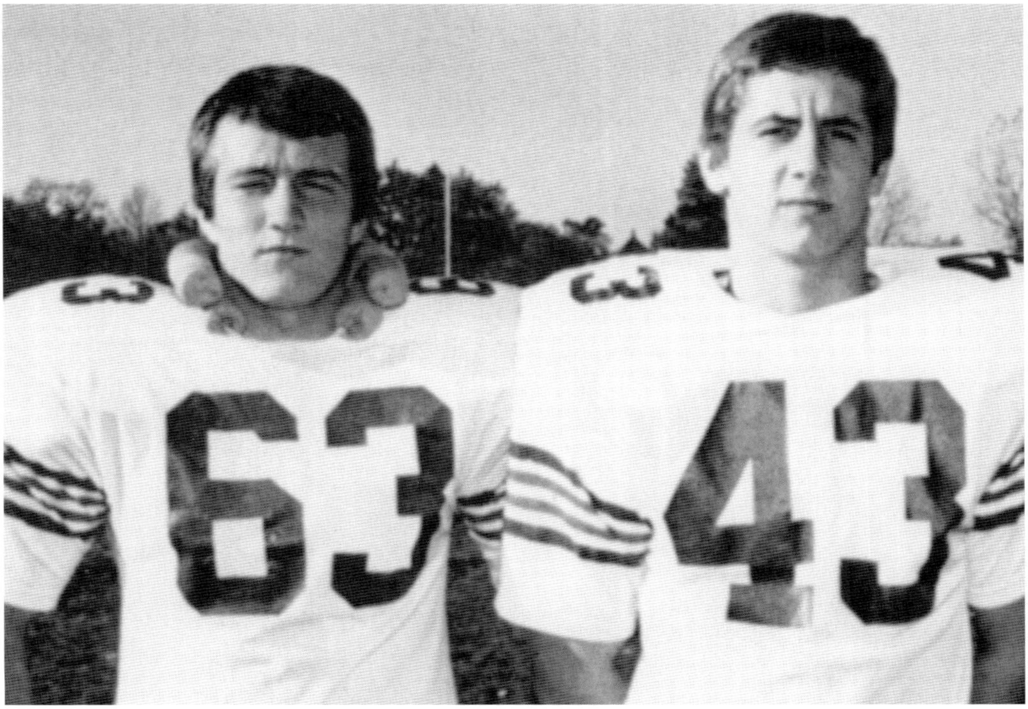

Jeff McMahon and Jeff Schlosser were captains of the Highlands team that captured the Class 3A state championship in 1975. McMahon started at the monster man position on defense and at wingback on offense. He won All Conference and All State honors. Jeff Schlosser played guard, tackle, and linebacker, and earned All Conference and First Team All State honors. Schlosser played in the Kentucky East-West All Star Game and went on to play on the defensive line at Centre College, where he was the team captain.

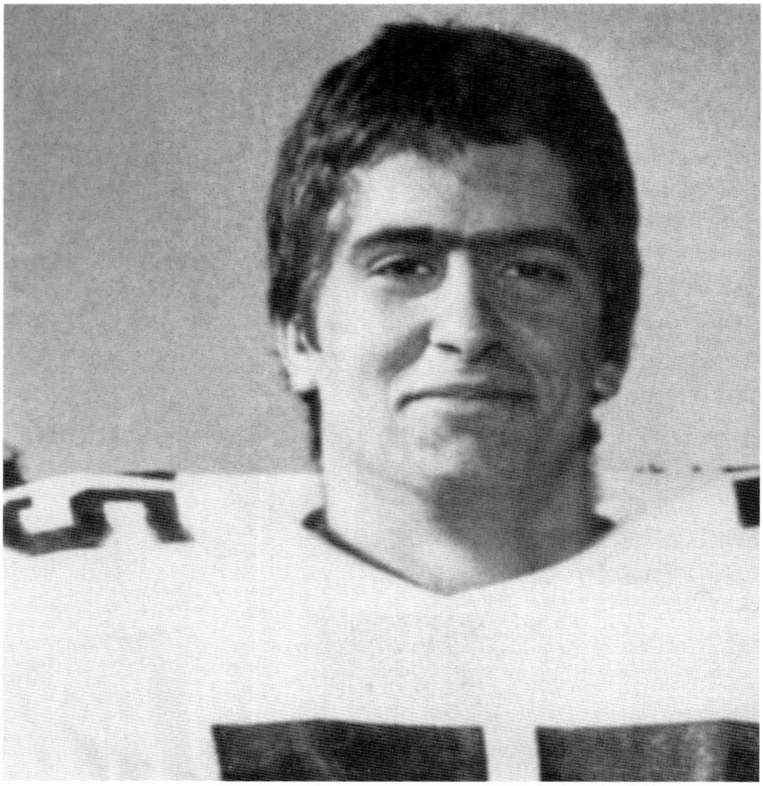

Brad Wendel played on the defensive line for Highlands in 1975 when Highlands won the Class 3A state championship. Wendel won the Best Defensive Lineman award and was named to All Conference and All State teams.

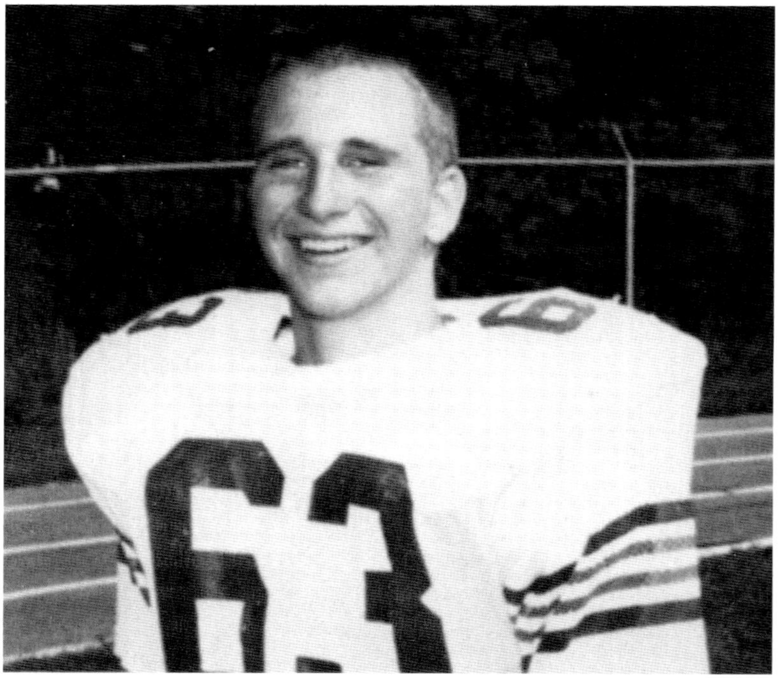

Jeff Theiss played down lineman and offensive guard on the 1975 Class 3A state championship team. Theiss was named Best Defensive Lineman and made the All Conference team. He was a member of the Kentucky All State team at down lineman and Honorable Mention All State at offensive guard.

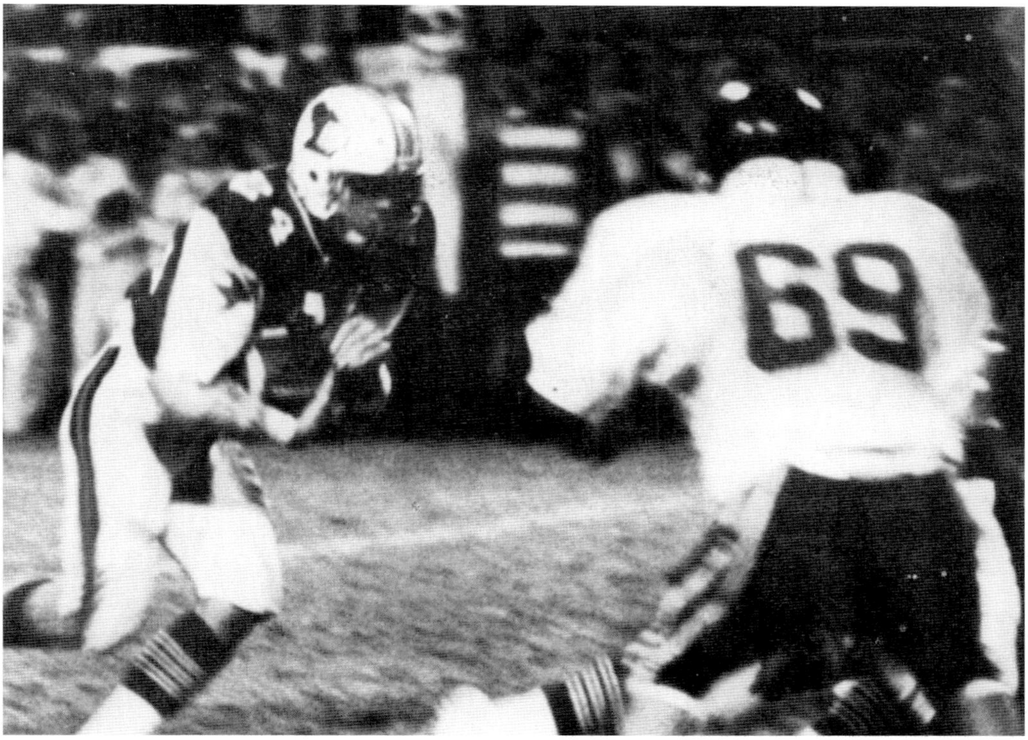

John Bankemper was a running back on the 1981 and 1982 Highlands teams that won back-to-back state championships. Bankemper was named Second Team All State his senior year after leading the state in scoring with 182 points and rushing for over 1,800 yards. He rushed for 254 yards against Elizabethtown in the 1981 state championship victory.

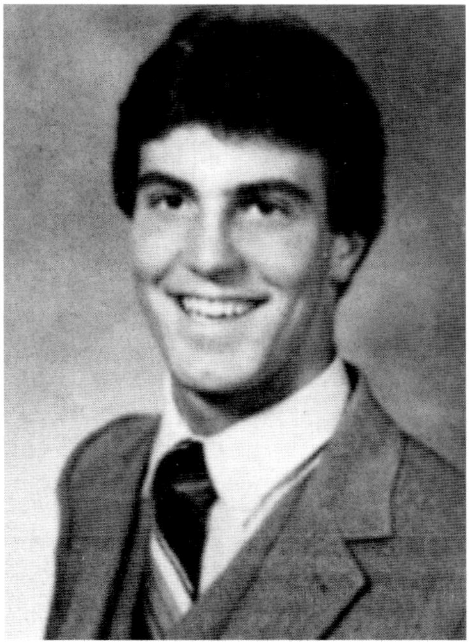

Jeff Kremer was the starting safety for Highlands in 1981 and the starting safety and quarterback in 1982. Kremer intercepted 12 passes as a junior and eight more passes his senior year when he made First Team All State. Kremer was a star linebacker at the University of Kentucky and captain of the Wildcat team in 1987. He played briefly for the Dallas Cowboys.

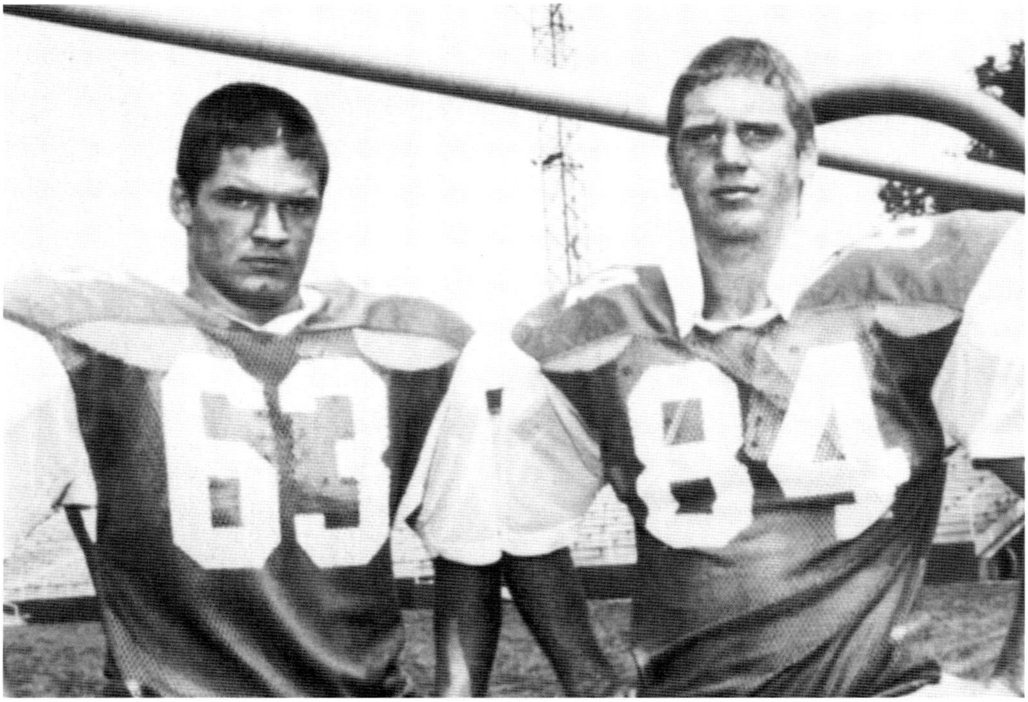

Jim Ulbricht (No. 84) and Dave Fischer (No. 63) were captains of the 1982 Highlands team that finished 15-0 and won the Class 3A state championship. Ulbricht was an All State tight end and defensive end, and Fischer was an All State nose guard. The two helped lead Highlands to six shutouts during the 1982 season.

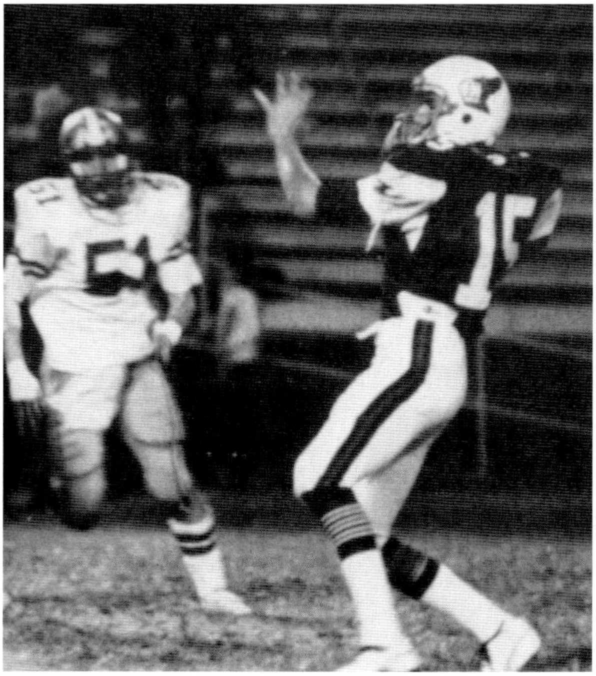

Jim Abner was quarterback of the 1981 state championship team at Highlands. He had an accurate arm and completed 87 passes for 1,612 yards and 26 touchdowns his senior year. Abner also was a standout baseball player at Highlands. His son was the quarterback of the freshman football team at Highlands in 2007.

Mike Dunn was Jim Abner's favorite receiver on the 1981 team that defeated Elizabethtown to win the Class 3A state championship. Dunn was a cocaptain of the team and an All Northern Kentucky selection. He was also an excellent defensive player for Highlands. Dunn was diagnosed with cancer in the spring of his senior year after breaking his leg during a baseball game. He passed away a few years later.

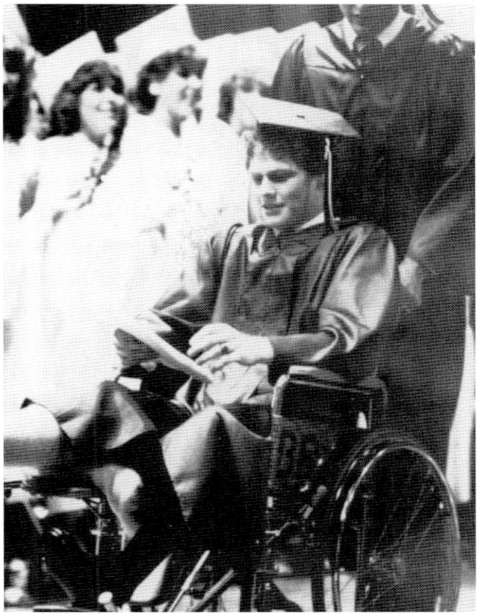

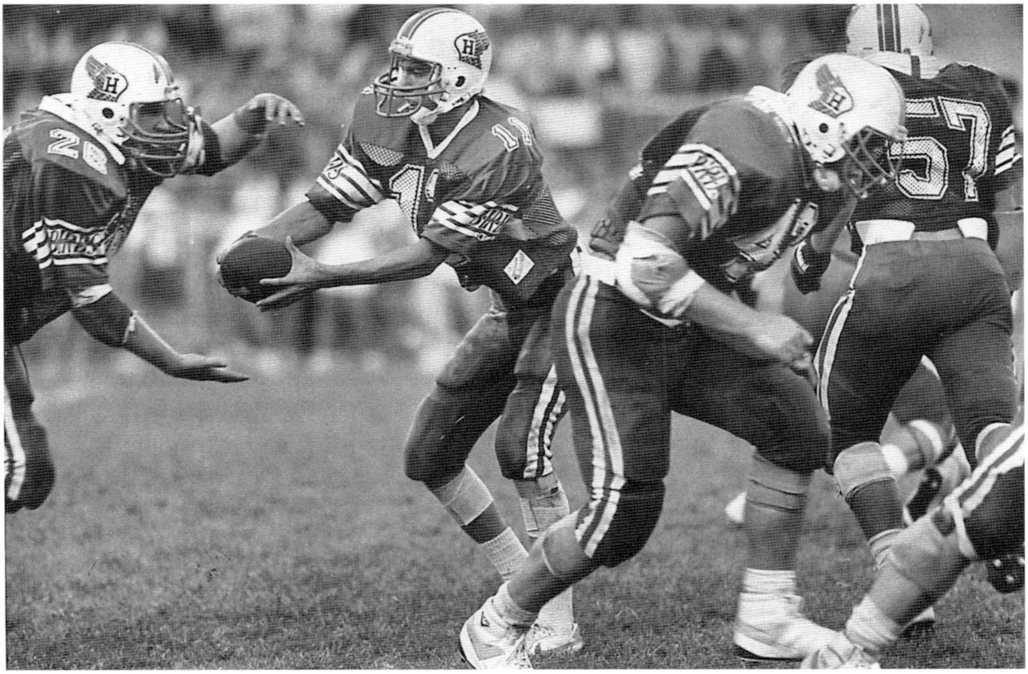

Marty Moore (No. 43) can be seen leading the blocking for Highlands' tailback in this photograph. Moore was one of the all-time best running backs and linebackers at Highlands. The All State selection went on to break school records at linebacker at the University of Kentucky and played eight seasons in the NFL. Moore was a top special teams player and linebacker for the New England Patriots for seven seasons and played one year for the Cleveland Browns. In 1997, he intercepted two passes and came up with one fumble recovery for the Patriots. He holds the University of Kentucky single season record for tackles with 183 in 1991. (Courtesy of the *Kentucky Post*.)

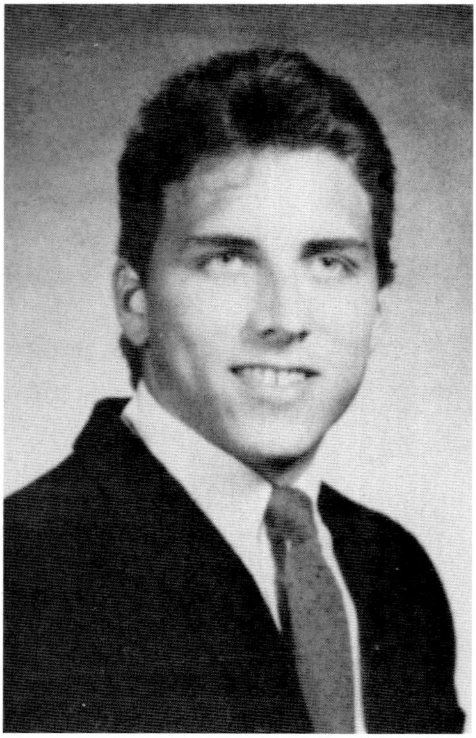

Kevin Hergott was a running back and linebacker on the 1986 Highlands team that finished the season with an 11-1 record. Coach Jack Eicher described Hergott as the "key to the offense" after he rushed for over 1,000 yards his senior year. Hergott played college football at the University of Indianapolis and lettered each year from 1988 to 1991. He was No. 10 on the school's all-time rushing list for a number of years.

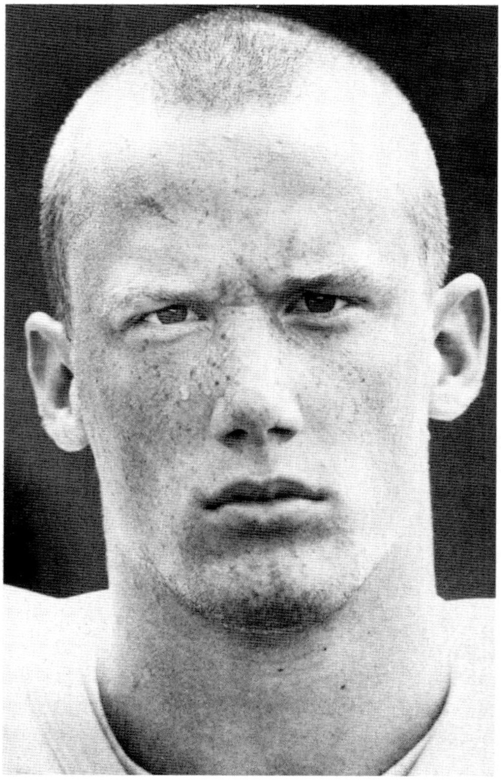

Rob Herfel was an All State player on coach Tom Duffy's first team at Highlands in 1988. (Courtesy of the *Kentucky Post*.)

Deron Blasingame played quarterback for Highlands in 1986 and 1987. He made All Conference and Honorable Mention All State as a senior. Blasingame was also an excellent basketball and baseball player for the Bluebirds. He went on to excel in basketball at Northern Kentucky University. (Courtesy of the *Kentucky Post.*)

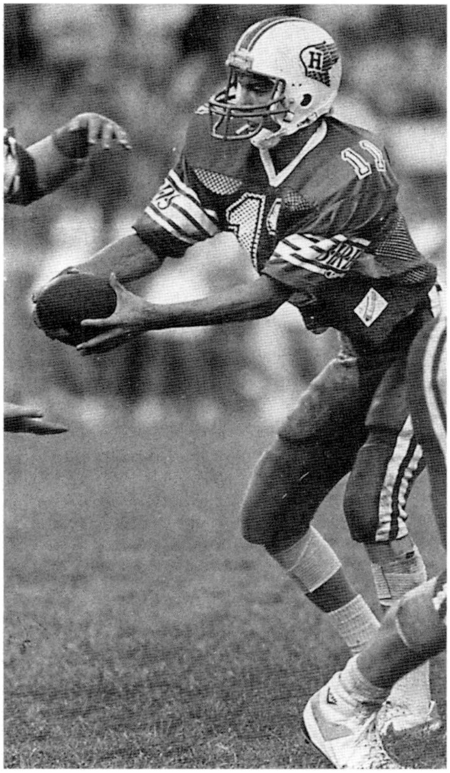

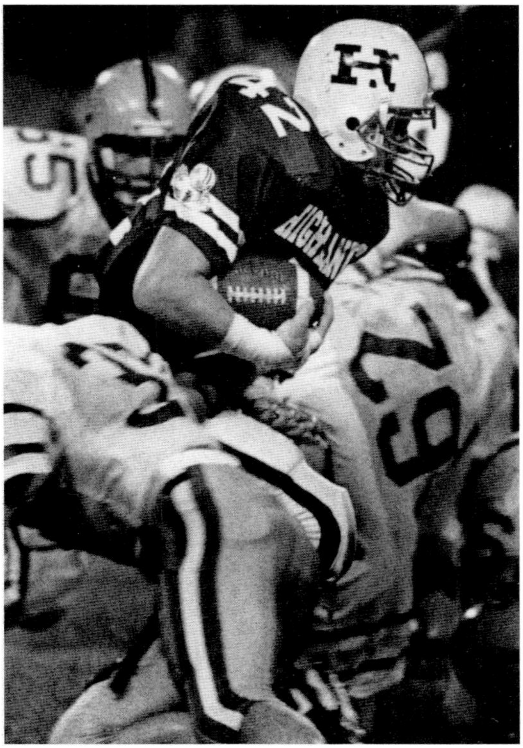

Corey Scarlato was a running back and linebacker for coach Tom Duffy at Highlands. Scarlato went on to play at Youngstown State University and also played fullback in 1997 for the University of Cincinnati. (Courtesy of the *Kentucky Post.*)

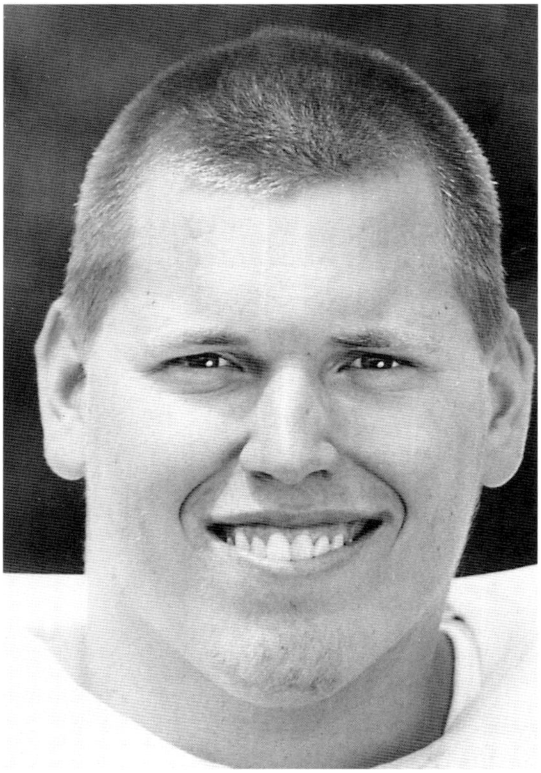

John Schlarman was an outstanding lineman for Highlands and earned All State honors his senior year. Schlarman went on to become a four-year starter on the offensive line at the University of Kentucky. He was named to the Freshman All Southeastern Conference Team in 1994 and was named Kentucky's most outstanding offensive lineman in 1995 and 1996. In 1997, Schlarman earned First Team All Southeastern Conference honors. Schlarman has coached at the University of Kentucky, Campbell County High School, and Newport High School, and is now the offensive line coach at Troy University. (Courtesy of the *Kentucky Post.*)

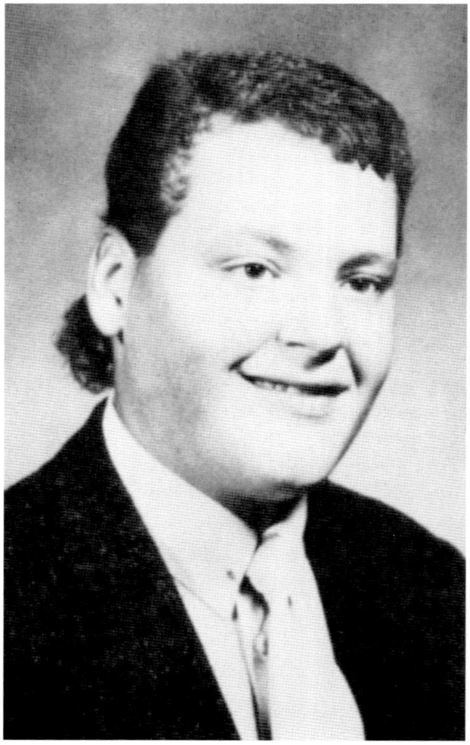

Jerry "Zeke" Reynolds played on the offensive and defensive lines for Highlands under coach Jack Eicher in 1987. He went on to play college football at the University of Nevada Las Vegas and professional football for the Cincinnati Bengals, Dallas Cowboys, and New York Giants.

Scott Kuhnhein (No. 70) is charging hard in a 1997 game. Kuhnhein was an All State offensive and defensive lineman for Highlands, and he went on to play offensive guard on the Ohio State team that won the 2002 National Championship. Kuhnhein was ranked as one of the Top 100 high school players in the country when he graduated from Highlands in 1998.

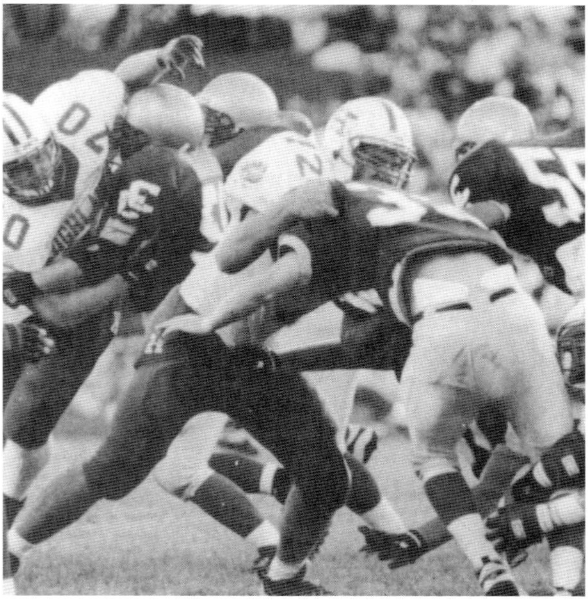

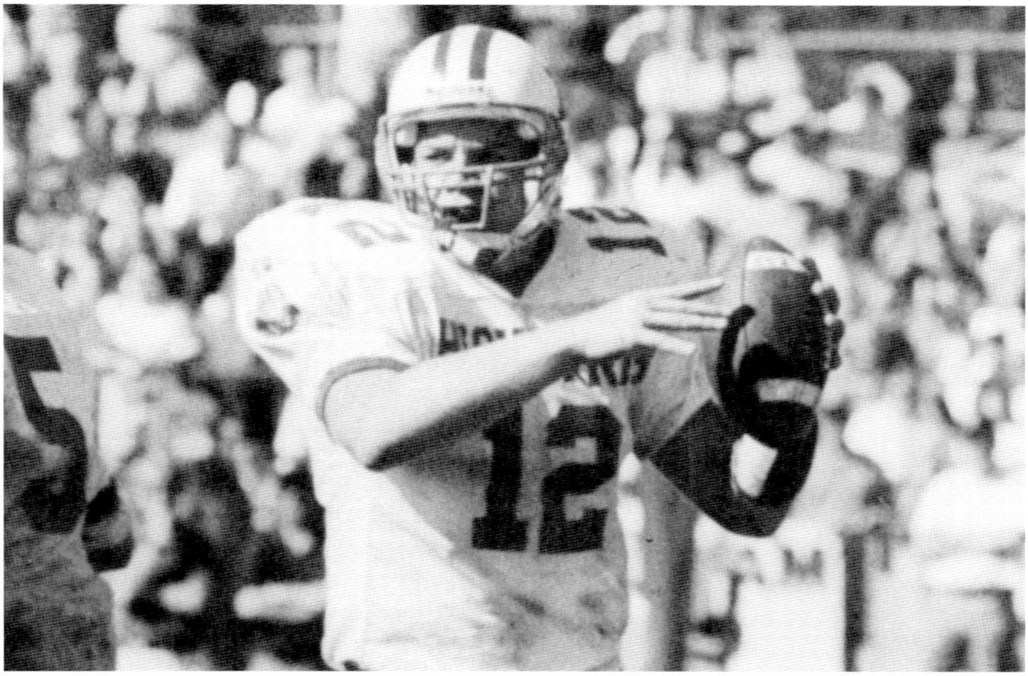

Jared Lorenzen played quarterback and led Highlands to a Class 3A state championship in 1998. Lorenzen was named Mr. Football in Kentucky after passing for 3,392 yards and 45 touchdowns. He holds University of Kentucky passing records for most passes attempted in a career (1,514) and a season (559), most passes completed in a career (862), most yards passing in a career (10,354), most yards passing in a game (528), and most touchdown passes in a career (78). Lorenzen holds six NCAA freshman records for passing and total offense. He is now the back-up quarterback for the 2008 Super Bowl champion New York Giants.

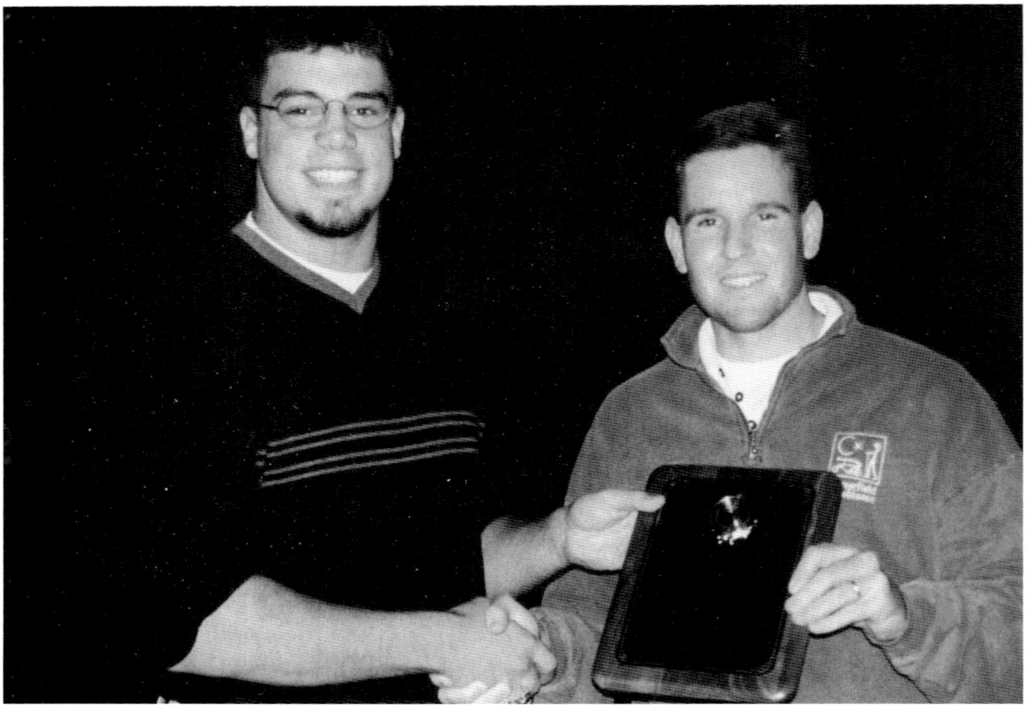

Derek Smith (left) is seen here receiving a Kentucky Player of the Year award during his senior year at Highlands. Smith was an outstanding tight end and defensive end at Highlands, and played on teams that won Class 3A state championships in 1996 and 1998. He caught seven passes for 304 yards in a game against Scott High School in 1998. Smith was an All State player who was the recipient of three different Kentucky Player of the Year awards his senior year. He went on to become an All Southeastern Conference tight end at the University of Kentucky and later was a member of the Cincinnati Bengal practice squad.

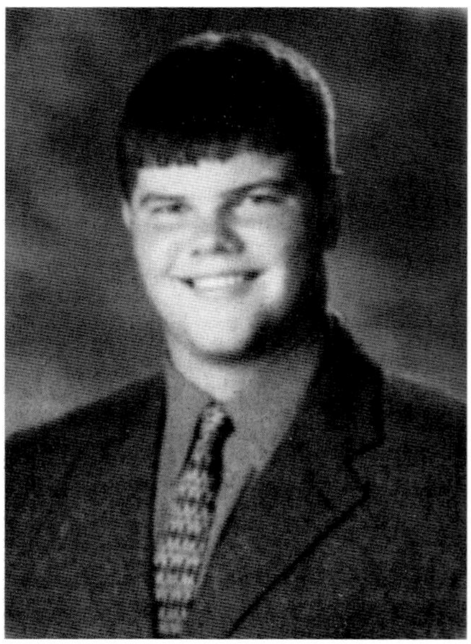

Rob Smith was a four-year letterman and three-year starter on the offensive line for Highlands. The 2002 graduate was an All State player and a member of the *USA Today* High School All American Team. He played college football at the University of Tennessee, and after a year with the Cleveland Browns, he is now on the practice squad of the Kansas City Chiefs.

Gino Guidugli led Highlands to two Class 3A state championships from his quarterback position in 1999 and 2000, and was named runner-up Mr. Football in Kentucky his senior year. Guidugli completed 260 of 404 passes for 4,367 yards and 51 touchdowns during his two years as a starter. Guidugli holds most of the passing records at the University of Cincinnati, where he completed 880 of 1,556 passes for 11,453 yards and 78 touchdowns. He signed with the Tennessee Titans in 2005 and is now a member of the B. C. Lions in the Canadian Football League.

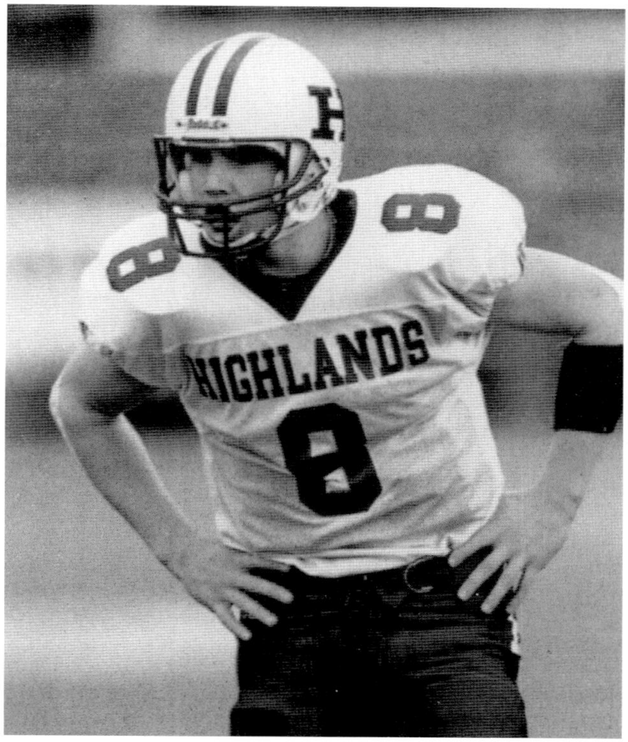

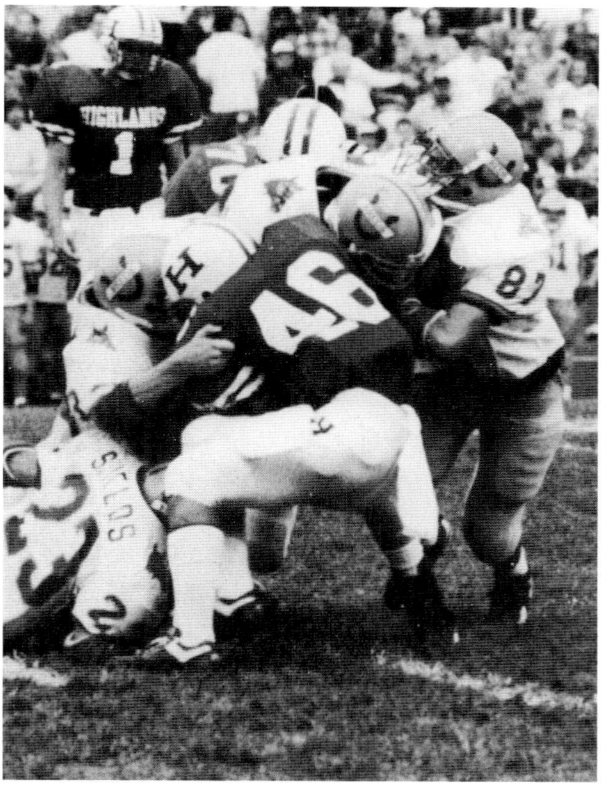

Justin Frisk (No. 46) has nowhere to run on this play. Frisk was a running back on the 1996 Highlands football team that won the Class 3A state championship. He rushed for 35 touchdowns and gained over 2,000 yards on the ground in 1996. An All State selection, Frisk went on to play football at a junior college in Arizona and finished his career at Thomas More College.

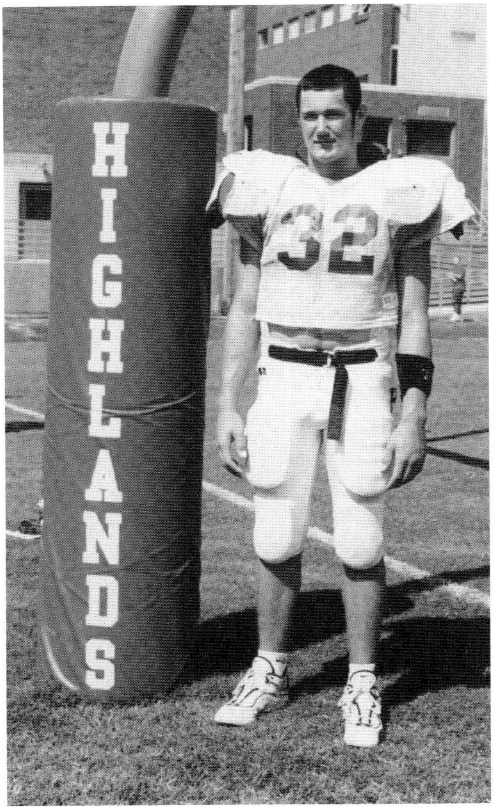

Brent Grover was ranked the No. 7 linebacker in the nation by SuperPrep during his senior year at Highlands in 2000. An All State middle linebacker, Grover amassed 226 tackles, including 44 for a loss, and 15 sacks as a senior. He was selected to play in the National East-West High School All Star Game in Dallas. Grover was a four-year starter at defensive tackle for Purdue University. In 2002, Grover was named by the *Sporting News* to the Big Ten All-Freshman Team.

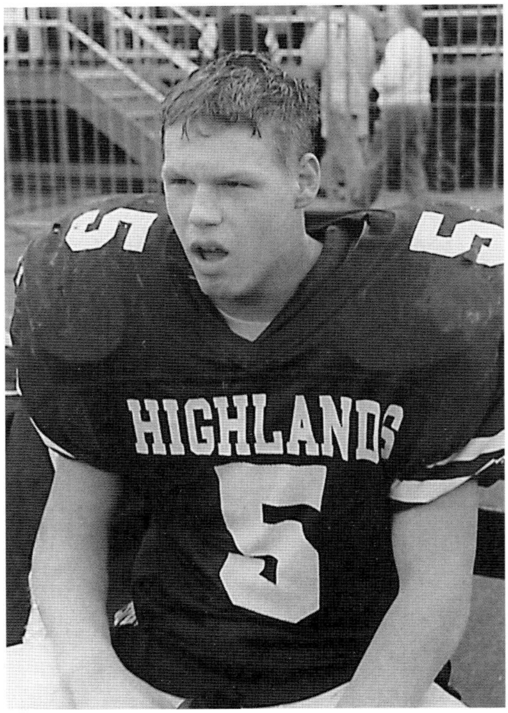

Brian Ulbricht was a running back and inside linebacker on the 1998 Class 3A state championship team. Ulbricht was an All State selection his senior year and went on to play at Cornell University, where he was the team's leading rusher.

Phil Scherrer played offensive tackle and tight end on the 1997 Highlands team that finished the season with an 11-2 record. He made the All Northern Kentucky team and went on to play on the defensive line at Harvard University. He was an All Ivy League performer.

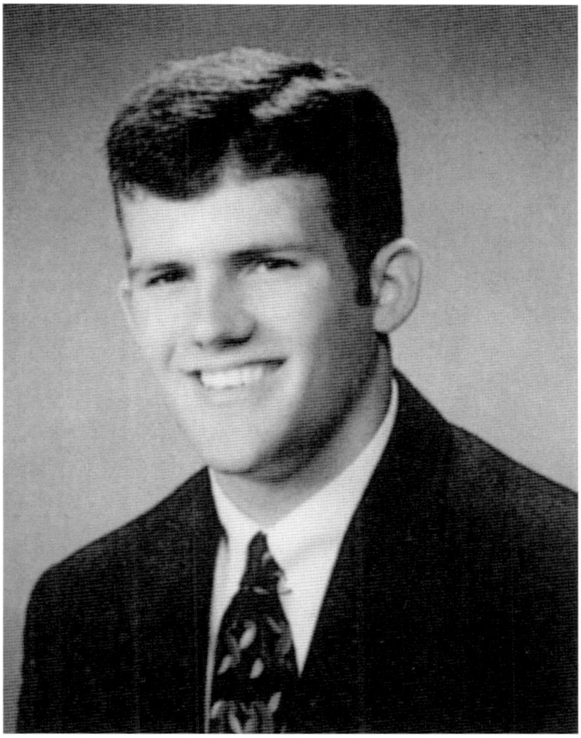

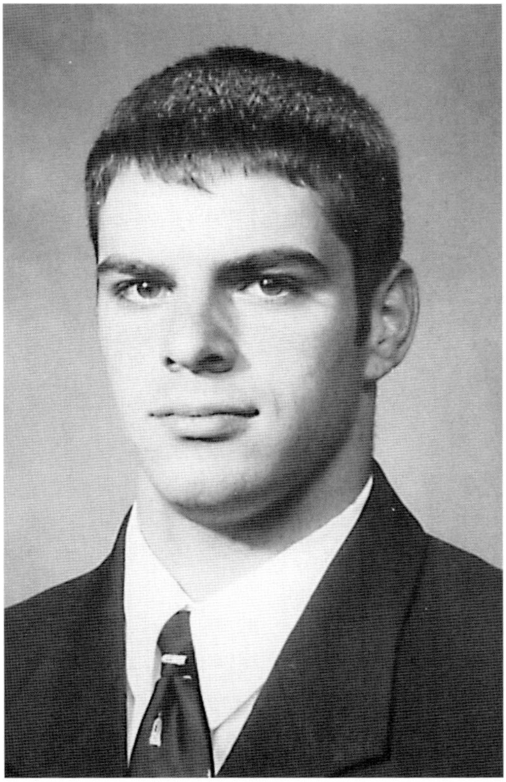

Randy Stegman was a wide receiver for Highlands in 1996 and 1997. His 70-yard touchdown reception in the state championship game in 1996 helped fuel a Highlands comeback that led to a victory. Stegman walked on at Miami University and earned a scholarship and a starting position at flanker. His quarterback at Miami was Ben Roethlisberger, now a member of the Pittsburgh Steelers. (Courtesy of Bev Stegman.)

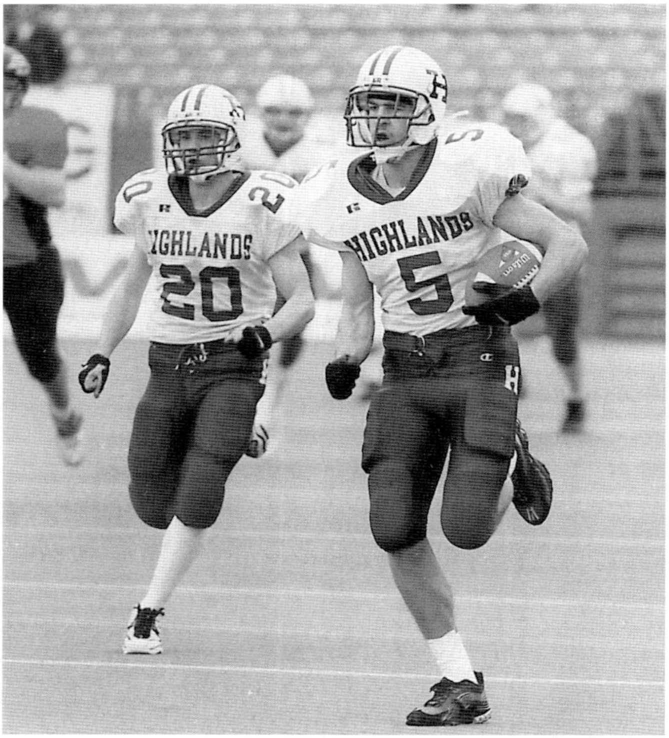

Brett Hamblen (No. 5) was a wide receiver, defensive back, and punt and kick-off return specialist when Highlands won Class 3A state championships in 1999 and 2000. Hamblen holds the state record with six touchdown receptions in one game. He caught 140 passes for 3,071 yards and 47 touchdowns in his career at Highlands. Hamblen was an All Conference and All State player, and received the Johnny Unitas Award as the best Class 3A player in Kentucky his senior year. He played football for one season at the University of Kentucky. (Courtesy of Mark Majors.)

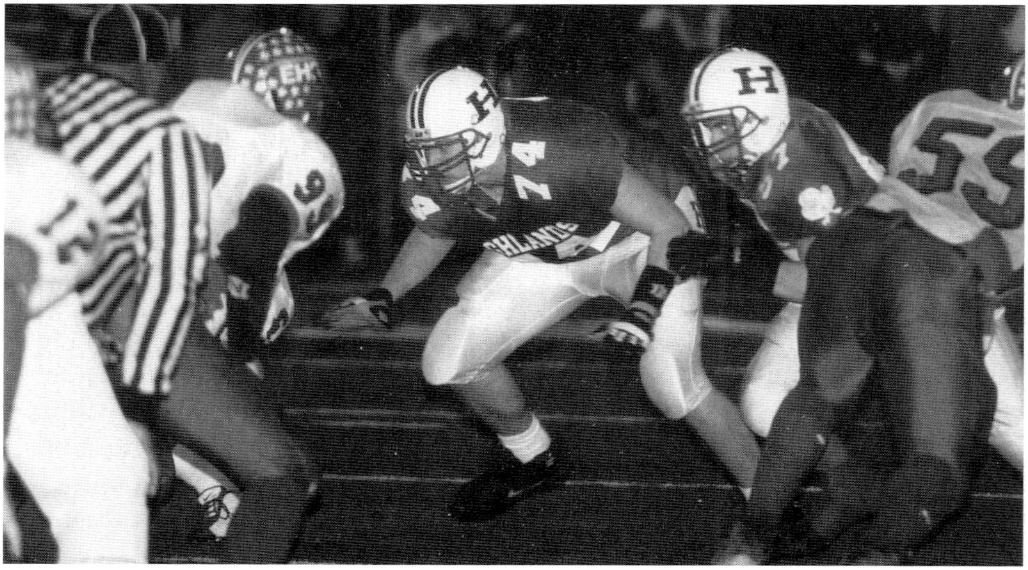

Sean Sester (No. 74) was an All State offensive tackle at Highlands, and he helped lead the Bluebirds to a 12-3 record and a trip to the state finals in 2003. Sester has been the starting right tackle in every game for the last three seasons at Purdue University. In 2005, CollegeFootballNews.com named Sester First Team Freshman All-American, and the *Sporting News* named him to the Big Ten All-Freshman team. At 6-foot-8-inches tall and 330 pounds, Sester has a good chance to be the next Highlands graduate in the NFL.

Jordan Nevels was an outside linebacker and running back on the 2004 Class 3A state championship team at Highlands. Nevels possessed great quickness and was a big hitter on defense. He is playing cornerback at the University of Kentucky.

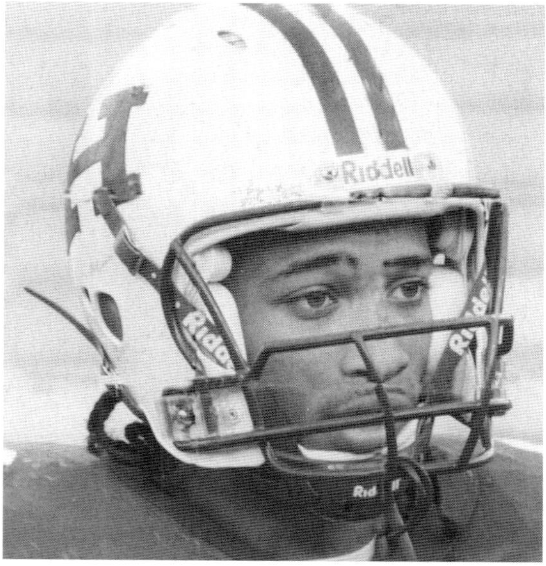

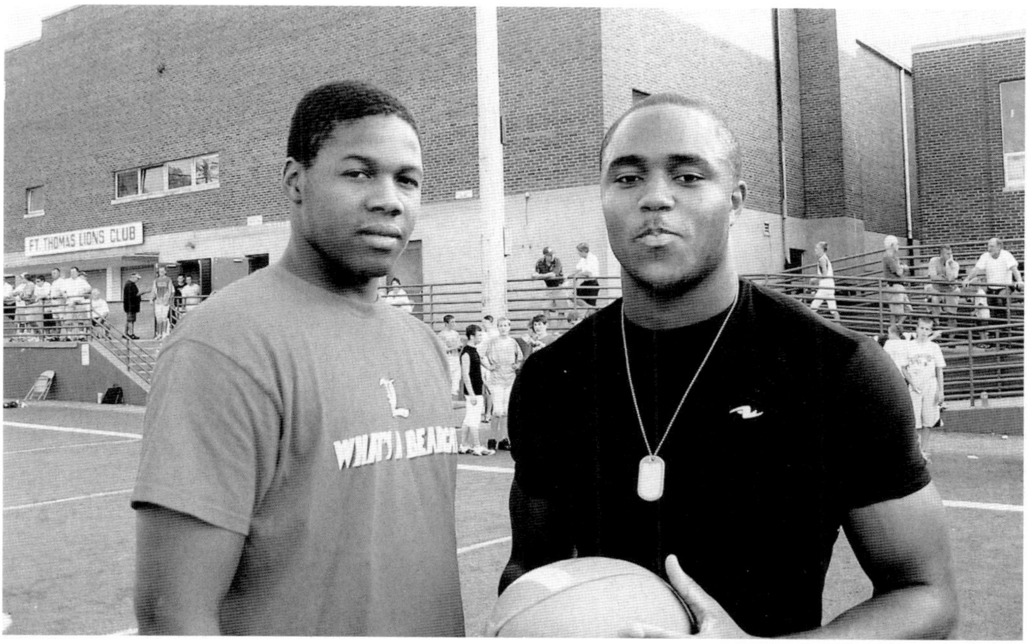

Michael Mitchell (right) returned to his alma mater over the summer to watch a scrimmage game before heading off to Ohio University to prepare for the 2007 season. Mitchell played running back and defensive back on the Highlands team that captured the Class 3A state championship in 2004. Mitchell scored both touchdowns in Highlands playoff win over Covington Catholic and scored the winning touchdown in the playoffs against Bell County. An All Northern Kentucky selection, Mitchell is the starting safety on the Ohio University football team. He finished his sophomore year tied for fourth on the team with 55 tackles and 2 pass interceptions. He was involved in 74 tackles and had 2 pass interceptions in 2007. At 6-foot-1-inches tall and 217 pounds, Mitchell has the size and talent to play professional football.

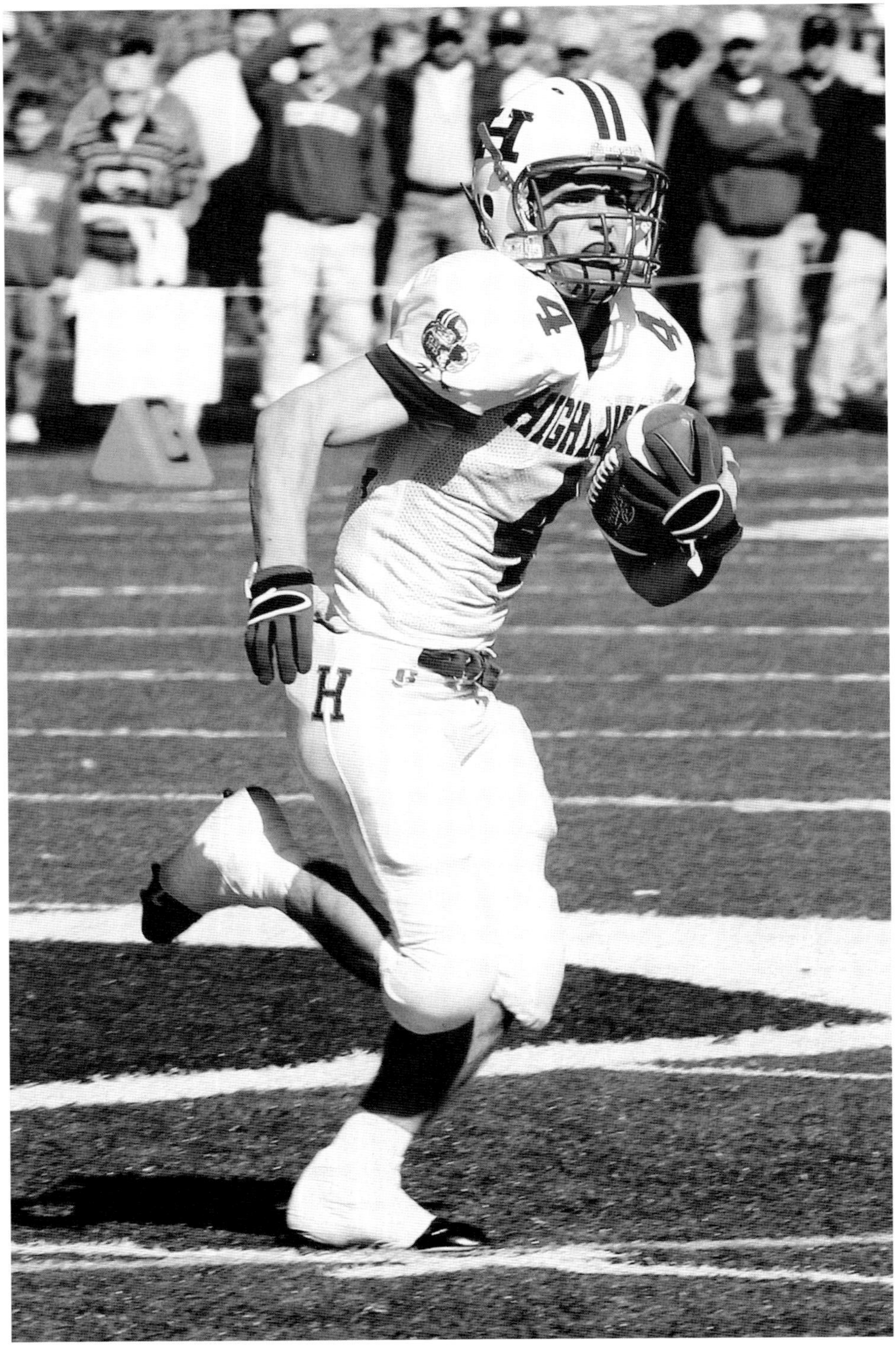

Jordan Kramer was the leading running back for Highlands in 2005 and 2006. He holds the school record for rushing in a single game with 324 yards. Kramer is playing college football at Georgetown College. (Courtesy of Tanner Johnson.)

8

Highlands Football Through the Years

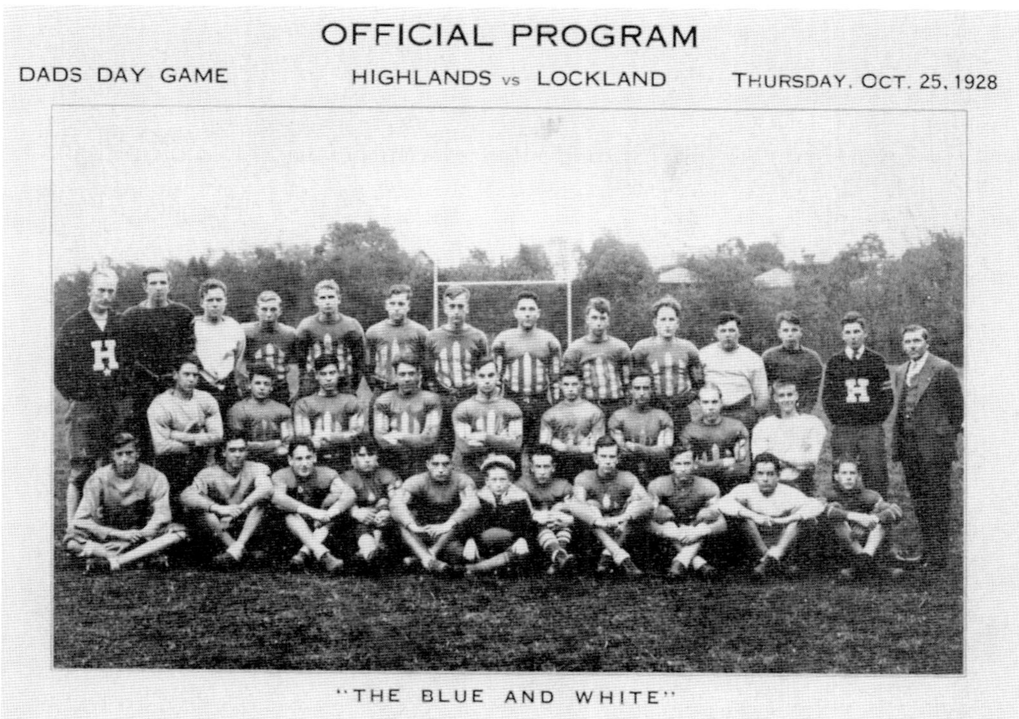

A special four-page program was printed in 1928 for the Dads Day Game against Lockland on a Thursday afternoon. Highlands crushed the Cincinnati team by a score of 59-2 en route to a 7-1 season. Highlands shutout five of its opponents and lost only to Ohio Military Institute by a score of 6-0. (Courtesy of Bert Thomas.)

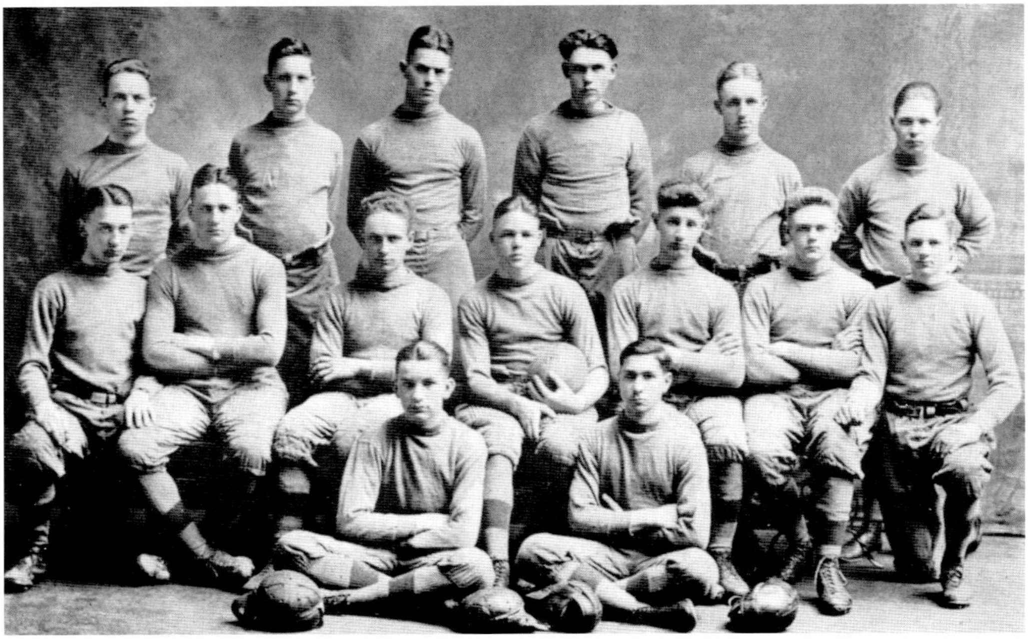

The 1918 Highlands team played only three games because of the influenza epidemic. An estimated 675,000 Americans and 20 to 40 million people worldwide died of influenza during the 1918–1919 pandemic.

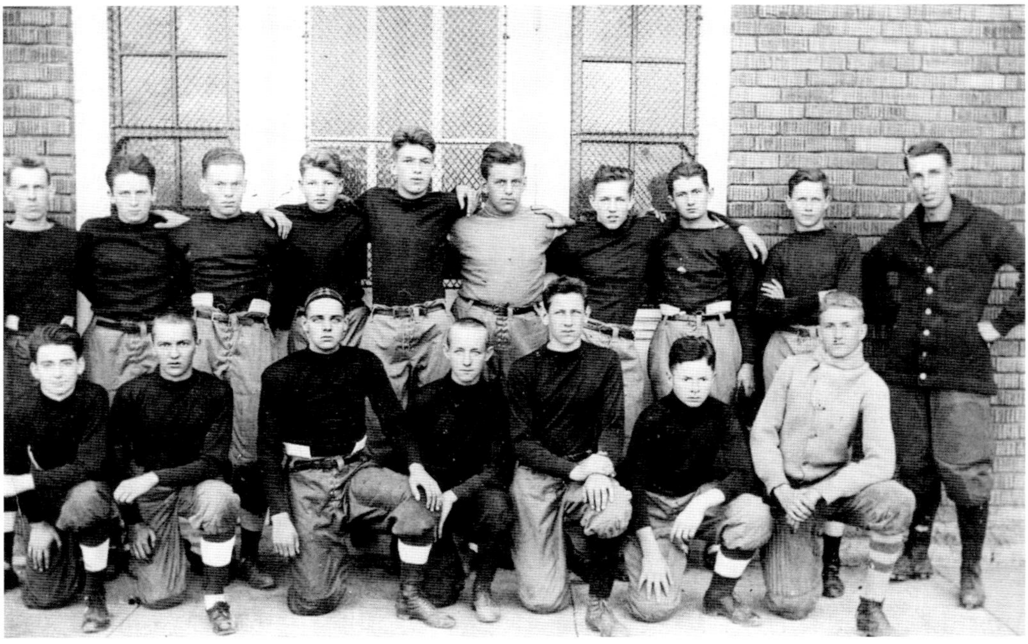

Highlands fielded its first football team in 1915. The team finished the season with a 4-5-2 record that included a huge win over rival Newport. One loss came at the hands of a team made up of Highlands alumni. Highlands' first coach was Thomas Lewis. (Courtesy of Jean Mettens.)

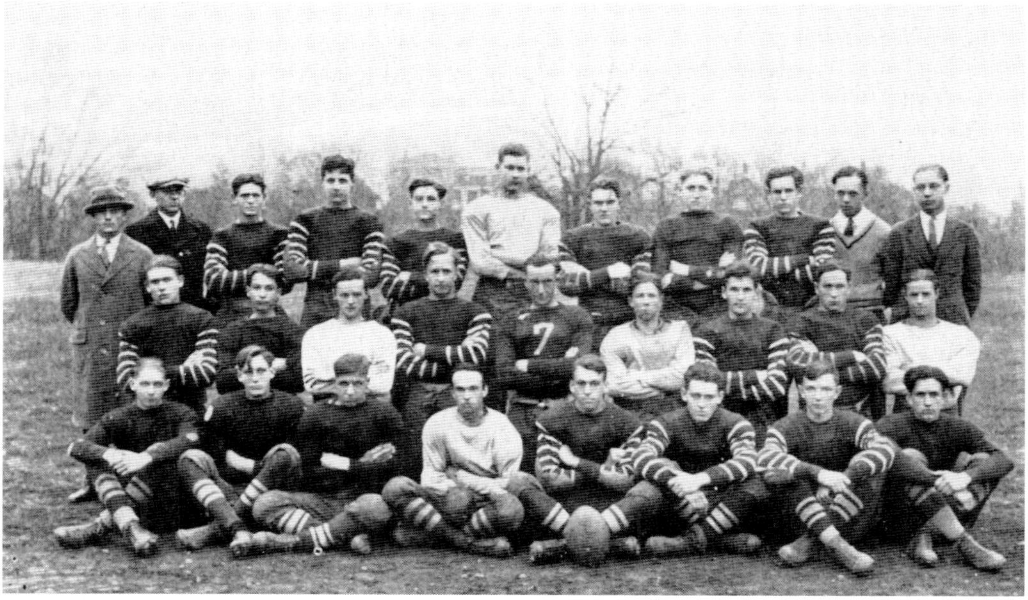

The 1924 Highlands Blue Devils finished the season with a 6-3 record against a schedule that included only two Kentucky teams, Ludlow and Richmond Madison.

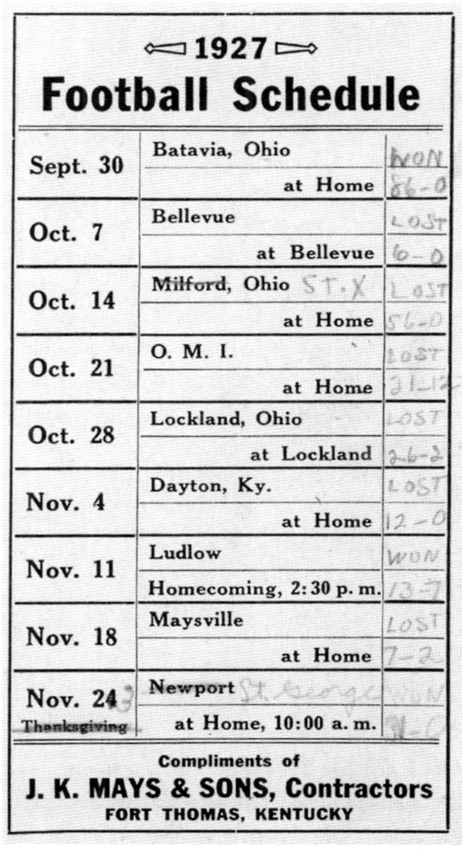

1927

Football Schedule

Date	Opponent	Site	Result
Sept. 30	Batavia, Ohio	at Home	WON 86-0
Oct. 7	Bellevue	at Bellevue	LOST 6-0
Oct. 14	~~Milford~~, Ohio ST. X	at Home	LOST 56-0
Oct. 21	O. M. I.	at Home	LOST 21-12
Oct. 28	Lockland, Ohio	at Lockland	LOST 26-2
Nov. 4	Dayton, Ky.	at Home	LOST 12-0
Nov. 11	Ludlow	Homecoming, 2:30 p. m.	WON 13-7
Nov. 18	Maysville	at Home	LOST 7-2
Nov. 24 Thanksgiving	Newport St. George	at Home, 10:00 a. m.	WON

Compliments of
J. K. MAYS & SONS, Contractors
FORT THOMAS, KENTUCKY

Highlands student Pat Johnson kept a record of every Highlands game during the 1927 season. The season went downhill after Highlands whipped Batavia by a score of 86-0 in the opening game on September 30. The team finished with a 3-6 record. (Courtesy of Bert Thomas.)

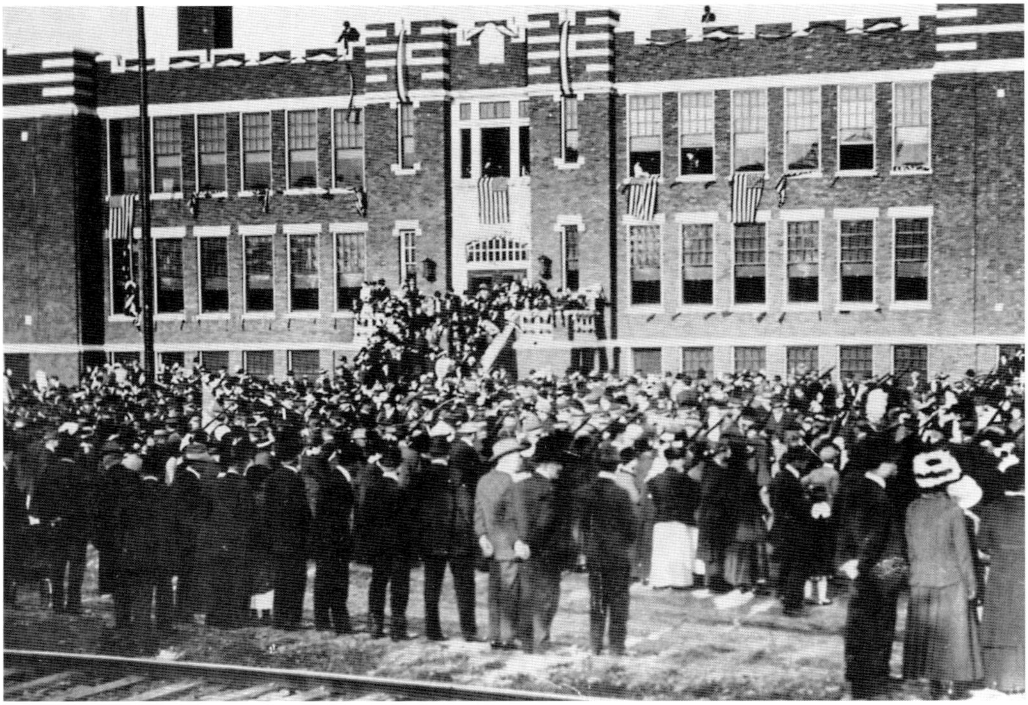

A community ceremony was held in 1915 for the opening of the new Highlands High School building. The building was destroyed by fire in 1962. The school's first football games were played on a field at the Fort Thomas military post. A few years later, a field and stadium were constructed behind the school.

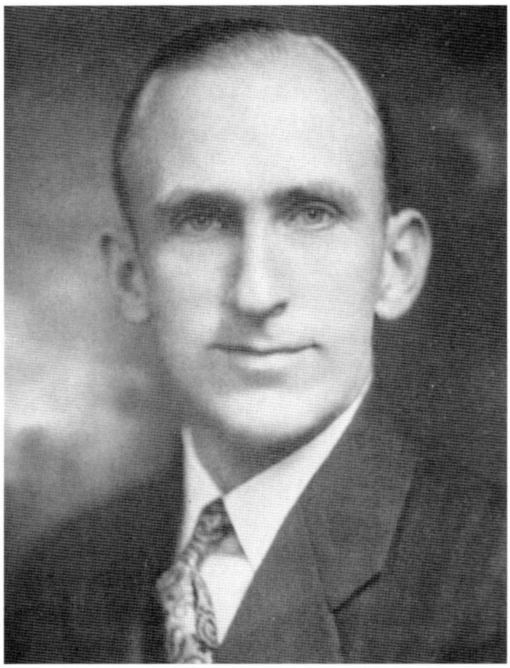

Homer Jackson, the football coach at Highlands in 1930, led the Blue Devils to an undefeated season and a Greater Cincinnati championship. John Hosking and Bill Fleming were named All State and All Cincinnati. Team captain Bob Stegeman also made the All Cincinnati Team.

Bud Rohrer was captain of the 1925 Highlands football team that finished the season with a 6-2 record. The Blue Devils (the mascot was changed a few years later to Bluebirds) were crowned Class B Cincinnati champions for the third year in a row. Rohrer was quarterback of the team.

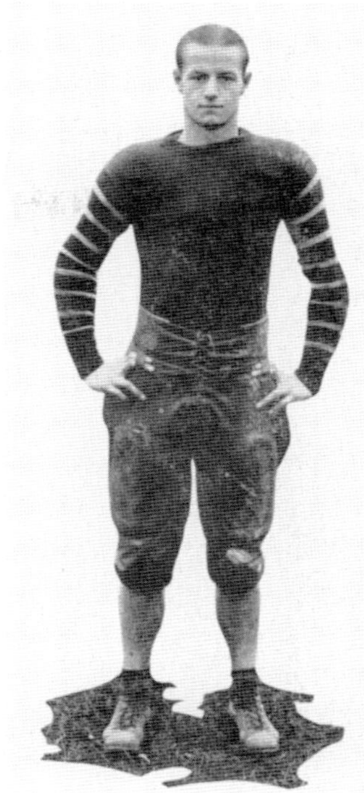

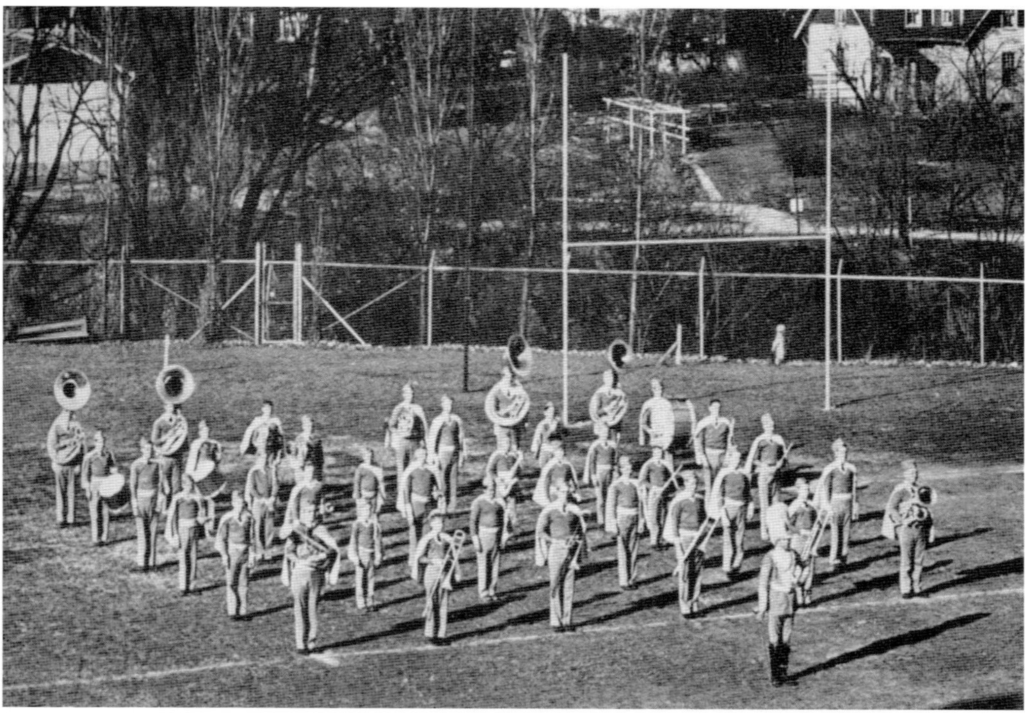

Highlands' marching band practices on the football field during the 1933 football season. Highlands finished the season with only one loss. Highlands and Dayton shared the Little Five Conference championship after the teams played to a 0-0 tie in the season finale.

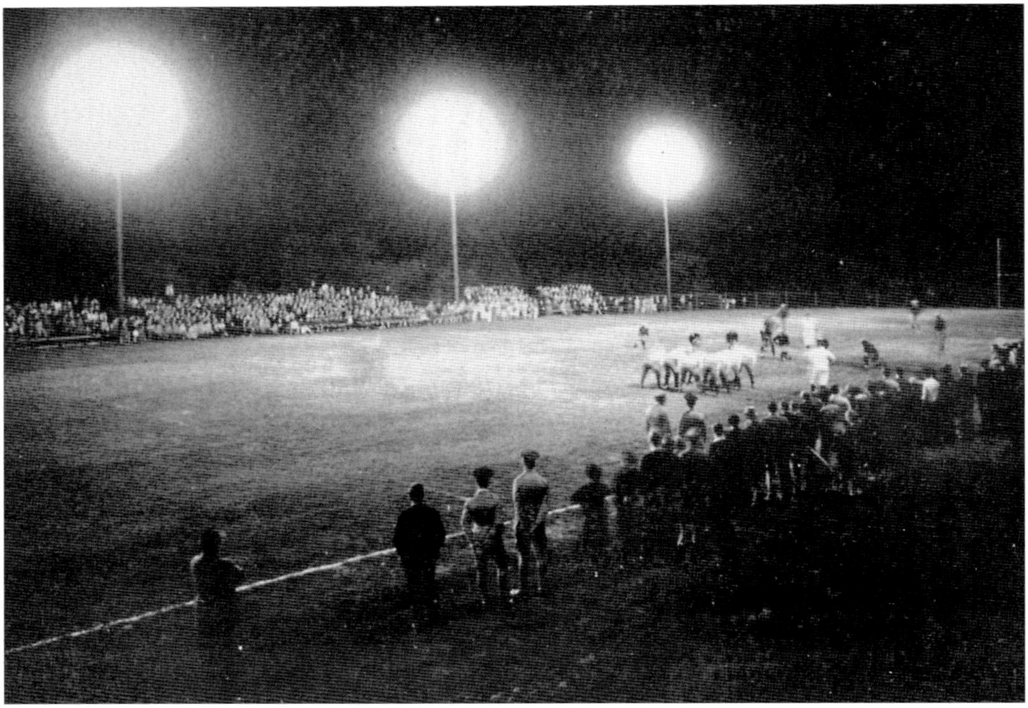

Highlands opened the 1934 season with new "spotlights" around the field. Games could now be played in the evening instead of during the afternoon. The field had been reseeded that summer with the best turf available for athletic fields. Highlands captured the Little Five Conference championship with a 6-2 record.

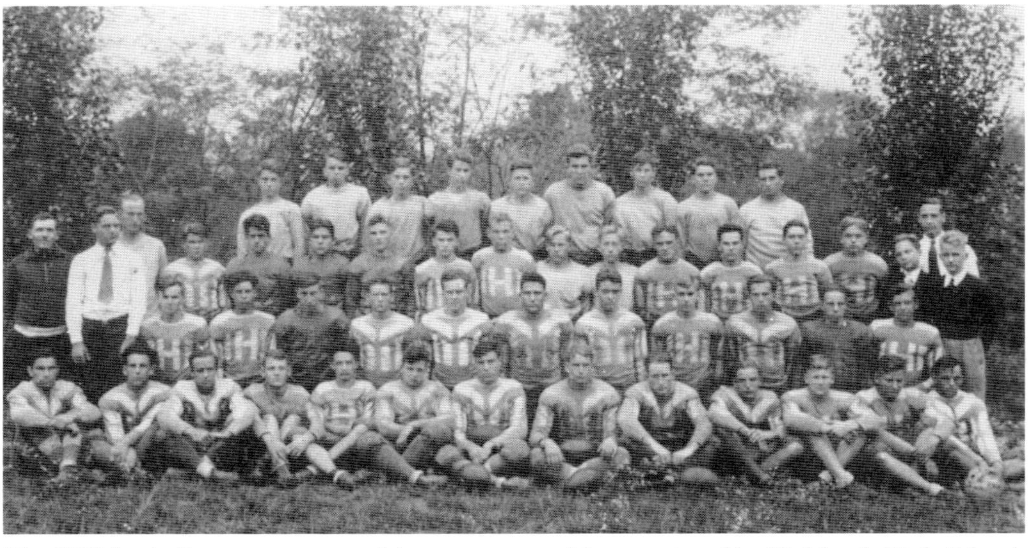

The 1930 football season was one of the most successful ever enjoyed by Highlands High School. The team captured the Greater Cincinnati championship for the first time, finished the season with a perfect 10-0 record, and finished No. 1 in the state with wins over Covington Holmes, Maysville, Ludlow, Bellevue, and Dayton.

Highlands coach Walter "Rip" Van Winkle was considered a shrewd tactician and a true Southern gentleman. He coached from 1932 through 1936 and compiled a 24-14-4 record.

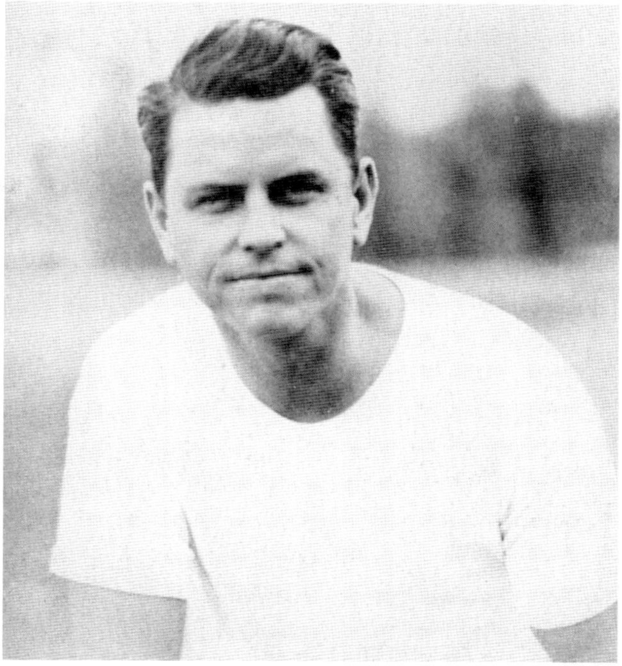

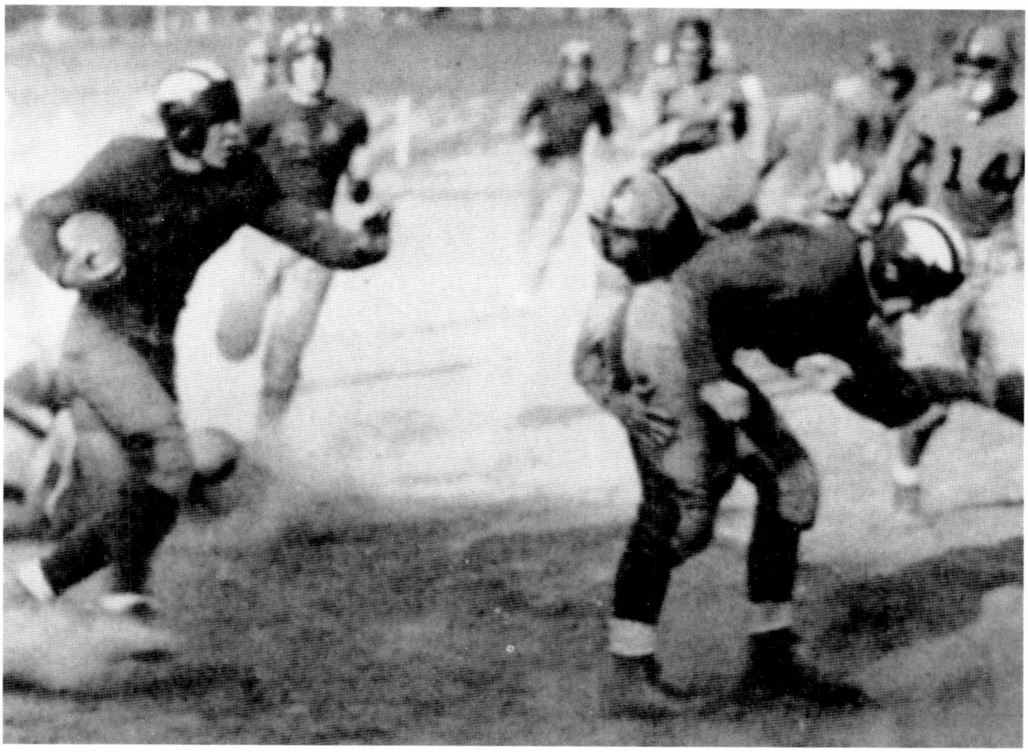

Rich Carothers was a halfback on the 1937 Highlands team that finished the season with a 7-1-1 record and won the Northern Kentucky championship. The team's only loss was to the defending state champion, Louisville DuPont Manual High School.

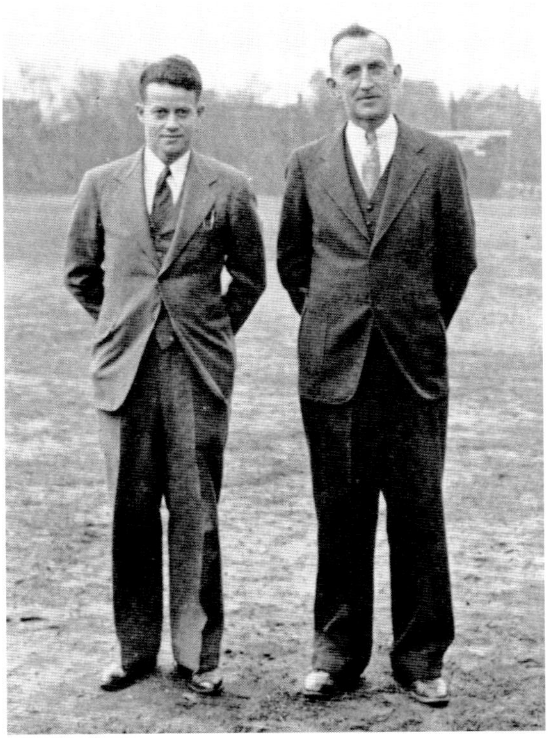

Bernie Sadosky and Al Rader were the coaches of the 1938 Highlands team that won the Little Six Conference championship and a second successive Northern Kentucky championship. Coach Rader resigned after the season, and Sadosky took over as head coach.

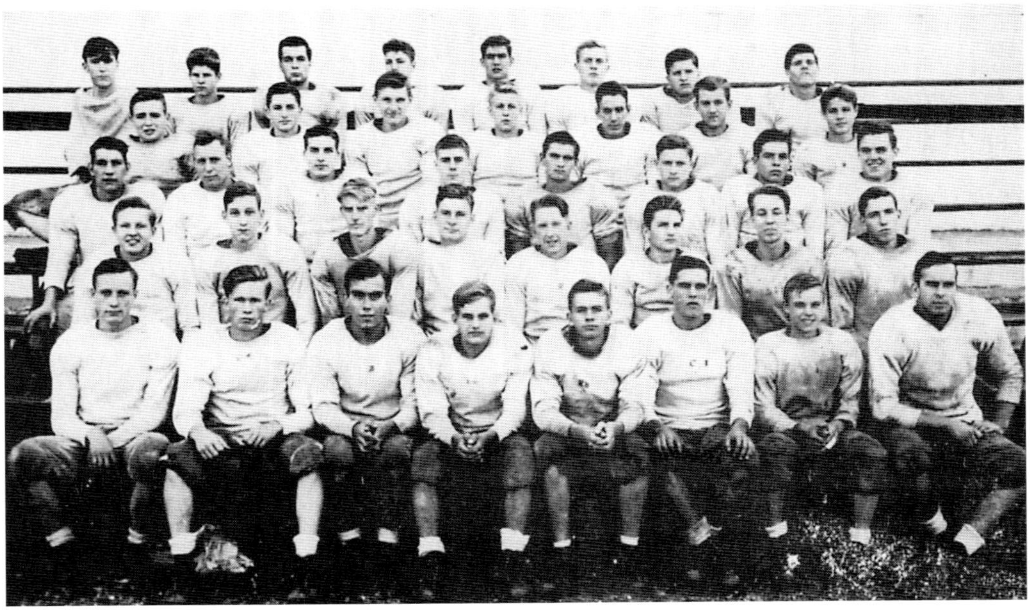

The 1942 Highlands football team finished the season with a 7-2 record after shutting out the first six opponents of the season. A victory souvenir program praised the coaching staff of the team that was playing games soon after the start of World War II. It read: "Hats off to Sadosky, Law, Waddell and Bridges through whose leadership the young men of Highlands football team have typified the fighting, courageous spirit of American Youth."

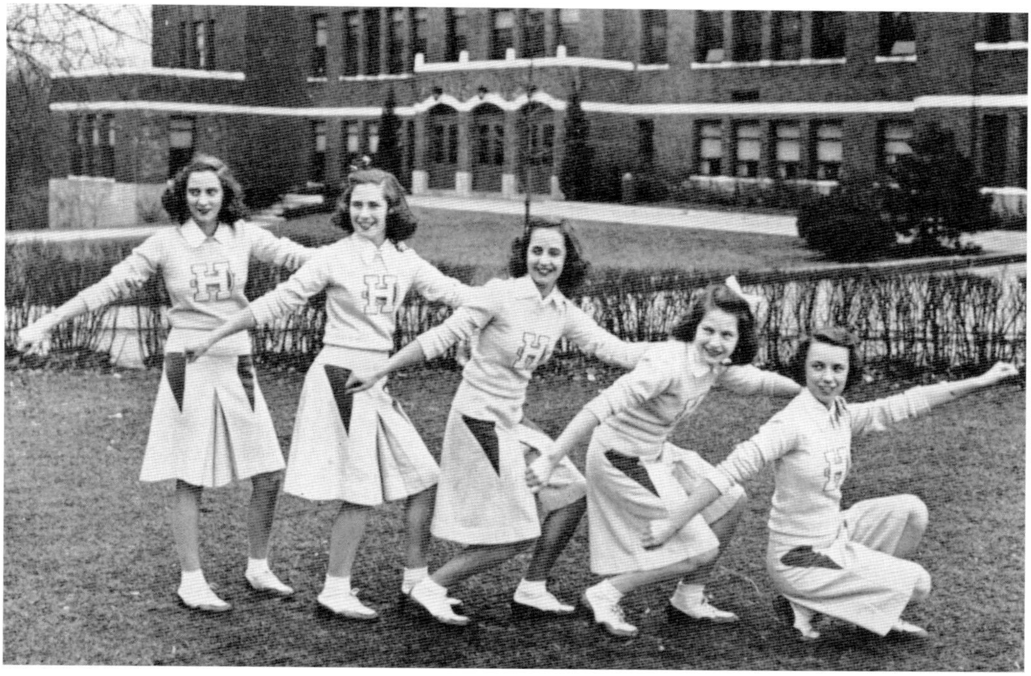

Highlands' cheerleaders supported the team at every game during the 1940 season. Highlands finished the season with a 5-3-2 record. The last names of the cheerleaders are, from left to right, Ellett, Henry, Schmidt, Ziegler, and Borden.

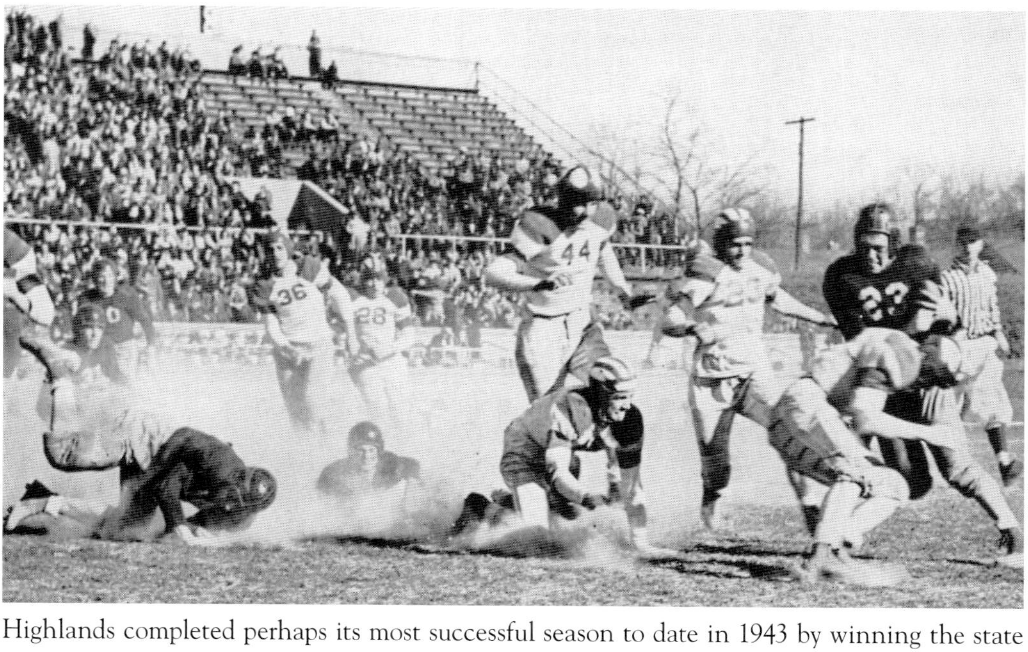

Highlands completed perhaps its most successful season to date in 1943 by winning the state championship and finishing the season with a 10-1 record. The Bluebirds defeated Ashland 19-0 in a post-season game at the University of Kentucky. In this photograph, Highlands' defense stops Ashland's top running back for no gain.

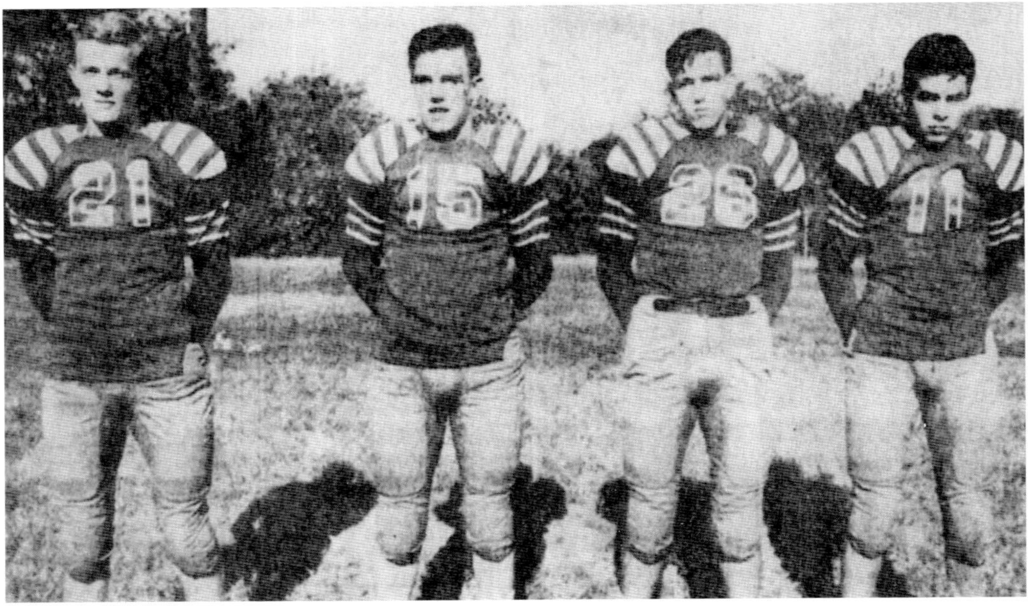

A newspaper article marveled at how big Highlands' running backs were in 1940. They ranged in weight from 150 to 170 pounds. The running backs are, from left to right, Morris Cecil, Red Kruer, Jack Pogue, and Bo Carothers. (Courtesy of Hank Pogue.)

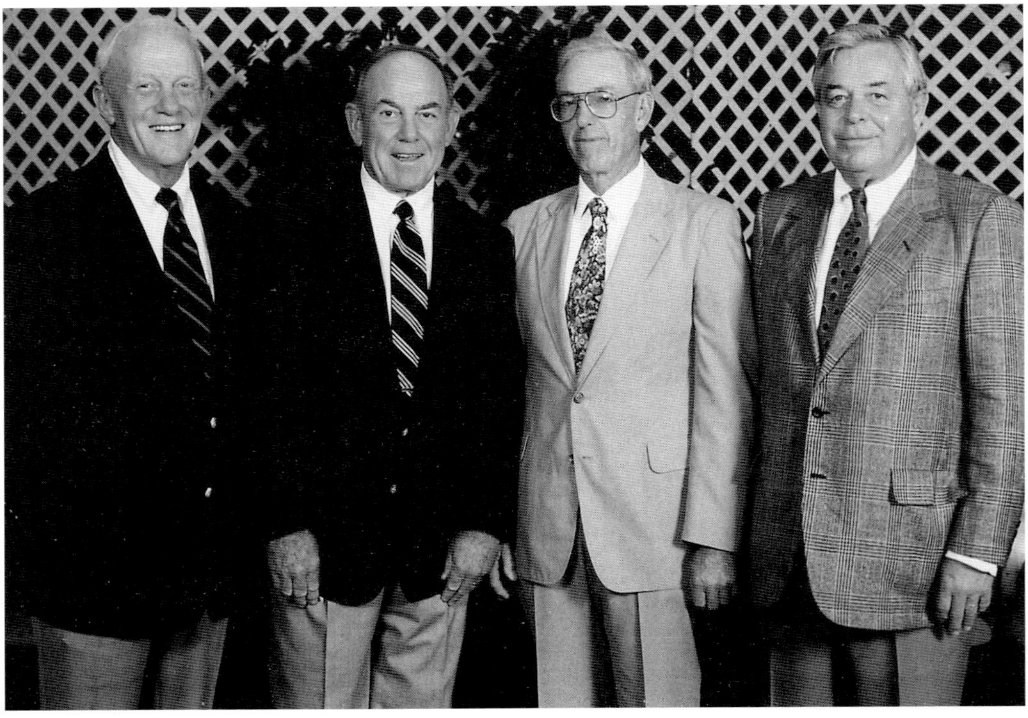

The running backs in the photograph above pose for this reunion photograph decades later. Pictured from left to right are Morris Cecil, Red Kruer, Jack Pogue, and Bo Carothers. (Courtesy of Hank Pogue.)

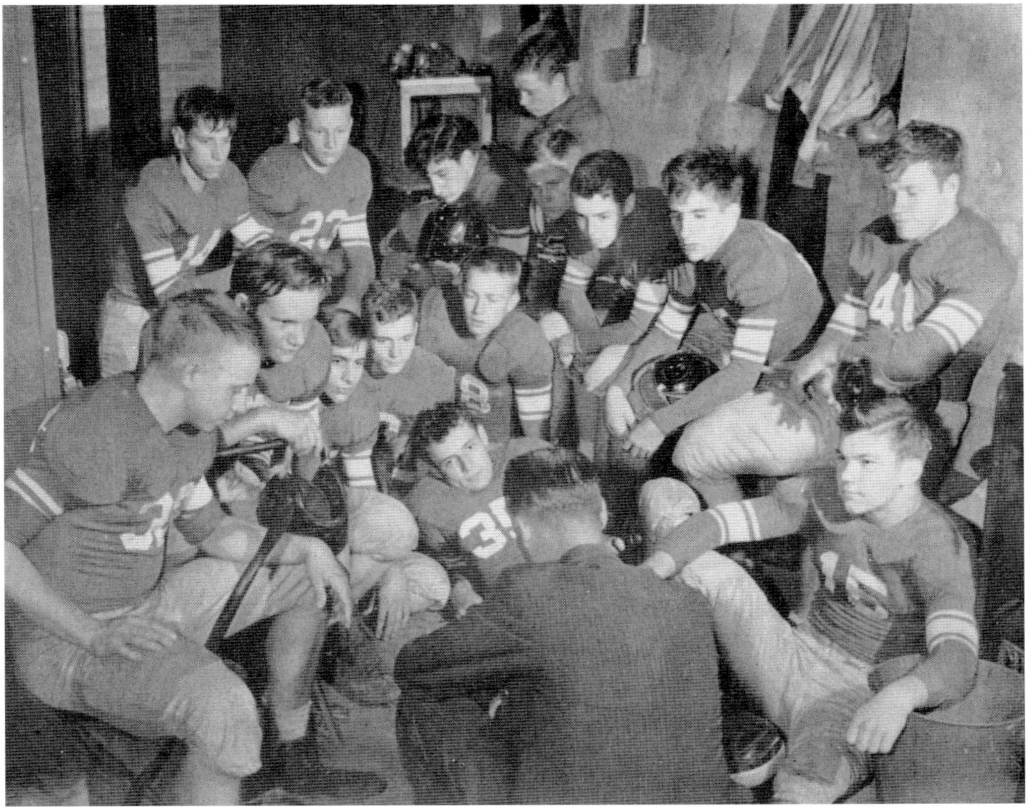

Members of the 1946 Highlands football team listen closely to instructions from coach Ewell Waddell in the locker room before a game.

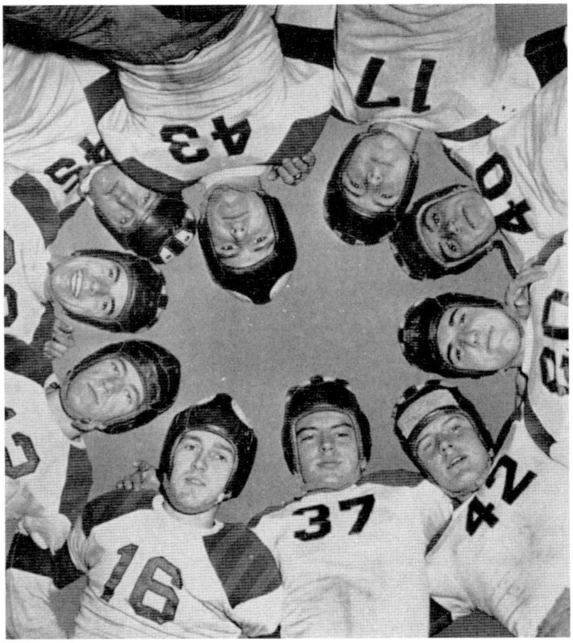

The offensive unit is in the huddle at a practice during the 1945 season. Highlands finished the season with a 6-5 record.

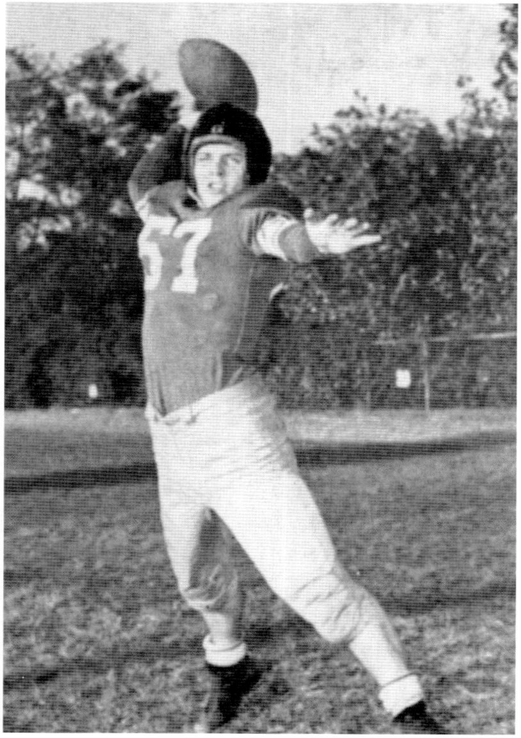

Halfback Fred Erschell is photographed in a classic passing position at the beginning of the 1947 season. Erschell would later serve as mayor of Fort Thomas for a number of years.

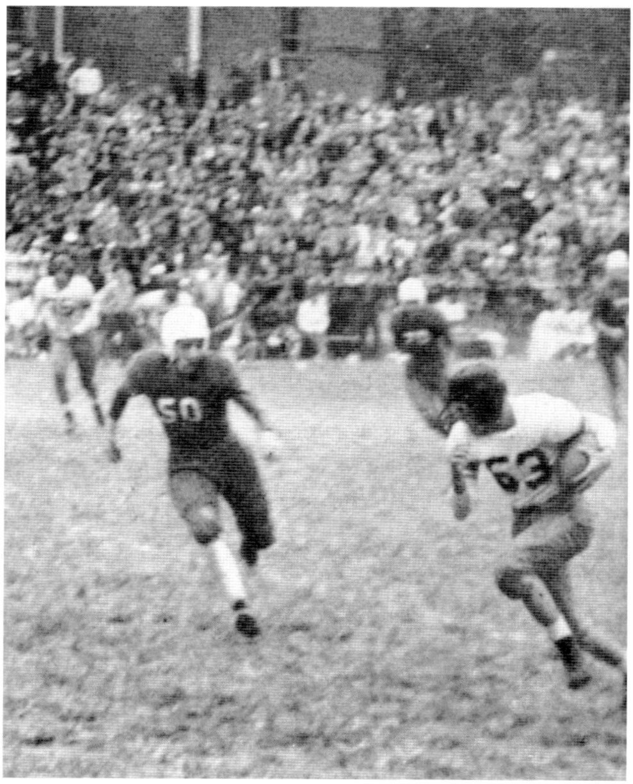

Quarterback Gene Waltrip sprints past a Lexington Lafayette player in 1948. The season ended with four consecutive losses and a 3-8 record. Lafayette beat the Bluebirds by a score of 21-14.

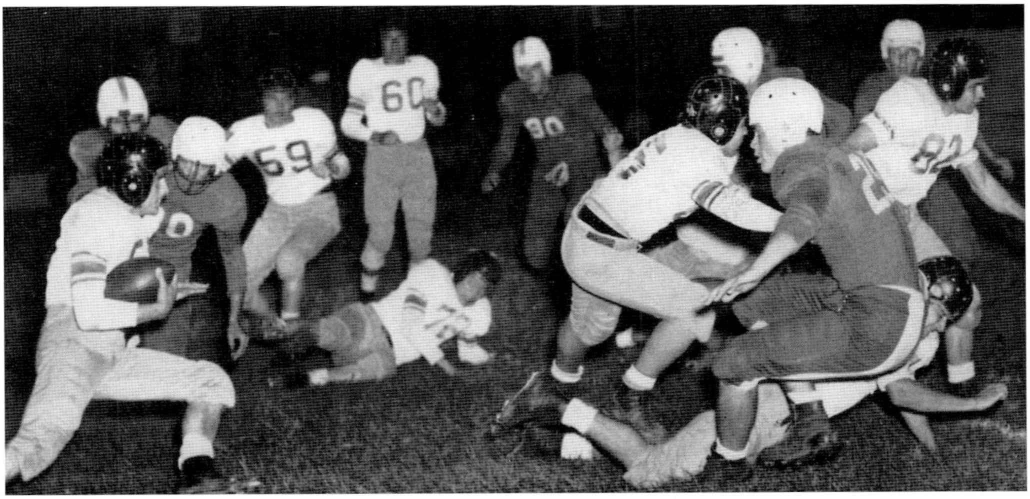

Milt Walz, a junior, searches for running room in Highlands' 13-0 victory over Dayton in 1949. Highlands finished the season with a 6-5 record.

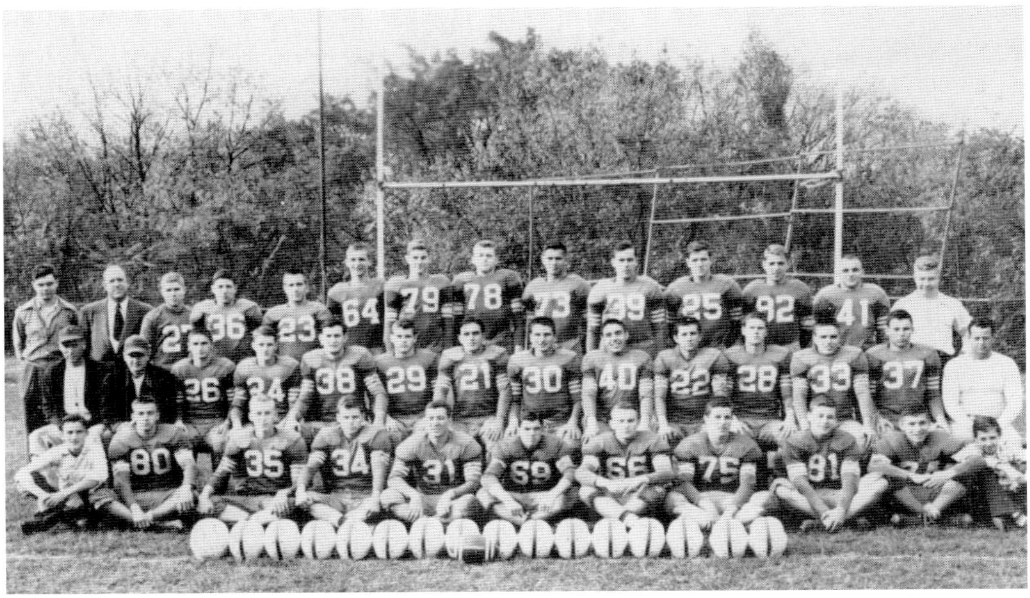

Highlands finished the 1950 season with a 12-1 record and won the Northern Kentucky Athletic Conference championship. The only loss came at the hands of Louisville St. Xavier by a score of 20-13 in the post-season Shrine Bowl in Lexington. Highlands' biggest rival in the 1950s was Newport, and the Bluebirds defeated the Wildcats by a score of 26-14 in 1950.

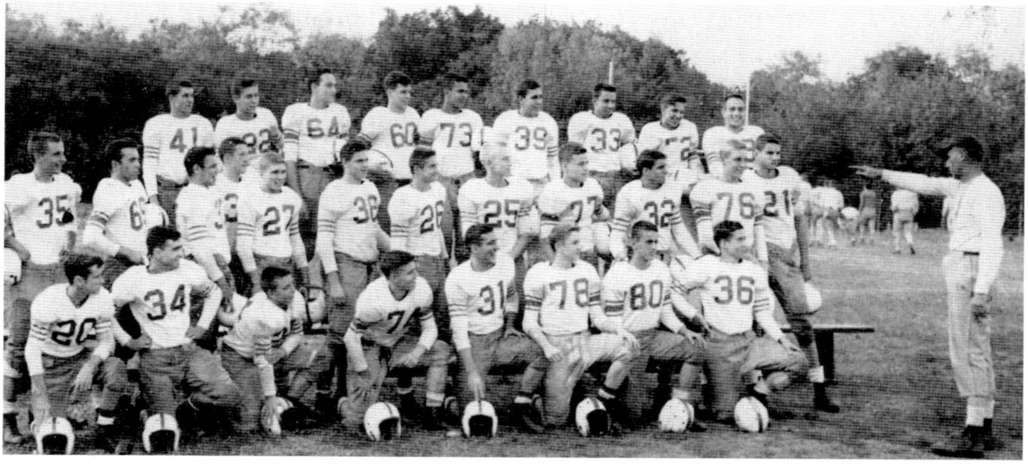

Coach Ewell Waddell gives instructions to his 1951 varsity team en route to a 9-1 record and second place finish in the Northern Kentucky Athletic Conference.

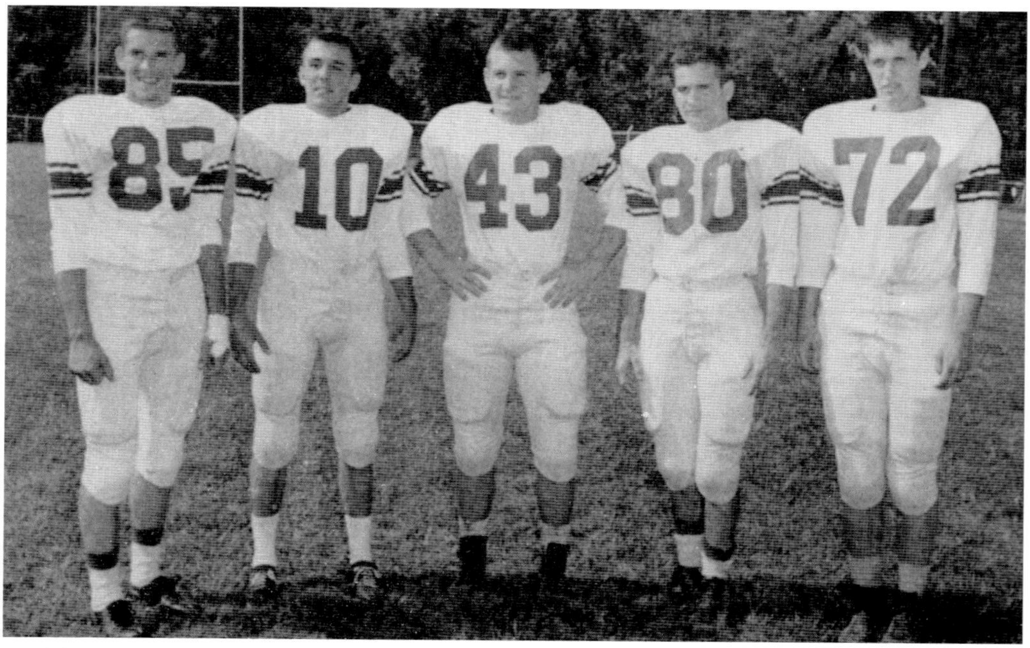

Highlands' team captains in 1957 are, from left to right, Denny McAtee, Billy Straub, Gary Cochran, Doug Martin, and Bill Waddell. Highlands finished the season with a perfect 10-0 record and a post-season victory over Danville in the Rotary Bowl.

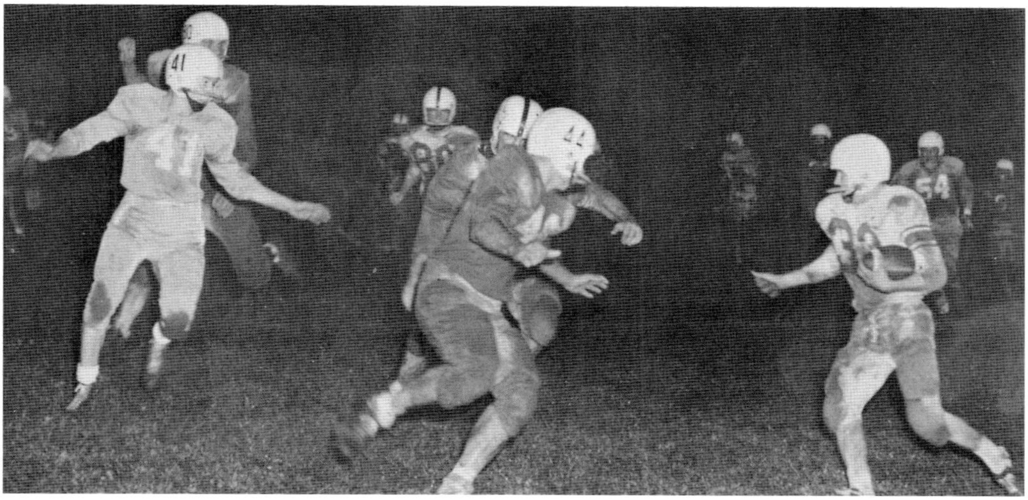

Fred Crawford carries the ball in a 1957 win over Boone County. Highlands finished the season with a 10-0 record and was ranked No. 1 in the state.

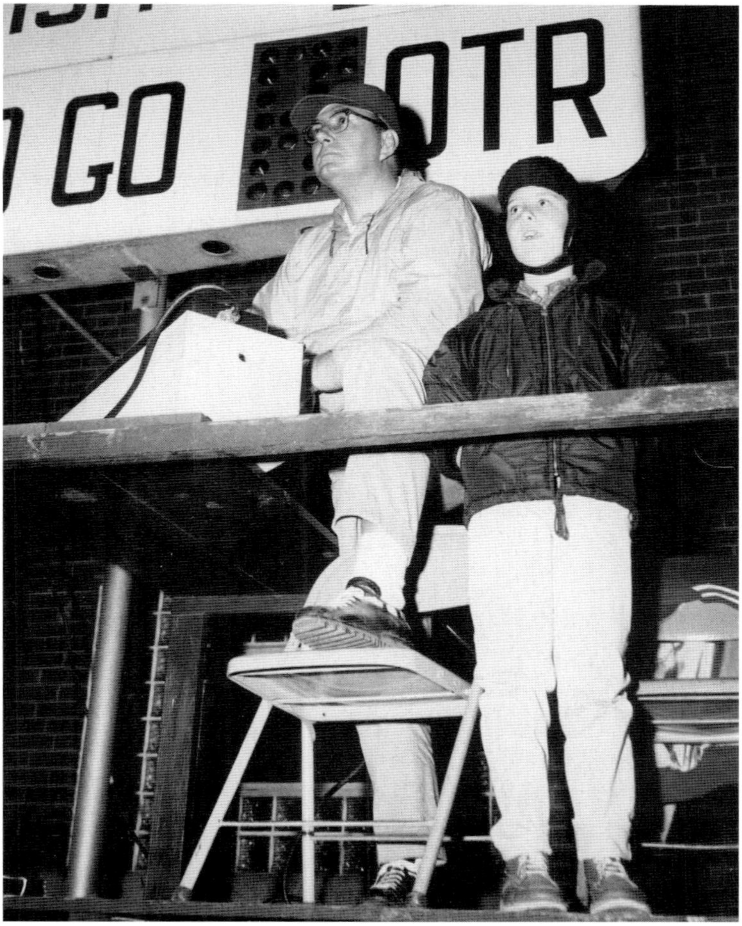

Ted "Bear" Englehard and his son Jon work the football scoreboard during Highlands' 68-0 victory over Bellevue in 1964. Englehard helped coach the football team for a number of years and later coached the tennis teams at Highlands. (Courtesy of Jon Englehard.)

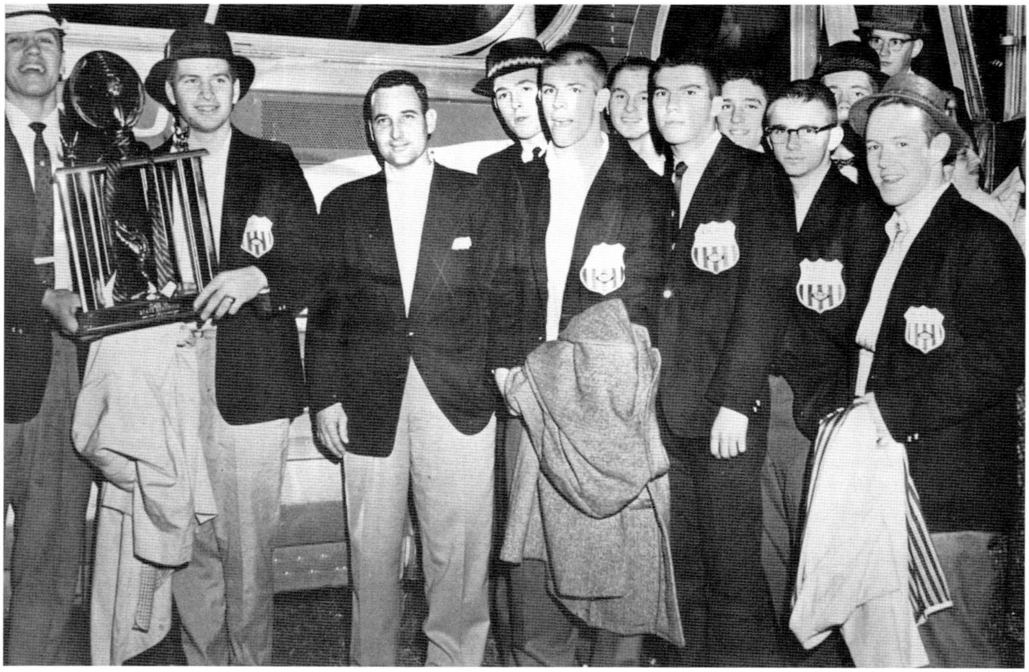

Legendary coach Homer Rice (third from left) arrives in Fort Thomas with the Highlands football team after capturing the school's first state playoff championship in 1960. Pictured with the trophy are John Burt and Bob Steinhauser. Bill Gibson, wearing a hat, is fourth from the left. Other players include, from left to right, the following: (first row) Joe Ross, Jack Gish, Roger Walz (glasses), and Jim Borches (hat). The 1960 team beat Bowling Green (the best team in the West), Louisville Male (the best team in Louisville), and Ashland (the best team in the East). Rice went on to be head coach at Rice University, the University of Cincinnati, and the Cincinnati Bengals.

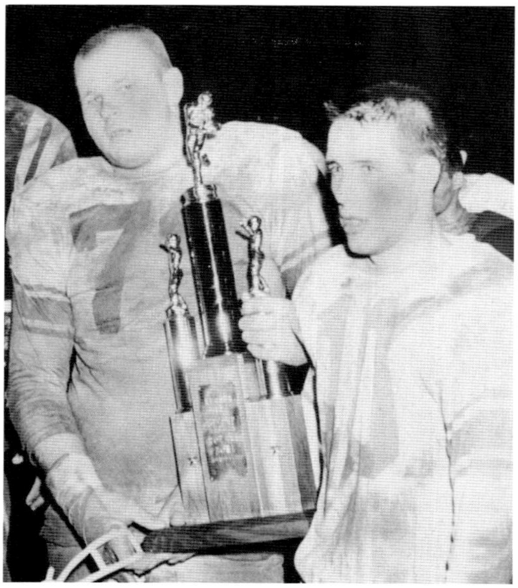

Paul Finneseth (left) and Richie Emmons (right) hold the 1958 Rotary Bowl runner-up trophy after Highlands' loss to Louisville Flaget by a score of 20-9. (Courtesy of Ken Honchell.)

George Ratterman helped organize the Fort Thomas Junior Football League in the late 1950s. Ratterman lived in Fort Thomas at the time and had played quarterback for the Cleveland Browns.

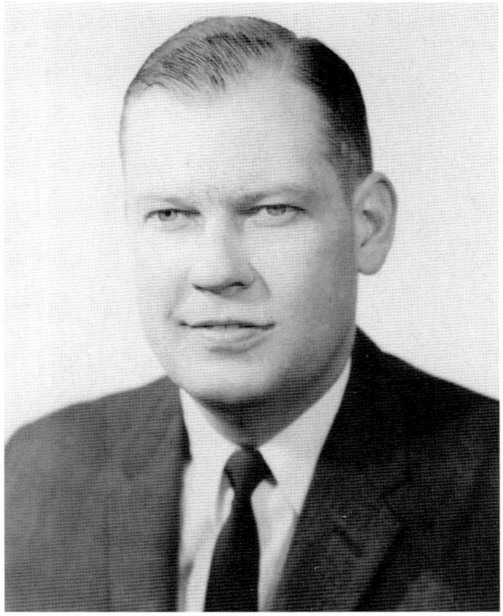

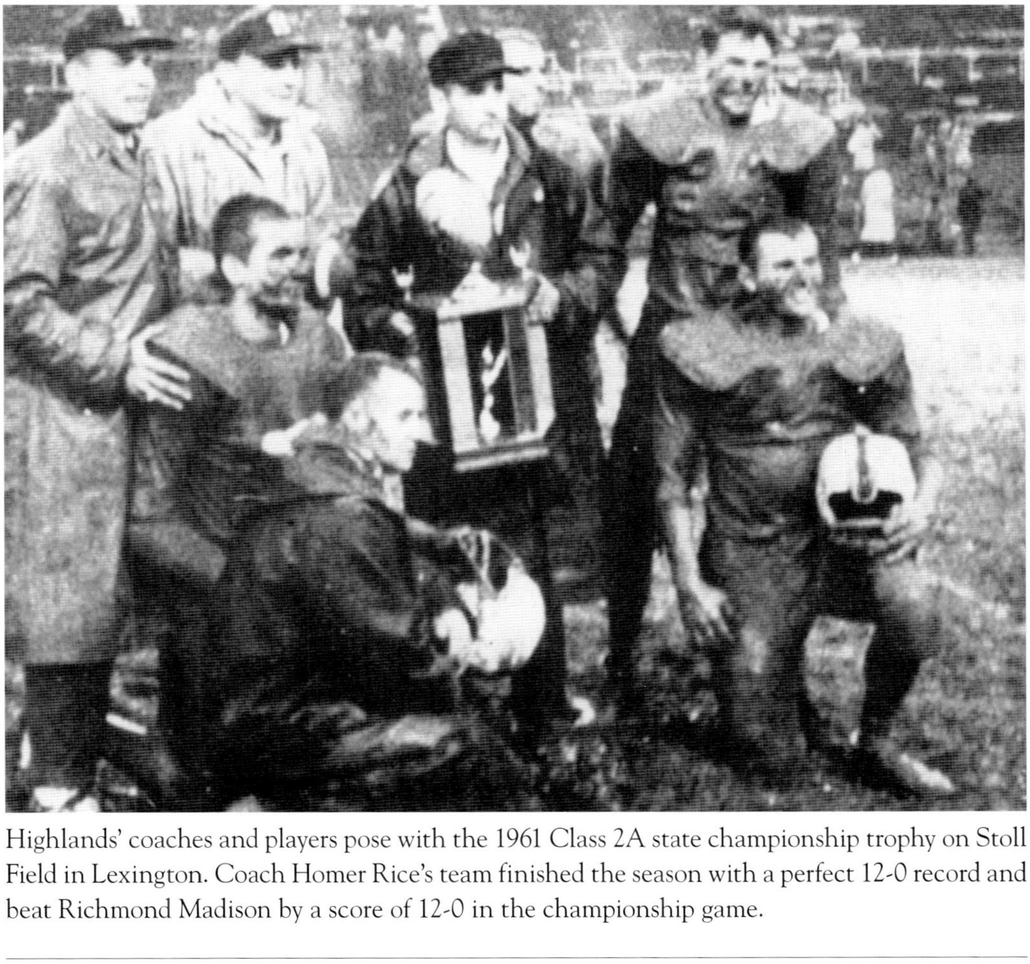

Highlands' coaches and players pose with the 1961 Class 2A state championship trophy on Stoll Field in Lexington. Coach Homer Rice's team finished the season with a perfect 12-0 record and beat Richmond Madison by a score of 12-0 in the championship game.

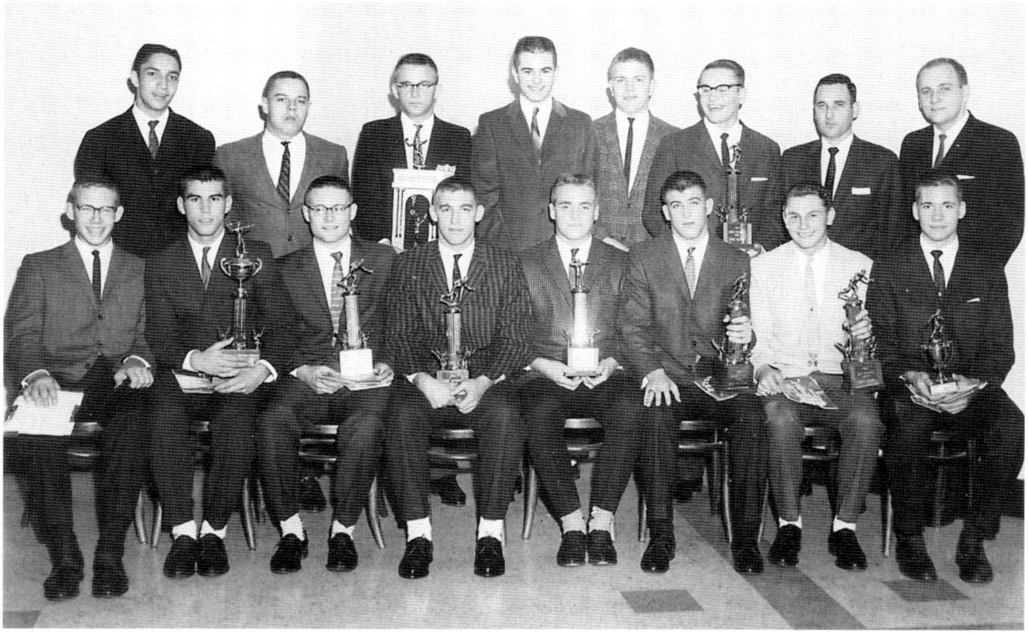

Pictured are the award winners at the Highlands football banquet in 1961. Players seated on the first row, from left to right, are Allen Law, Charlie Hoffman, Gary Carnan, Harry Reif, Bill Montfort, Dale Faulkner, Doug Moore, and Bob Heinze. Players standing on the second row, from left to right, are Bill Bradley, Mike Lawson, Roger Walz, C. R. Lyons, Powell Smith, and Mike McGraw. The coaches standing on the second row are Homer Rice (second from right) and Owen Hauck (far right). (Courtesy of Jean Mettens.)

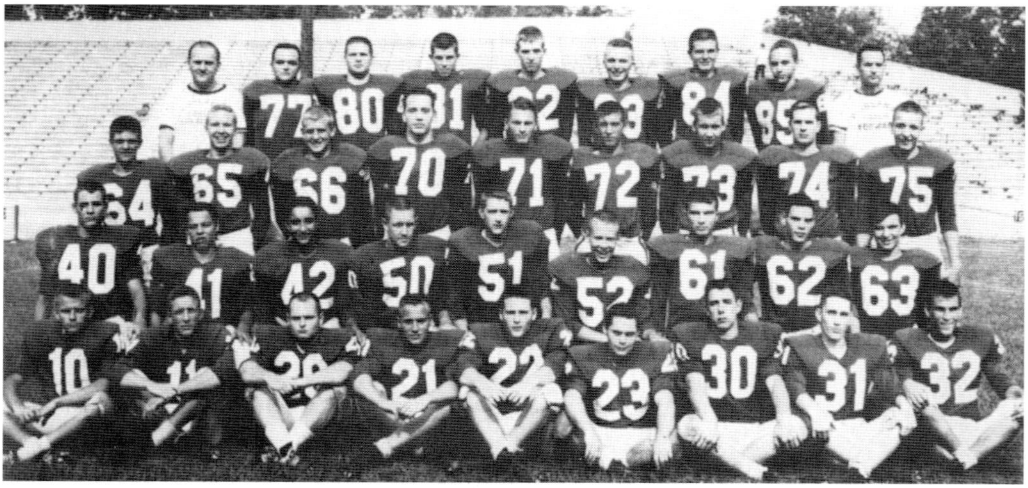

Highlands' football team in 1960 was loaded with college talent. Among the players that played on the collegiate level were Roger Walz (No. 10) at the University of Cincinnati and University of Kentucky, Jim Ullman (No. 20) at Wittenberg University, Jim Burt (No. 30) at Western Kentucky University, John Burt (No. 40) at Western Kentucky University, Alan Berry (No. 70) at Duke University, Bob Steinhauser (No. 80) at the University of Cincinnati, and Joe Ross (No. 81) at the U.S. Air Force Academy.

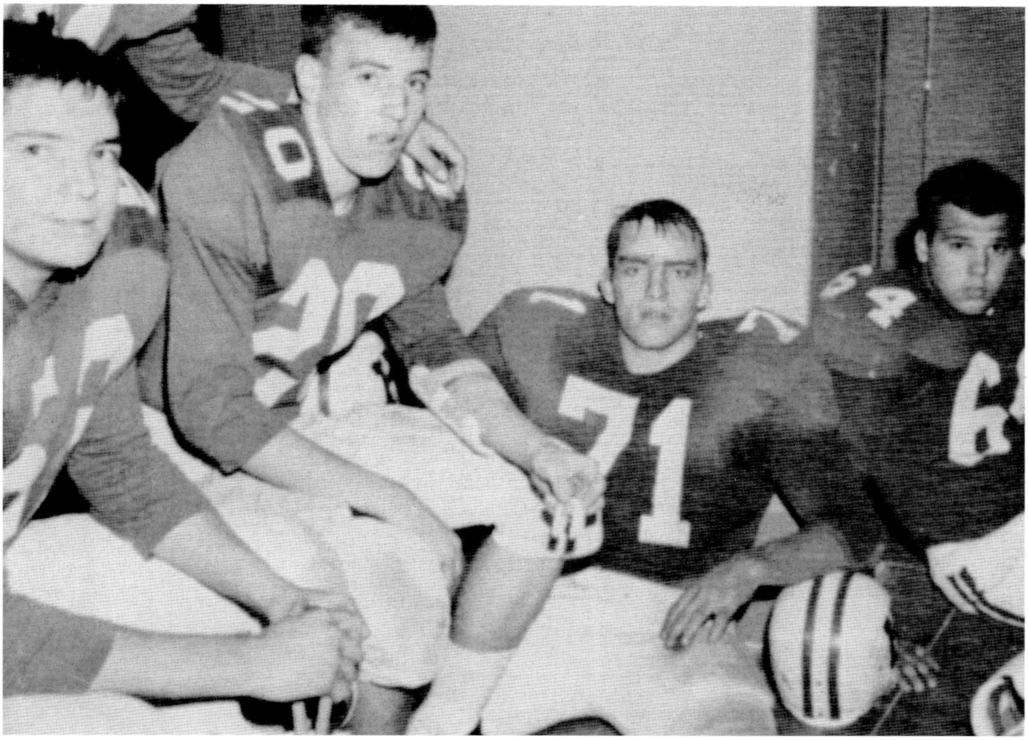

Highlands players take a break during halftime of the 1964 game against Covington Holmes. The players, from left to right, are Bob Oliver, Dave Crooks, Chuck Kyle, and Gerry Schweitzer. Kyle was a high school All American and went on to become an All American at Purdue University.

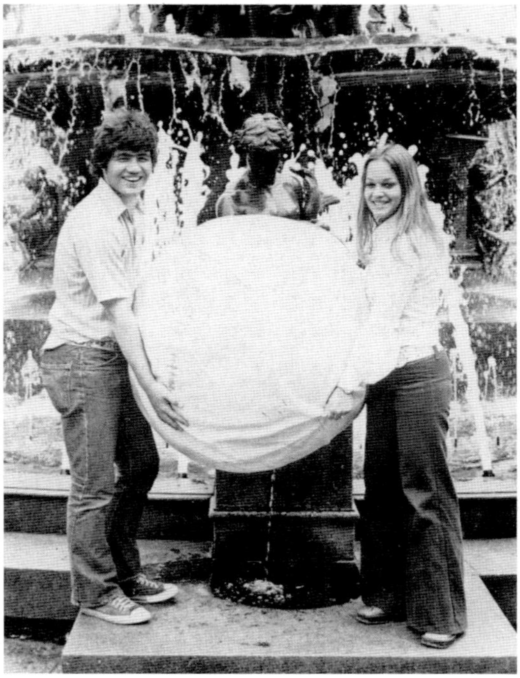

That is Dale Mueller on the left of this photograph honoring the "Most All-Around" students in the Highlands class of 1973. Lindsey Townsend was the female winner. Mueller has coached Highlands' football team for the last 14 years and has won six state championships. He is a Cornell graduate and was a head coach at Sycamore High School and Withrow High School before coming to Highlands in 1994. Mueller has compiled a 153-43 career record at Highlands and has had a major impact on the lives of many of his players. He is dedicated and well prepared, and is also the most enthusiastic and positive coach this writer has ever been around.

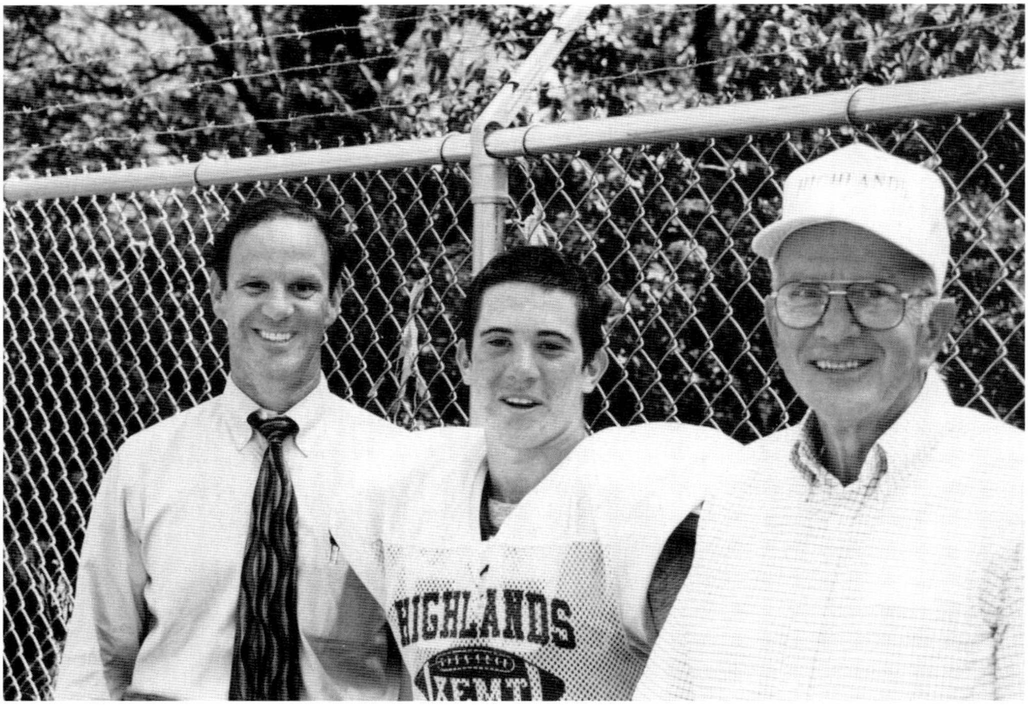

Three generations of the Fennell family have played football at Highlands. Clem Fennell Jr. (right) played on the 1943 Highlands team that finished as the No. 1 team in Kentucky; Clem Fennell III (left) played on the 1968 Highlands team that captured the Class 2A state championship; and Clem Fennell IV played on the Highlands team that won the 2000 Class 3A state championship.

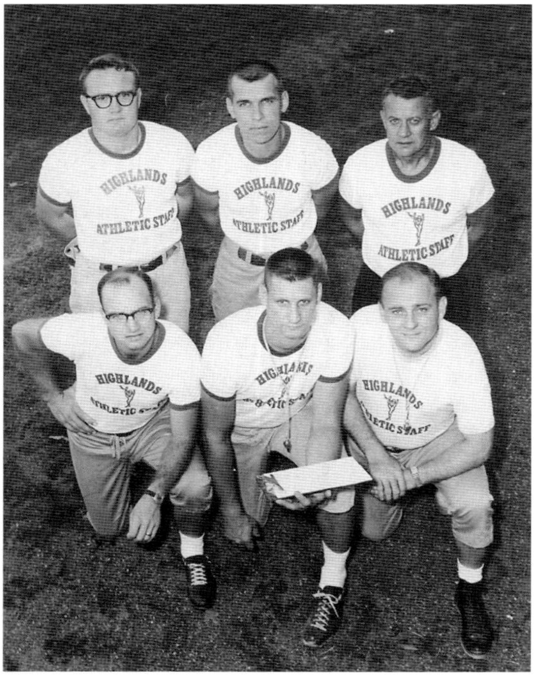

Six coaches guided the Highlands football team through the 1962 season. Kneeling, left to right, are Mike Murphy, Sig Lawson, and head coach Owen Hauck. Standing, from left to right, are Tom Condrom, Bill Herrmann, and Bernie Sadosky. Coach Hauck led Highlands to a state championship in 1964. Mike Murphy was head coach at Highlands when the school won state championships in 1968 and 1970, and Bill Herrmann guided the Bluebirds to state titles in 1977, 1981, and 1982. (Courtesy of Jean Mettens.)

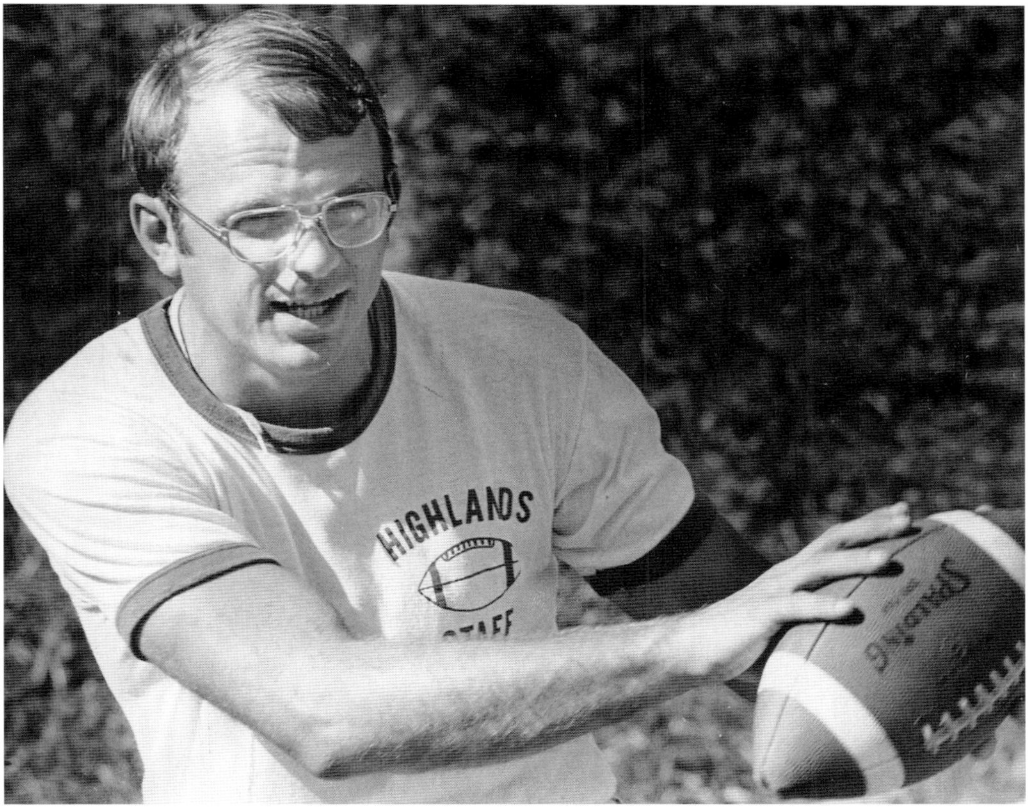

Roger Walz was one of Highlands' greatest football players and also coached the Bluebirds to a state championship in 1975. His 1975 team defeated Franklin-Simpson by a score of 21-0 at Western Kentucky University to win the Class 3A state championship. (Courtesy of the *Kentucky Post.*)

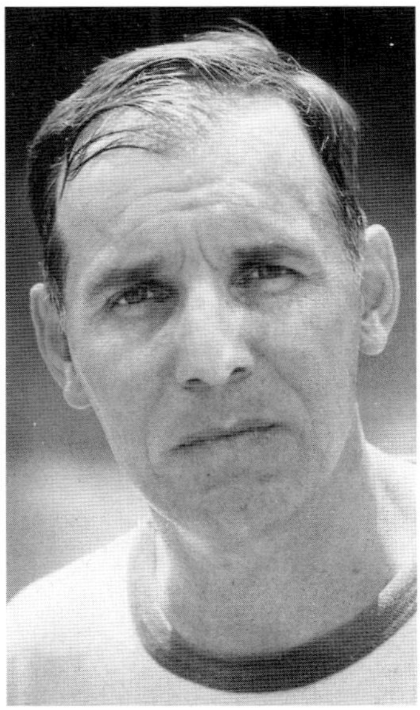

Bill Herrmann coached Highlands to state championships in 1977, 1981, and 1982. Herrmann's teams won 29 consecutive games between 1981 and 1983. He retired with a career record of 81-18 at Highlands. (Courtesy of the *Kentucky Post.*)

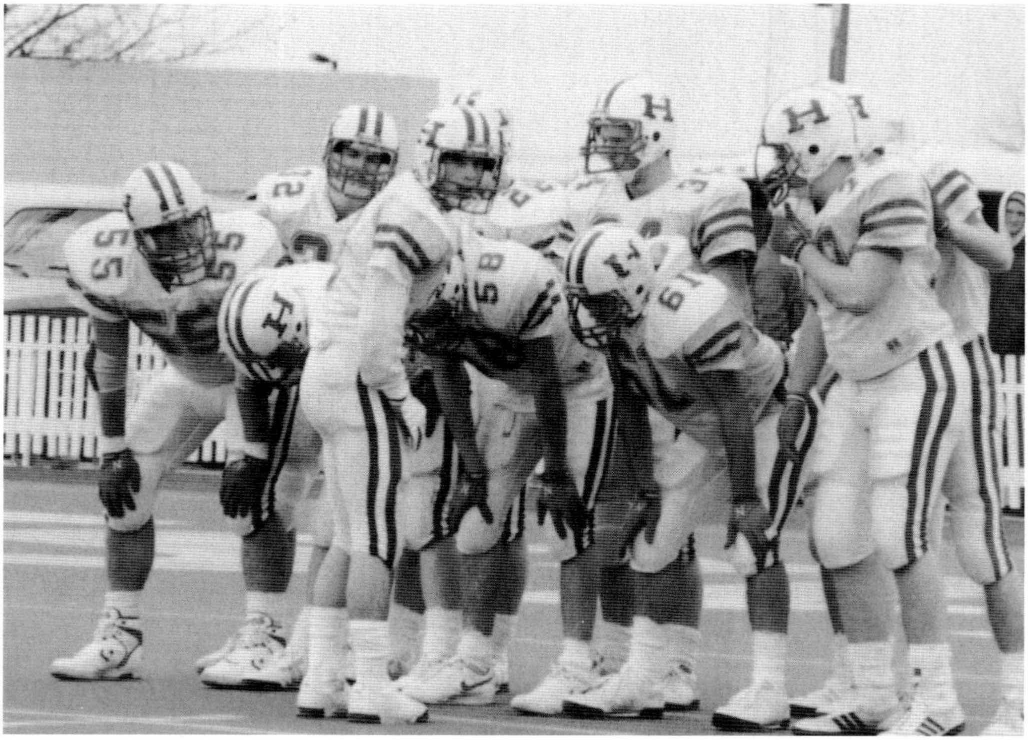

Quarterback Chris Gallichio prepares to call a play in the huddle during the 1989 state championship season. Gallichio was an excellent runner who completed 9 of 11 passes for 117 yards in the Class 3A state championship win over Paducah Tilghman.

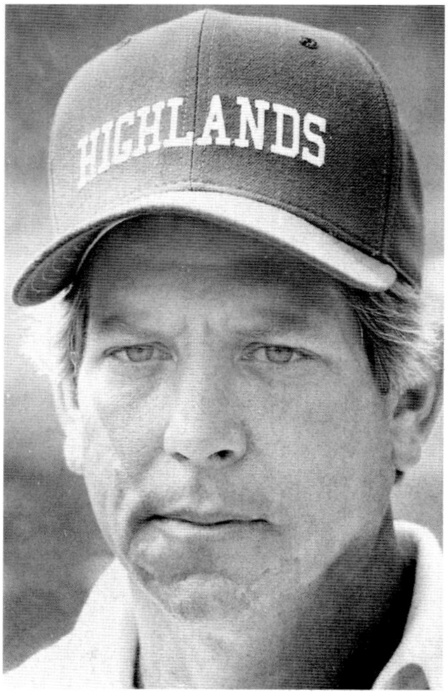

Coach Tom Duffy won two state titles at Highlands between 1988 and 1993. Duffy had a career record of 61-15 at Highlands. (Courtesy of the *Kentucky Post*.)

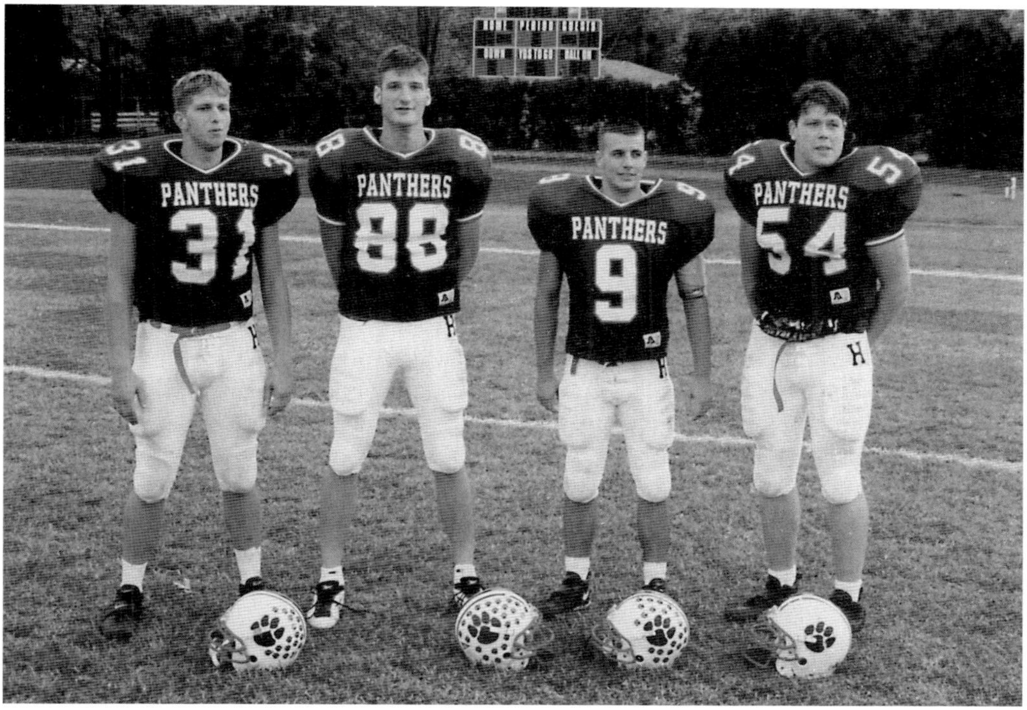

Four former Highlands football players suited up for Hanover College on Parent's Day a few years back. They are, from left to right, Brian Wenstrup, Jeff Fritsche, Jeff Hicks, and Jeff Barth. (Courtesy of Randy Fritsche.)

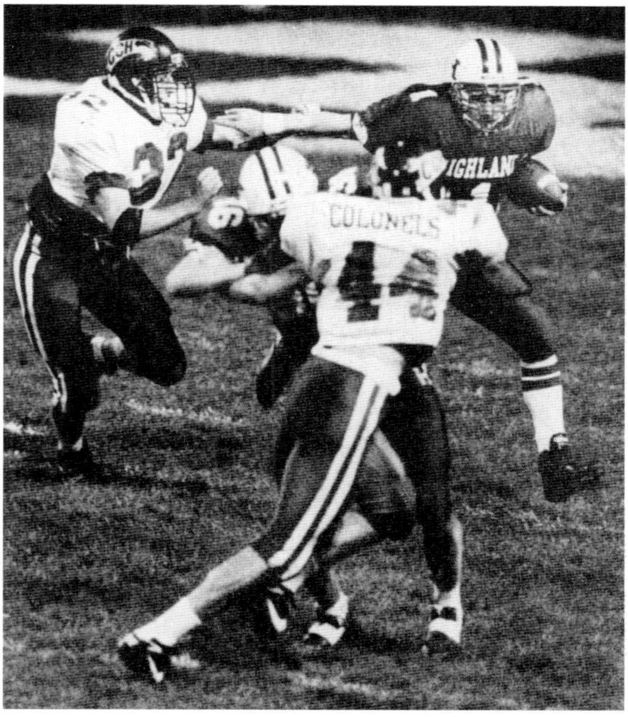

Highlands running back Steve Lickert cannot escape a swarming Covington Catholic defense in 1994. Lickert went on to play linebacker for a national championship Georgetown College team and is now the head football coach at Covington Holmes High School. (Courtesy of the *Kentucky Post*.)

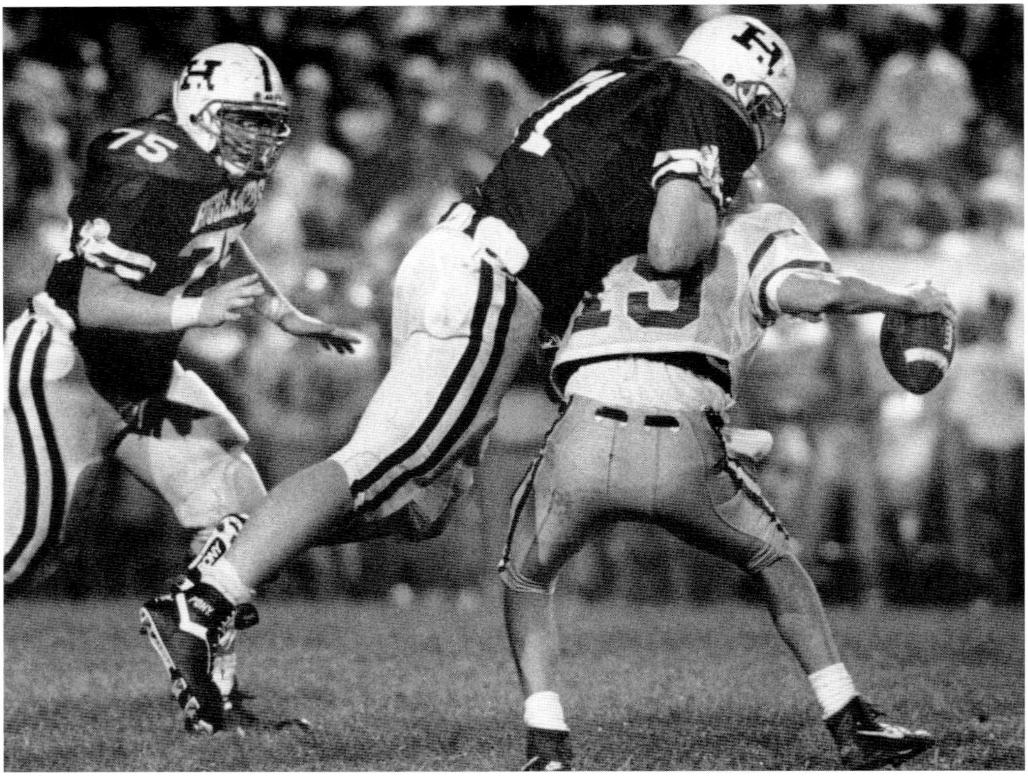

Highlands' Rob Reynolds pounces on Campbell County's quarterback as David Berringer (No. 75) moves in to help. (Courtesy of the *Kentucky Post.*)

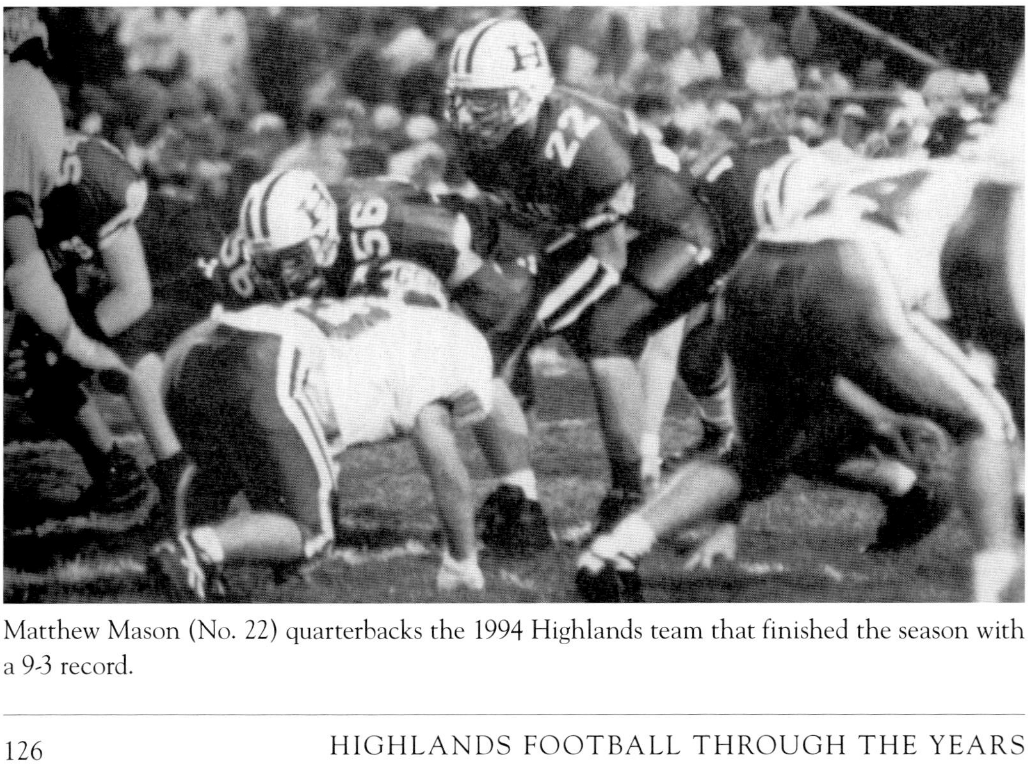

Matthew Mason (No. 22) quarterbacks the 1994 Highlands team that finished the season with a 9-3 record.

Quarterback Adam Crawford takes off around the right end looking for a receiver in 1992 action against Newport. Crawford helped lead Highlands to a Class 3A championship in 1992. Highlands defeated Newport by a score of 55-6.

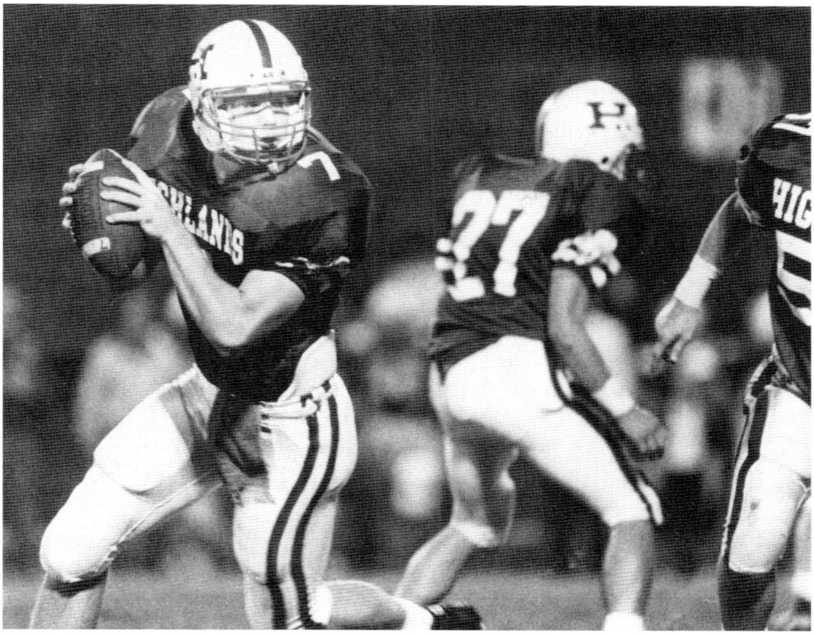

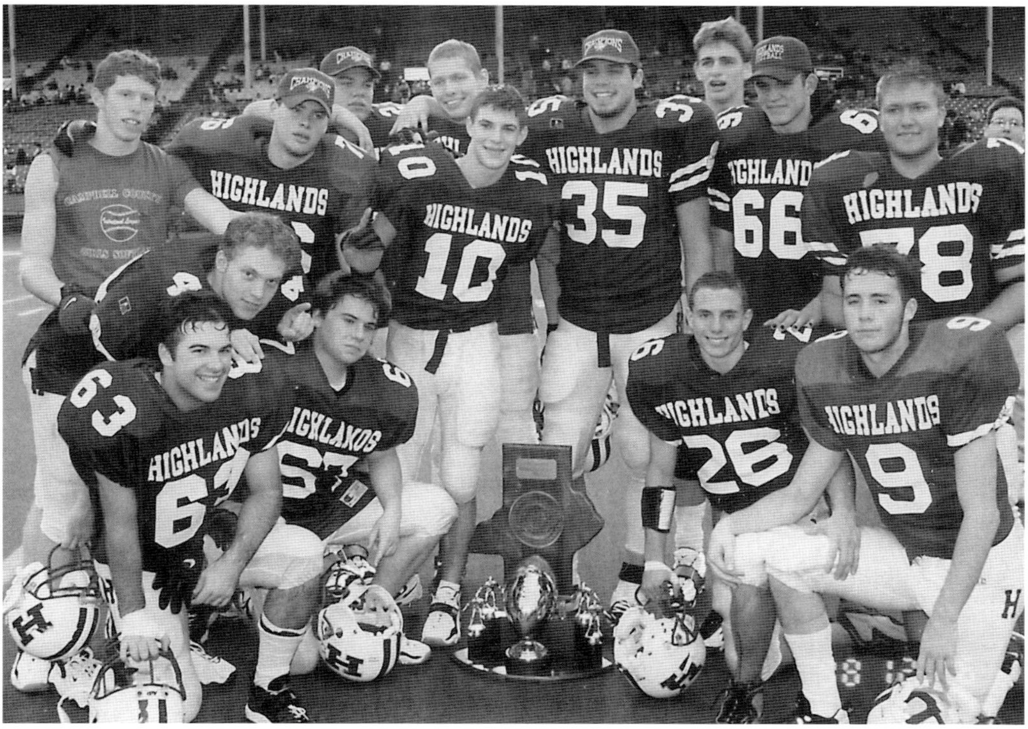

Highlands' seniors celebrate with the Class 3A state championship trophy after defeating Louisville Waggener by a score of 56-7 in 1998. Highlands finished the season with a perfect 15-0 record and was rated among the top 20 prep teams in the nation.